Modern Automotive HVAC: Electrical and Electronic Systems

BOOK 2

Electrical and Electronic Systems Operation Manual – including Fundamentals, Service, Diagnostics and Repair

This publication is protected under the copyright laws of the United States and all other applicable international laws and treaties. All rights are reserved, including resale rights. No part of this publication may be reproduced or transmitted in any form, by any means (electronic, photocopying, recording, or otherwise) without the prior written permission of Mobile Air Conditioning Society Worldwide (MACS Worldwide). Unauthorized use, reproduction or distribution of this publication, or any portion of it, may result in severe civil and criminal penalties, and will be prosecuted to the maximum extent possible under the law. If you received this publication from anyone other than MACS Worldwide, then you have received a pirated copy. We would appreciate it if you would notify us of the situation.

The publication is designed to help technicians improve and maintain their professional competence. The information contained in this publication is based on technical data and tests and is intended for use by persons with technical skill at their own discretion and risk. While the author(s) and publisher have made every reasonable effort to achieve the utmost accuracy in the information in this publication, they assume no responsibility for errors or omissions. Please remember that your particular situation may differ from any examples illustrated here; you should adjust your use of the information (and any recommendations in this publication) accordingly. MACS Worldwide makes no representations or warranties concerning the information contained herein or the applications described or referred in this publication. MACS Worldwide specifically disclaims any implied warranties including the warranties of merchantability or fitness for any particular purpose. MACS Worldwide shall in no event be liable for any loss of profit, business interruption or any other commercial damage, including without limitation, special, incidental, consequential, or other damages arising out of the use or inability to use the presentations or applications described or referred to herein.

The identification of any products, techniques or firms referred to in this publication does not constitute an endorsement by MACS Worldwide. Further, any use of product names and services that are trademarks or service marks are the marks of their respective holders and are used in this publication solely in an editorial fashion.

If, for any reason, you wish to contact MACS Worldwide about this publication, please refer to the information listed at right.

For more information, contact:

MACS Worldwide™
P.O. Box 88
225 S. Broad Street
Lansdale, Pa, 19446
Voice: 215-631-7020
Fax: 215-631-7017
E-mail: info@macsw.org

MACS® and the MACS® logo are registered trademarks of
the Mobile Air Conditioning Society Worldwide™
All Rights Reserved. Printed in the U.S.A.

© 2012, Mobile Air Conditioning
Society Worldwide™

TABLE OF CONTENTS

Table of Contents i
Introduction iv
   Preface iv
   Safety and Precautions v
   Going Green vi

Section 1: Electrical Basics 1
   Electrical Theory 1
      Ohm's Law 3
      Watt's Law 5
   Electricity and Magnetism 5
   Section 1 Review Quiz 7

Section 2: The Multimeter and Circuit Designs 9
   Meters 9
      Meter checks on circuits 9
      Meter scaling 10
      The voltmeter 13
      The ammeter 14
      The ohmmeter 15
   Circuit Designs 16
      Series circuits 16
      Parallel circuits 18
      Series-parallel circuits 21
      Circuit Faults 22
      Testing for voltage drop 24
      Digital multimeter tips 30
   Worksheet 1 – Section 2 31
   Section 2 Review Quiz 32

Section 3: Wiring Diagrams and Service Information 33
   Wiring Diagrams 33
      Using wiring diagrams to trace a circuit 37
      Circuit troubleshooting procedures tips 44
   Worksheet 2 – Section 3 46
   Section 3 Review Quiz 48

Section 4: Basic Computer Operation & Function 49
   Controlling Modern HVAC Systems 49
   Computer Communication 51
   Computer Components 52
      Computer interfaces 54
      Communications 55
   Electrical/Electronic Components that Affect System Operation 56
      Engine management modules 56
   HVAC Module Definitions 58
      HVAC control head 58

TABLE OF CONTENTS

    Body control module (BCM) 58
    Powertrain control module (PCM) 59
  Engine Management Operation 62
    Computer inputs. 63
      Potentiometers 63
      Variable resistors 63
      Voltage generators 64
      Frequency generators 64
      Variable pressure sensor (transducer) 65
      Switches. 66
      Switch circuits 66
    Serial data 67
  Computer Outputs & Output Devices 68
    Relays 69
    Solenoids 70
    Motors 71
    Controller modules 73
    Diagnostics 73
  Serial Data Outputs 74
    Controller area network (CAN). 74
  Semiconductors. 78
    Diodes 78
    Resistors 79
    Capacitors 81
    Transistors 81
  Integrated Circuits 82
  Worksheet 3 – Section 4 83
  Section 4 Review Quiz 84

Section 5: Electrical/Electronic Troubleshooting and Diagnosis **85**
  Types of Circuit Failures 85
  Electrical/Electronic Test Equipment. 85
    Diagnostic procedures 87
    Preliminary diagnosis 89
    Charging system tests 91
    Charging system voltage drop tests 91
    Analytic steps. 93
    Scan tool checks 94
    Multimeter testing 97
    Compressor clutch relay checks 98
    Checking switches and sensors with a multimeter 101
    Powertrain control module (PCM) check 103
  Worksheet 4 – Section 5 105
  Section 5 Review Quiz 106

TABLE OF CONTENTS

Section 6: HVAC Control Systems 107
Compressor Clutch Controls..107
Introduction 107
Clutch cycling designs 108
Air conditioning pressure sensor (ACP) 111
Evaporator temperature sensing devices 112
Variable displacement compressors 115
Worksheet 5 – Section 6 117
Section 6 Review Quiz 118

Section 7: Blower Motors and Cabin Filters 119
Blower Motor Designs 119
Power modules and pulse width modulation 122
Pulse width modulation 123
Blower motor diagnostic tips 124
Cabin air filters 124
Worksheet 8 – Section 7 125
Section 7 Review Quiz 126

Section 8: Air Delivery Systems 127
The Impact of Electronics on HVAC Systems..127
Manual Control Systems 127
Operator interface 130
Mode controls 131
Actuator motors 132
Actuator diagnosis 134
Actuator calibration 136
Automatic Temperature Control Systems (ATC)..138
Additional inputs...143
Data lines..143
Air delivery 144
Blower controls 145
Common ATC designs..146
ATC diagnostics and calibration 149
Hybrid HVAC...153
Worksheet 7 – Section 8 156
Section 8 Review Quiz 157

Section 9: Glossary..159

Introduction

PREFACE:

Welcome! This book is aimed at a broad section of automotive repair professionals, including students, entry-level, and seasoned technicians. It is designed to educate, develop and maintain professional level skills to make you efficient and effective in your shop.

The purpose of this book is to educate the reader about the importance of the electrical system in relation to the HVAC system. Often a technician will install refrigeration-related components, only to find that the compressor clutch will not engage or the cooling fans will not operate. Another scenario could be that the A/C system has a full refrigerant charge but the compressor clutch will not engage, or the A/C control panel will not change blower speeds or distribute air from the proper duct. This book will cover the fundamentals of electricity, required test equipment and test procedures. It will also address the electronics utilized in HVAC systems, including the inputs from the power train electronics that affect A/C operation.

With the increased use of electrical and electronic controls and sensors, it is important that all persons involved with vehicle repair have at least a working knowledge of electricity and electronics. The image below shows an example of the electronics used on today's vehicles. While this book is not a complete electrical and electronics course, it provides basic information and is a starting point for further study.

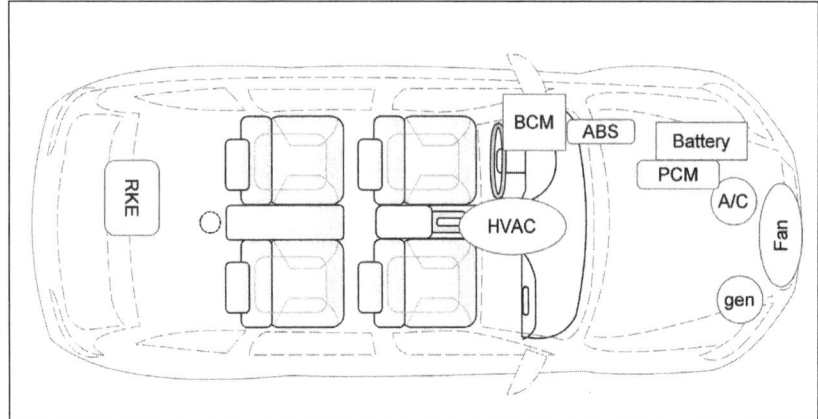

The Operation of Modern Mobile HVAC Systems Involves Many Different Electronic Control Modules

Notes:

INTRODUCTION

SAFETY AND PRECAUTIONS

All testing and repair procedures must be performed in accordance with recommended service and diagnostic manuals. All warnings, cautions and notices must be observed and followed to prevent personnel injury and vehicle damage. The following is a list of general guidelines:

- Always wear safety eye protection when working on a vehicle or vehicle components.
- Always work in a well-ventilated area and use exhaust venting equipment.
- Set the parking brake and use safety stands whenever working under a vehicle.
- Be sure the ignition is in the OFF position unless a particular procedure requires another setting.
- Keep clear of moving parts when the engine is running, especially drive belts and fans.
- Avoid contact with hot metal, exhaust components, and the cooling system, all of which can cause serious burns.
- Never wear rings, watches or jewelry while working on a vehicle.
- Do not wear loose clothing and keep long hair secure behind your head.
- Always follow the manufacturer's instructions when using test or service equipment.
- Always use a fused jumper wire and a direct ground wire to the battery ground post.
- Use caution when removing components and dash panels.
- Disable airbag systems before removal or when working in proximity of it to perform system tests.
- Prevent Electrostatic Discharge by grounding yourself to the vehicle frame or wear an anti-static strap.
- Never touch connector pins or soldered components on ECUs.

Typical Warning Symbol

INTRODUCTION

GOING GREEN

The automotive repair industry has always been in the forefront of environmental issues beginning back in the early 1960's when the PCV valve was mandated. As the decades rolled on more emission control components were added and more regulations were implemented.

In 1974, chlorine based chemicals (CFC) refrigerants were tied to environmental concerns with regard to ozone depletion. In 1987, steps were taken to phase out ozone depleting substances including the R-12 refrigerant used in mobile air conditioning systems. By 1995 the production of R-12 refrigerant in the USA ended and the switch to R-134a (which began in 1992) was completed on new production vehicles.

Increased concerns with regard to the global warming potential of R-134a lead the European Union to ban the use of R-134a in Mobile air conditioning systems beginning with new models in 2011. Presently a new refrigerant with less global impact than R-134a is being considered.

These global concerns regarding the release of refrigerants during the service of mobile A/C systems has resulted in revised standards for service procedures and equipment. To reduce refrigerant emissions during service, new equipment and servicing procedures have been developed. Additionally, improved system designs will result in reduced refrigerant emissions and increases in system operating efficiencies.

Notes:

SECTION 1 • ELECTRICAL BASICS

Notes:

Section 1: Electrical Basics

ELECTRICAL THEORY

What is electricity? In simple terms it is the movement of electrons in a conductor. Although electricity itself cannot be seen, its effects can be seen and often felt.

The number of electrons flowing past any point in a circuit in a unit of time is called current and is measured in amperes.

The external force pushing the electrons through the circuit is known as electromotive force, usually called voltage.

The third factor in electricity is resistance, which is the opposition to current flow.

To summarize, voltage is the pressure that moves the current, current does the work, and resistance is what slows down the current flow.

The flow of electrons must have a path to follow. This path is called a circuit. A circuit consists of: a power source, a form of circuit protection (a fuse or circuit breaker), a control (switch), wiring (the conductor), and a load.

The load is a device that changes the electrical energy into light, heat, or movement. *motors, relays, solenoids*

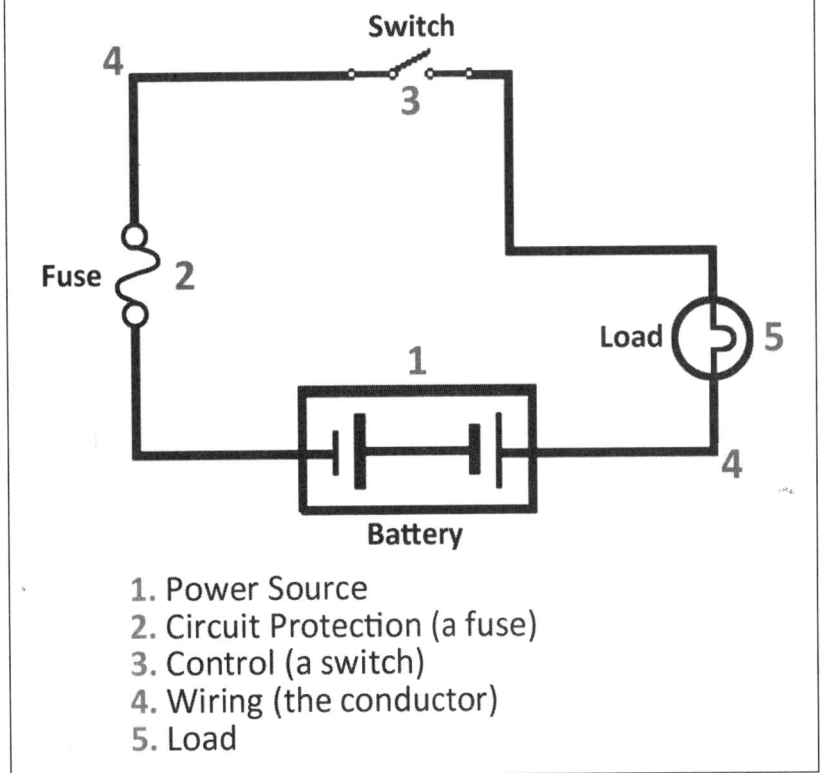

1. Power Source
2. Circuit Protection (a fuse)
3. Control (a switch)
4. Wiring (the conductor)
5. Load

A Typical Circuit

Three types of circuits are found on vehicles:

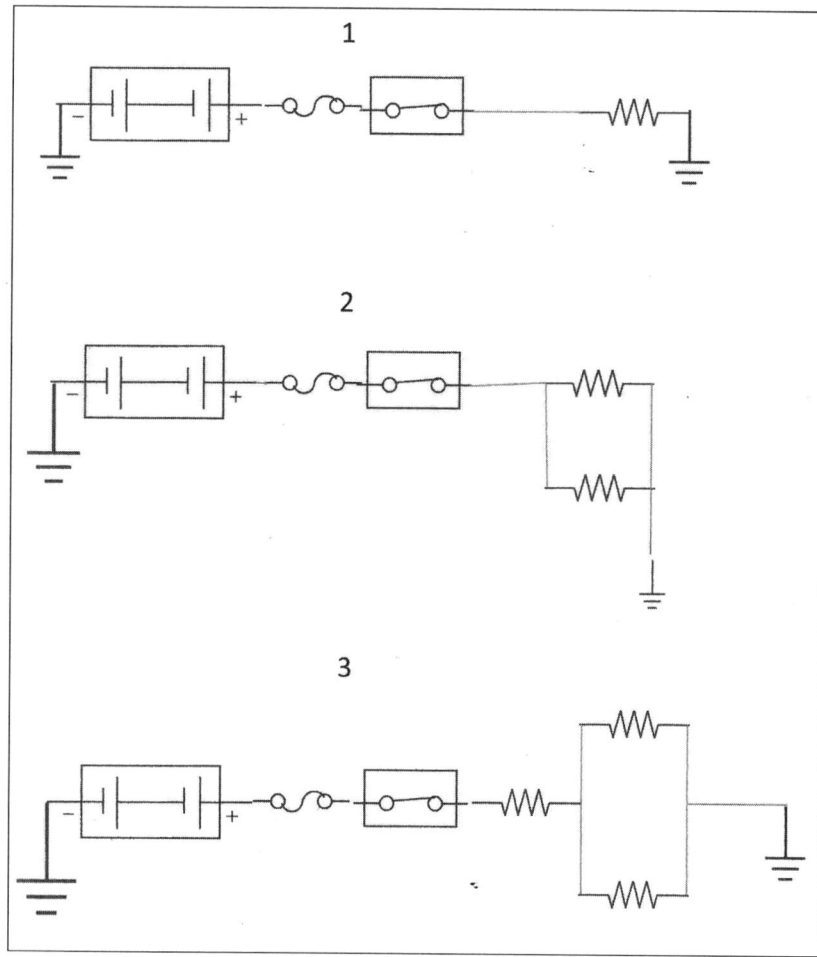

Automotive Circuit Designs

1. **Series:** This type of circuit provides only one path for current flow. There may be more than one load in the circuit. <u>The same current flows through the entire circuit.</u> A characteristic of a series circuit is that a break anywhere in the circuit will entirely stop electrical flow everywhere.

2. **Parallel:** A parallel circuit provides <u>two or more paths for current flow</u>. The current flowing in each path is determined by the electrical resistance of that path. <u>The total current flowing in the circuit will be equal to the sum of the currents flowing in the individual paths.</u> If the circuit is broken in one leg of the circuit, current will still flow in the other legs.

3. **Series Parallel:** <u>Some of the loads are in series and some are in parallel</u> with each other, so the characteristics of both types of circuits are found here.

On a motor vehicle, because <u>the frame and body are metal,</u> they serve as the <u>return path</u> that the electricity uses to get back to its source. This simplifies the wiring. Also, a drawing of a circuit uses a simple symbol that represents that return path as a "ground."

Notes:

Total circuit resistance is always less than value of the lowest ohms resistor

Switch will be in series

SECTION 1 • ELECTRICAL BASICS

Notes: A/C two directions

major resistance is where you do the most work

In any circuit, there are factors that affect a conductor's resistance. They are: material, area, and length. Temperature also has an effect on resistance.

The type of electricity produced by a vehicle's battery is called direct current (DC). Direct current flows in one direction only and is used to power most of the circuits on a motor vehicle.

Ohm's Law governs the relationship between current, voltage, and resistance in a circuit. To simplify the discussion, the analogy of water will be used.

Voltage is the electrical force that causes the movement of electrons.
- Unit of measure: Volts
- Symbol: E
- Water analogy: pressure; pounds per square inch (PSI)

Current is the rate of electron flow.
- Unit of measure: Amps
- Symbol: I
- Water analogy: rate of flow; gallons per minute (GPM)

Resistance is the opposition to current flow.
- Unit of measure: Ohms
- Symbol: R
- Water analogy: the size of the pipe   amount of friction

Remember: Voltage is the pressure that moves the current, current does the work, and resistance opposes the current flow.

Ohm's Law

Ohm's Law, (ohm - symbolized by the greek letter Omega [Ω]), states that there is a relationship between volts, amps, and resistance: the amount of current flow in a circuit depends on how much voltage and resistance there is in the circuit. The current flow in a circuit is directly proportional to circuit voltage and inversely proportional to circuit resistance.

1. When resistance stays the same:
   a. If voltage increases, current increases.
   b. If voltage decreases, current decreases.
2. When voltage stays the same:
   a. As resistance increases, current decreases.
   b. As resistance decreases, current increases.

The easiest way to use Ohm's Law is to use the circle seen on the left. The **E** represents voltage, the **I** stands for Amps, and the **R** is Resistance.

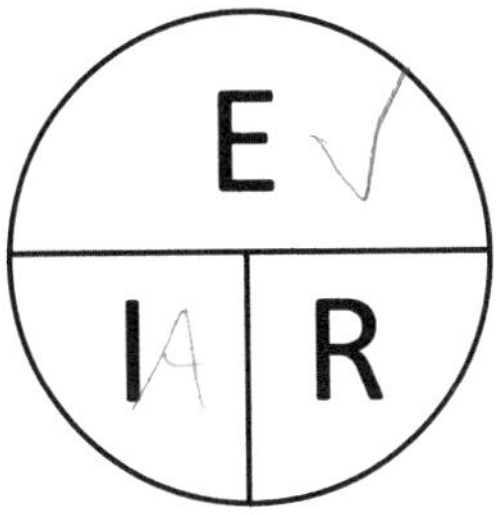

$E = I \times R$
$I = E \div R$
$R = E \div I$

Ohm's Law Circle

To determine any one of the three variables, we must know the other two. If values are known for any two factors, the third can be calculated.

For example, if the voltage and resistance values are known, cover the **I** (amps) in the circle to calculate current. In other words, to find amperage, divide voltage by resistance. This makes sense, since amperage is the result of the voltage pushing and the resistance opposing current flow.

PRACTICE APPLYING OHM'S LAW

Using the Ohm's Law circle, solve the problems below for the unknown:

1. E = 12v   R = 4Ω   I = _____   [answer: 3A]
2. R = 6Ω   I = 2A   E = _____   [answer: 12v]
3. E = 12V   I = 6A   R = _____   [answer: 2Ω]
4. E = 12V   R = 90Ω   I = _____   [answer: 0.133A]
5. R = 60Ω   I = 0.2A   E = _____   [answer: 12V]

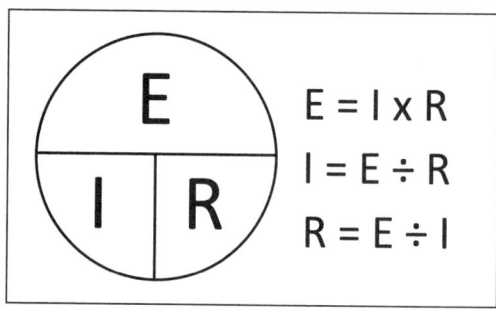

Ohm's Law Circle

The correct answers are in the parentheses. These values were found by covering the unknown on the Ohm's Law circle and performing the math needed.

Notice that the current flow changes as the resistance values change. An increase in resistance lowers the current flow when the voltage is held constant, while a decrease in resistance increases current flow. This is important to remember when diagnosing electrical problems.

An easy way to remember the relationships in Ohm's Law is to think of a teeter-totter. With voltage always constant, if current increases, resistance decreases. If resistance increases, current decreases.

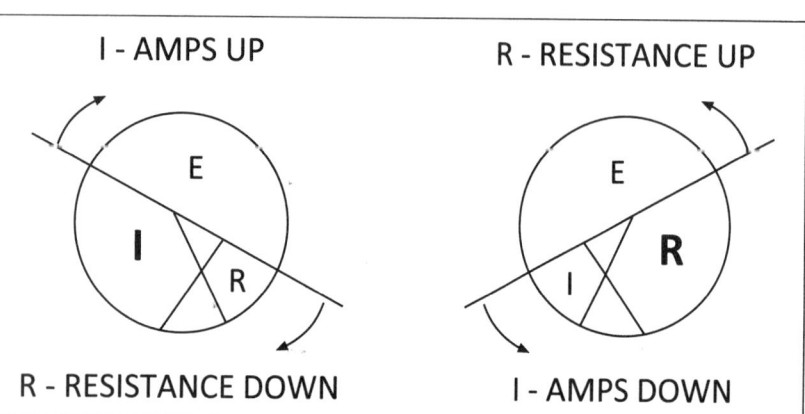

Seesaw

Ohm's Law Relationships

SECTION 1 • ELECTRICAL BASICS

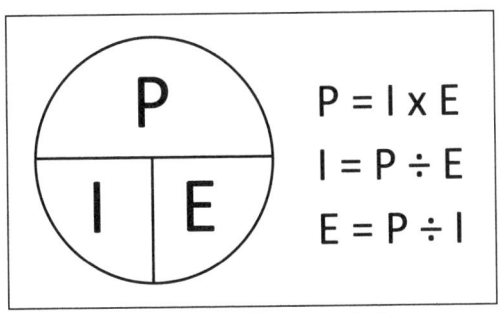
Watt's Law of Power Circle

Watt's Law

Just as Ohm's Law governs the relationship of voltage, current and resistance, Watt's Law pertains to power. Power measures the rate at which work is done, or the rate at which heat is generated. Voltage represents the pressure or force that causes current to move in a closed circuit. Work is done whenever a force causes motion. In an open circuit, where there is voltage present but there is no current flow, no work is done. A closed circuit is carrying current and voltage causing electrons to move, so work is done. The unit of measure for electric power is the watt.

The Power circle is used like the Ohm's Law circle: **P** represents Power (in watts), **I** represent amps, and **E** represents voltage. Simple math is used to find the watts value of a component. For example, a cooling fan may be rated at 150 watts, and an ammeter can be used to determine current flow. The voltage is 12 volts. To find the correct current value, the Power Law is applied: Cover the unknown (I) and do the math. With the I covered, the correct procedure is to divide Power (150) by Volts (12); the current should be 12.5 amps.

ELECTRICITY AND MAGNETISM

When current flows through a wire it creates a magnetic field around the wire. If the wire is formed into a coil, the magnetic field grows in strength and can become useful. The magnetic field cannot actually be seen, but its effects can be observed. Here are some common devices that rely on the principle of electromagnetism:

- Electromagnet – By inserting a steel rod into a coil of wire, and connecting the coil's wire leads to a battery, the steel rod will become a powerful magnet.
- Electromagnetic Clutch – Used to drive the compressor in an air conditioning system.
- Solenoid – When power is applied to the wire coil, a metal rod inserted into the coil will be pulled in.
- Motor – By placing one magnet inside another, then passing current through one of them, the opposite poles of each magnet will attempt to line up. Since opposite poles attract, motion will be created, thus turning the motor's shaft
- Relays – A relay is made up of an electromagnetic coil, a contact point set, and an armature. The armature is a movable device that allows the contacts to open and close.

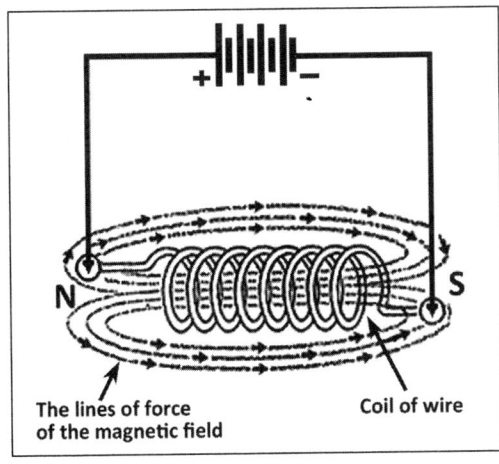
Magnetic Field

Magnetism provides a link between mechanical energy and electricity. Magnetism is very useful for many automotive systems, including controls and instrumentation.

Another principle relating to magnetism is induction. When an electrical conductor is passed through a magnetic field, current flows in the conductor. This principle is put to use in the generator, which is used to create the electricity used to charge the battery on a vehicle.

A side effect of induction is self-induction, which is usually undesirable. When current flow through a coil of wire (such as the air conditioning electromagnetic clutch or a solenoid) is suddenly stopped by opening a switch, the collapse of the magnetic field around the coil induces a voltage that opposes the change in current flow. This induced voltage is capable of producing an arc across the switch, damaging it. To prevent this, a diode is wired in parallel with the electromagnetic clutch or a solenoid. This "clamping diode" provides a path to ground for the induced voltage, preventing any damage due to arcing.

Notes:

SECTION 1 • ELECTRICAL BASICS

Section 1 Review – Electrical Basics

1. Technician A says voltage causes current to move through a circuit and resistance opposes the flow of current. Technician B says the load converts electrical energy into increased resistance. Who is correct?
   A. Technician A
   B. Technician B
   C. Both Technician A and Technician B
   D. Neither Technician A nor Technician B

2. True or False: A typical automotive electrical circuit contains a power source, a circuit protection device, a control device, conductors and a load.
   A. True
   B. False

3. Regarding the following statements:
   A. Ohm's Law states that as circuit resistance increases, current flow in the circuit also increases.
   B. Ohm's Law states that as circuit resistance increases, circuit source voltage also increases.
   Which statement(s) is/are correct?
   A. Statement A is correct
   B. Statement B is correct
   C. Both statements are correct
   D. Neither statement is correct

4. If the voltage in a circuit is 12 volts and the resistance of the circuit is 4 ohms, what is the current value?
   A. 16 amps
   B. 48 amps
   C. 3 amps
   D. 8 amps

5. Technician A says a conductor that has current flowing through it will develop a magnetic field. Technician B says the clamping diode used with the A/C compressor clutch increases the current flow through the clutch circuit. Who is correct?
   A. Technician A
   B. Technician B
   C. Both Technician A and Technician B
   D. Neither Technician A nor Technician B

Notes:

Notes:

SECTION 2 • THE MULTIMETER & CIRCUIT DESIGNS

Section 2: The Multimeter and Circuit Designs

METERS

There are two types of multimeters: analog and digital.

An analog meter uses a needle that "sweeps" the scale on the meter. This type of meter should never be used on a computer circuit. When an analog meter is connected, it essentially changes the value of the circuit, and can do damage to a computer circuit. Also, the reading produced is less accurate than that given by most digital meters.

A digital multimeter (DMM) is actually a computer itself, and typically has a very high input impedance, on the order of 10 million ohms (10 megohms). Thus, when it is used on a computer circuit, there is no risk of circuit damage, and its reading will be quite accurate.

A digital multimeter is one of the most important tools for HVAC electrical and electronics testing and diagnosis. There are many DMMs on the market, and price should not be the key factor in meter selection. Choose one that provides the functions needed.

Test lights, which are very popular, have far less impedance, and actually add a load to the circuit, or could shut the circuit down. The advantage of a DMM is that it will not harm the vehicle and its reading constantly updates concerning the data on the circuit or the component being tested.

Meter Checks on Circuits

Accurate diagnosis of problems in electrical circuits requires the ability to use meters to measure voltage, voltage drop, current and resistance. The digital mulitmeter has all these functions built in.

To measure DC voltage, set the DMM to the DC voltage scale, and place the leads in the proper jacks.

1. Set the voltage scale to the highest level.*
2. Connect the negative lead of the DMM to the negative battery terminal or another good ground.
3. Touch the positive lead of the DMM to the battery (positive) side of the load.
4. Operate the circuit.
5. If needed, adjust the scale to the setting that gives voltage reading for that circuit.*

*Note: Many DMMs contain an "auto-range" feature.

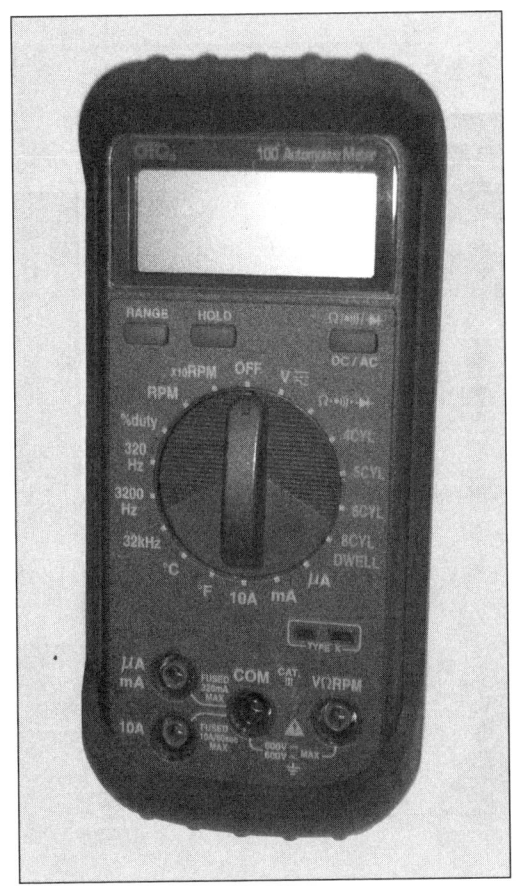

Digital Multimeter

6. The DMM will indicate the available voltage at that point in the circuit.

7. If the voltage reading is not equal to source voltage, work back point by point toward the battery until the voltage reading is correct. This will indicate where more testing is needed. With computer circuits, corrosion at connections can easily reduce the voltage available in a circuit and produce problems.

Meter Scaling

In many instances, the basic units of electricity (volts, amps, and ohms) are too "large" (or small) to allow accurate measurement in an automotive circuit. Smaller (and larger) units of measure are available.

Digital multimeters work on the base number of 10, making it possible to change the unit by moving the decimal point. The decimal point moves three places with each prefix. The most common prefixes are micro, milli, kilo, and mega. The meter will display which unit it is reading on the face of the meter.

The common prefixes (and the value of each) are shown below:

Prefix	Symbol	Multiplier
Meg, Mega	M	1 million
Kilo	K	1 thousand
milli	m	One thousandth 0.001
micro	µ	One millionth 0.000001

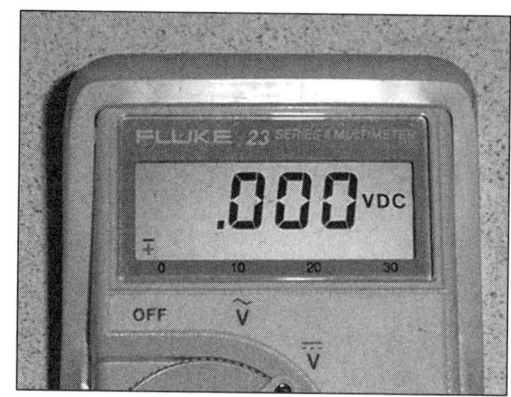

Digital Meter Display

Notes:

SECTION 2 • THE MULTIMETER & CIRCUIT DESIGNS

The following table shows examples of basic values and also displays them with an appropriate prefix. The most common ranges that will be used during diagnosis and troubleshooting are from mega to micro.

3,500 Ω	=	3.5 KΩ
1,200 Ω	=	1.2 KΩ
120 KΩ	=	120,000 Ω
3,500,000 Ω	=	3.5 MΩ
6.3 MΩ	=	6,300,000 Ω
0.000355 A	=	355 µA
0.000355 A	=	0.355 mA
863 mV	=	0.863 V
657 Ω	=	0.657 KΩ
35 µA	=	0.000035 A
10 KΩ + 1000 Ω	=	11,000 Ω
500 KV	=	0.5 MV
7,500,000 µA	=	7.5A

Many DMMs have an "autorange" feature. This means the meter will automatically select the range, or setting, that provides the highest accuracy. However, in some instances, it may be necessary for the user to select the desired scale.

The digital multimeter is designed to perform multiple functions. Care must be taken when using the meter for various tests to protect the meter from damage and to get the correct information from the device or circuit being tested.

For example, when measuring resistance (ohms), the circuit must not be energized.

Also, when using the meter to measure current (amps, milliamps) the meter must be in series with the circuit. If a meter set to amps is mistakenly placed in parallel with the circuit, the fuse built into the meter will blow, preventing meter damage. Perhaps the easiest way to measure current is to use what is called an inductive pickup, which is clamped around a cable or wire, thus eliminating the need to "open" the circuit.

THE MULTIMETER & CIRCUIT DESIGNS • SECTION 2

The diagram below shows the different hookups used to measure resistance, voltage, and current using a DMM.

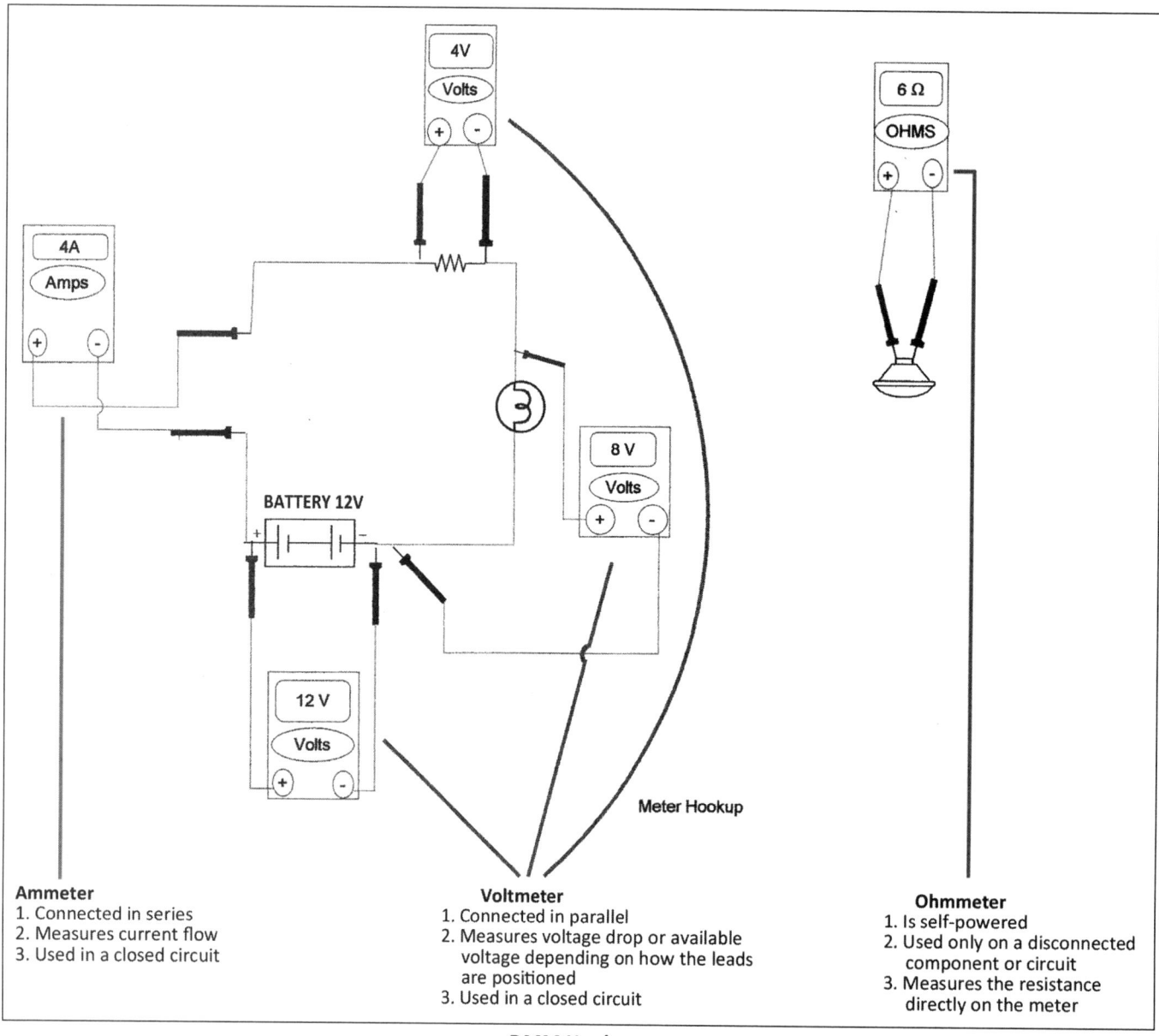

Ammeter
1. Connected in series
2. Measures current flow
3. Used in a closed circuit

Voltmeter
1. Connected in parallel
2. Measures voltage drop or available voltage depending on how the leads are positioned
3. Used in a closed circuit

Ohmmeter
1. Is self-powered
2. Used only on a disconnected component or circuit
3. Measures the resistance directly on the meter

DMM Hookups

Notes:

SECTION 2 • THE MULTIMETER & CIRCUIT DESIGNS

The Voltmeter

A voltmeter measures the difference in voltage between two points in a circuit. The two leads are polarity sensitive. The red lead connects to the positive side of the circuit, and the black lead to the negative or ground side. However, if a DMM is hooked up backward, the meter will display a "-" (minus) sign in front of the reading.

The voltmeter is always connected in parallel with the circuit or the component being tested. Think of the voltmeter like a pressure gauge; when using a tire pressure gauge, the purpose is to read the tire pressure, not change it. It is the same with the voltmeter; the meter should read the value without changing it. The high impedance of a DMM allows this to happen. If an analog meter is used, the reading may differ from the actual value, due to the low resistance of the meter.

The meter hookup will determine if the reading is voltage drop or available voltage. The diagram below shows two hookups, both of which are parallel connections.

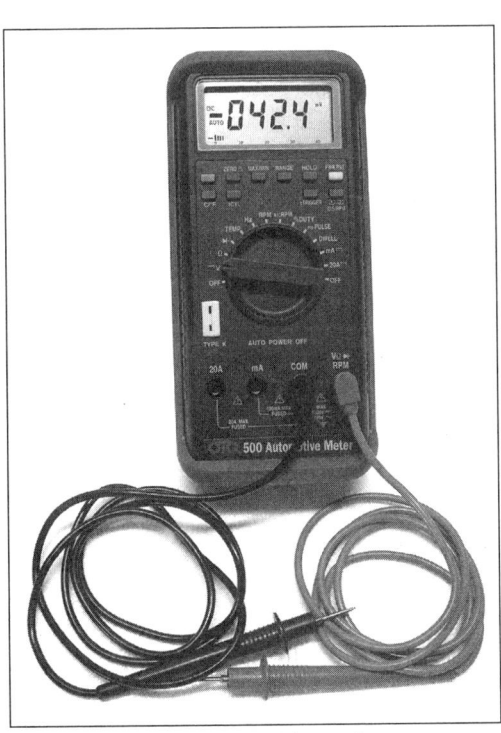

Voltmeter with Leads

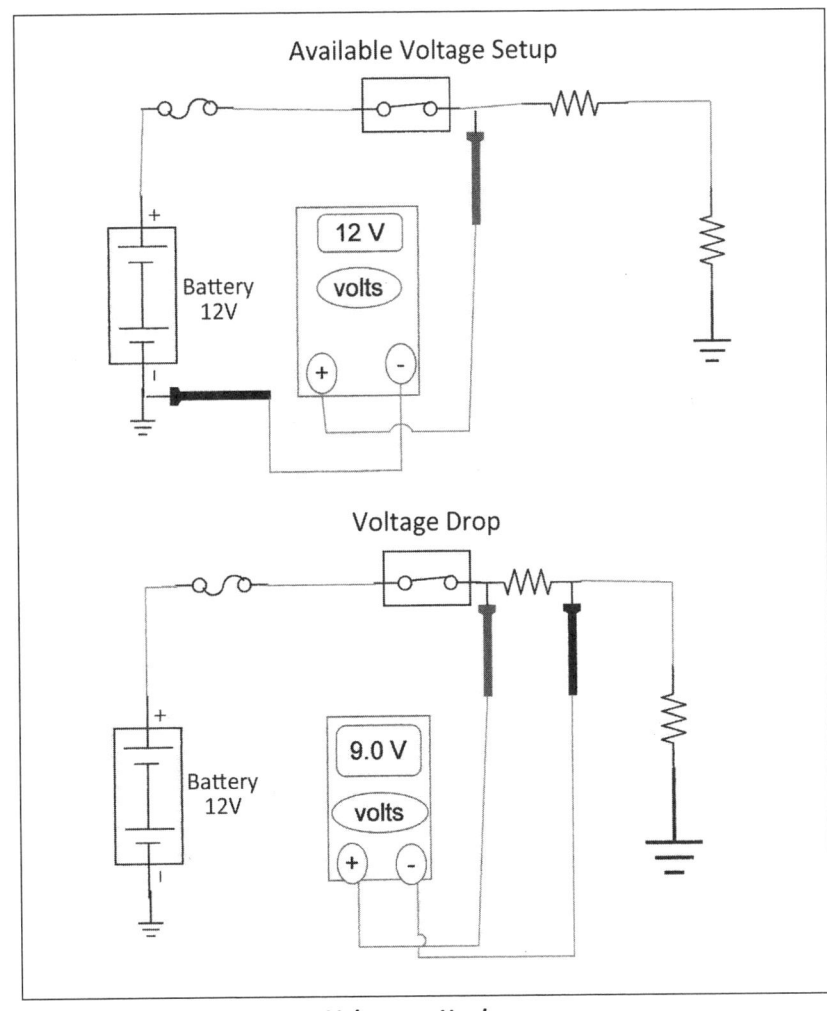

Voltmeter Hookups

The Ammeter

An ammeter measures the flow of current in a circuit. The ammeter is connected in series. The same two test leads are used, but the red lead is moved to the "A" jack. The maximum current flow through most meters is 10 amps. If 10 amps are exceeded, a fuse in the meter will blow. Although the replacement fuse may be costly, it certainly is less than the cost of meter replacement.

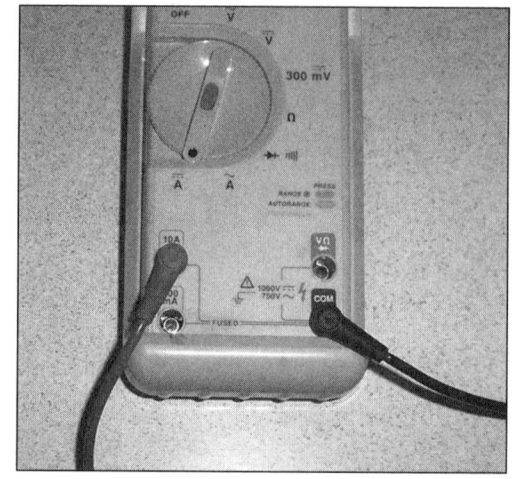

Ammeter with Leads

Since many current loads (such as a blower motor) will exceed 10 amps, an (inductive) amp clamp, mentioned earlier, which plugs into the meter is available. The clamp reads the strength of the magnetic field to determine the amount of current that is flowing.

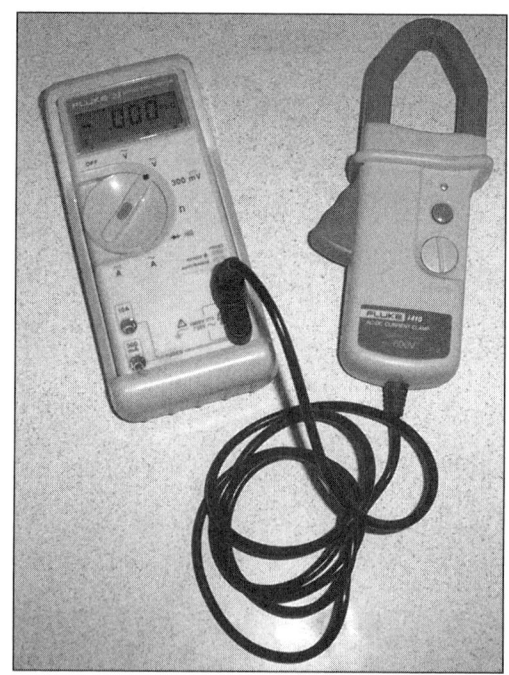

Ammeter with Amp Clamp

Notes:

SECTION 2 • THE MULTIMETER & CIRCUIT DESIGNS

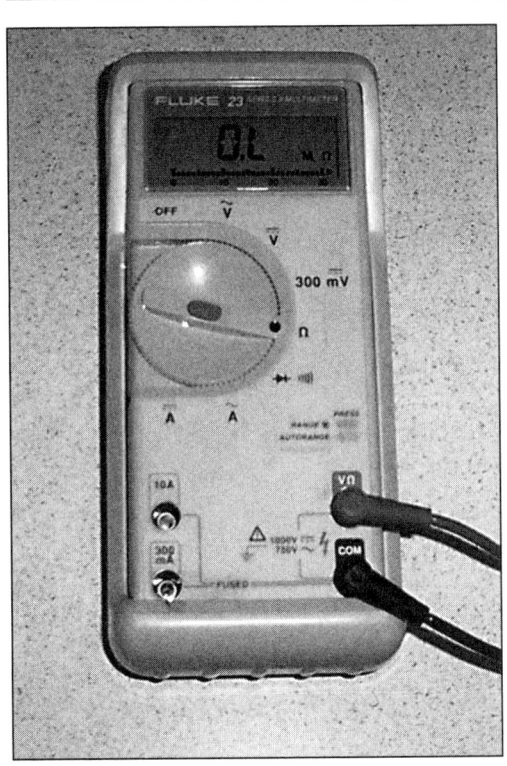

Ohmmeter with Leads

The Ohmmeter

An ohmmeter measures the resistance in a circuit or a component. The same two test leads, red and black, are used. The test leads are in the same jacks used for voltmeter testing, however the selector knob is moved to the "ohms" position.

The ohmmeter has its own power source. Therefore, the component or circuit wiring that is being tested must be disconnected or isolated from the rest of the circuit to be tested properly. The ohmmeter can be used to check a circuit for continuity. Some meters are equipped with a buzzer that will sound if the circuit is complete.

An ohmmeter can show a complete circuit even if one or more strands in a wire are broken. Because of this, it is recommended that a circuit be tested under load with a voltmeter to check for proper circuit operation.

Below is the ohmmeter being used to measure resistance in a circuit and measuring the resistance of a component.

Never connect an ohmmeter to a live circuit; the meter readings will be inaccurate and the meter can be damaged.

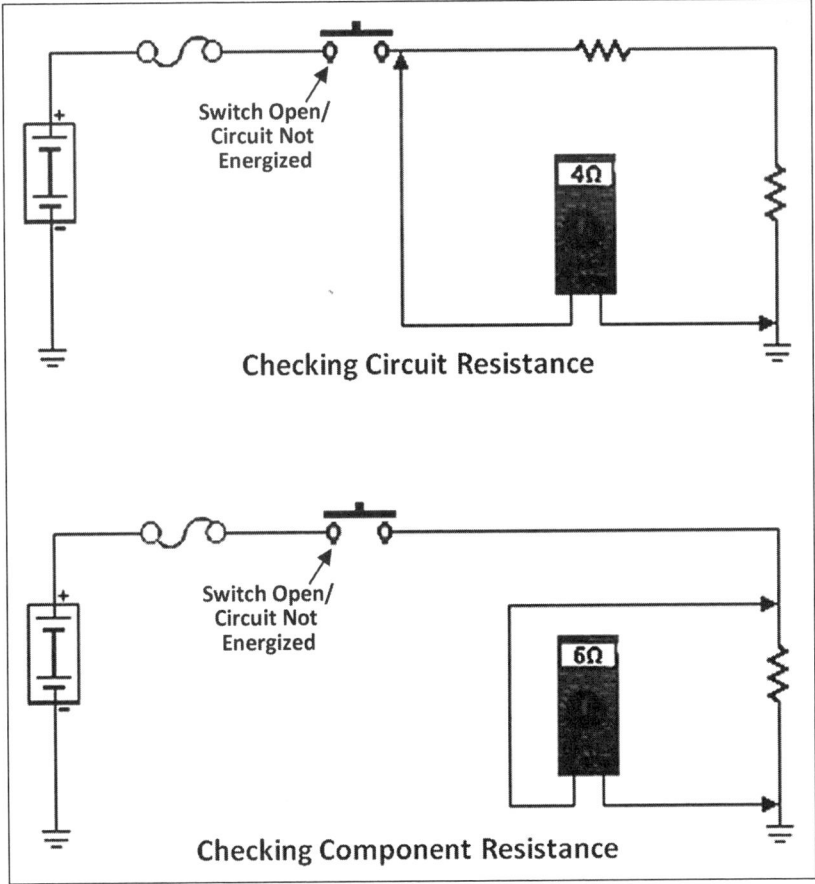

Ohmmeter Check of Resistance

CIRCUIT DESIGNS

For electrical devices to operate, there must be a complete path from the power source to the device and back. This circular path is a complete circuit. There are different circuit designs used depending on the circuit. As discussed earlier, the three basic design are series, parallel and series-parallel.

Power supply   load   ground

Series Circuits

Below is a diagram of a series circuit. In a series circuit, the components are connected end to end, and there is only one path for current flow. If any portion of the circuit becomes open, the entire circuit will be open, and no work will be done.

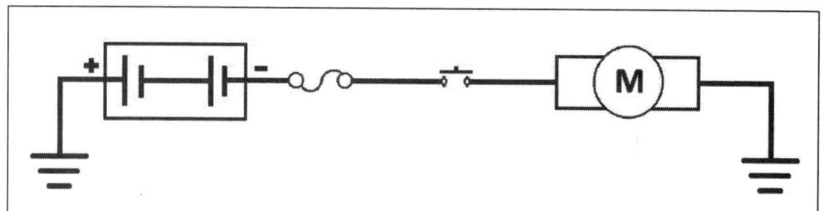

Series Circuit Diagram

SERIES CIRCUIT LAWS

- In a series circuit the current flow is the same at any point in the circuit.
- Total circuit resistance is equal to the sum of all individual resistances.
- The voltage drops across the resistances will be different if the component resistances are different.
- The sum of the individual voltage drops equals source voltage.

Notes:

SECTION 2 • THE MULTIMETER & CIRCUIT DESIGNS

Below, Ohm's Law has been used to calculate circuit values. Source voltage is divided by resistance to calculate current. As the laws of a series circuit state, total circuit resistance is the sum of the individual resistances. Current flow is the same at any point in the circuit, and the sum of the individual voltage drops equals source voltage.

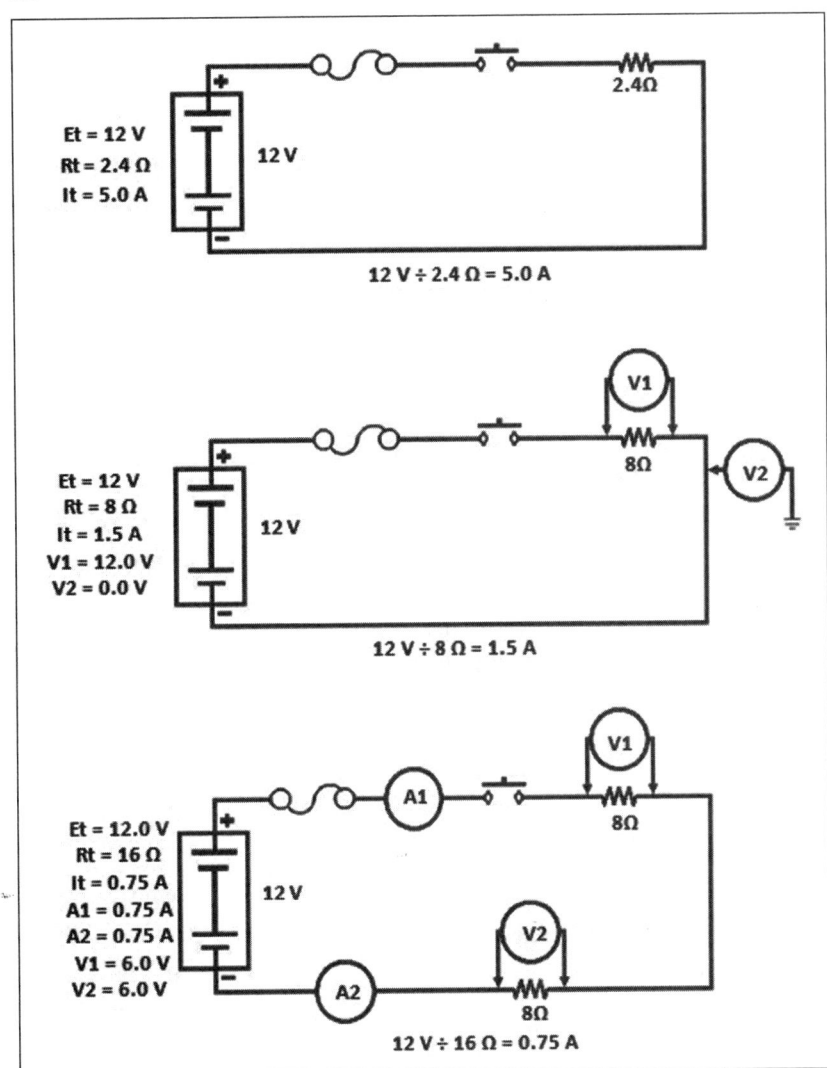

Ohm's Law Used

Parallel Circuits

Parallel circuits are connected to the same power source but have separate, independent paths for current flow. If one leg of a parallel circuit is open, the other legs will continue to operate. Parallel circuits share a common fuse; if it fails all the parallel legs will be affected. Parallel circuits will have a branching point; this is a terminal or connection where the circuits or components are connected.

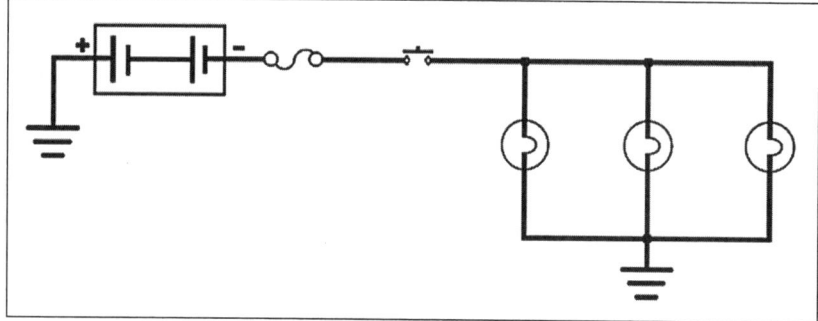

Parallel Circuit

PARALLEL CIRCUIT LAWS

- The voltage is the same across each branch.
- If any leg of the circuit consists of more than one resistance, the voltages across the individual resistances are in proportion to the resistance values.
- The total circuit current is the sum of the currents in the individual branches.
- Current flow through the legs of the circuit will be different if the resistances of the legs are different.
- Total circuit resistance is always less than that of the smallest branch. IR Drop

Notes:

SECTION 2 • THE MULTIMETER & CIRCUIT DESIGNS

PARALLEL CIRCUIT EXAMPLES

When working with parallel circuits, there are different formulas for calculating the total resistance. As shown in the image below, when there are only two parallel resistances, resistance total can be found by multiplying the two values, and then dividing that by the sum of the two values. In this example, 12 x 6 = 72. Then add: 12 + 6 = 18. Now divide 72 by 18 – the total resistance is 4 ohms.

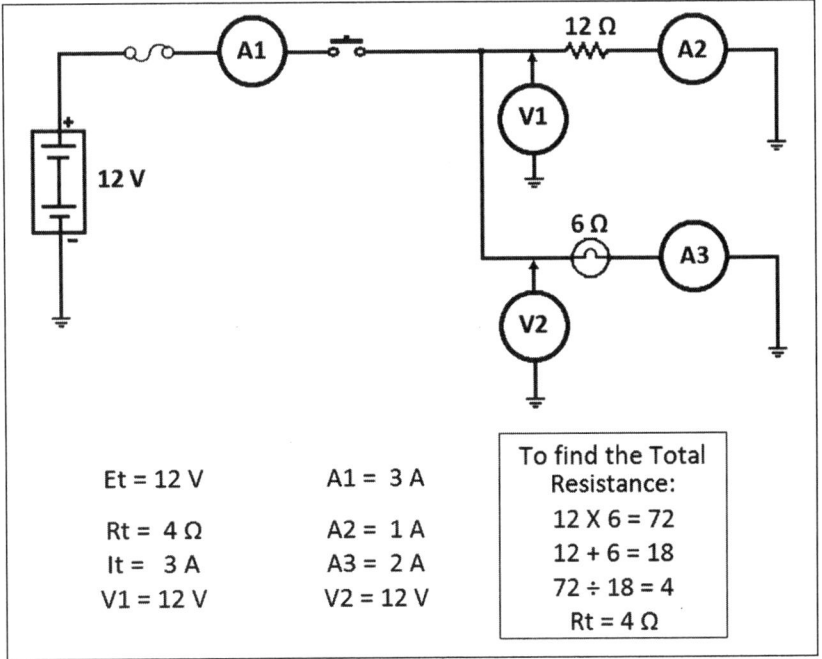

Parallel Circuit Example

Notes:

As shown in the image below, the reciprocal formula must be used when there are three or more different resistance values. A reciprocal is calculated by dividing the value of the individual resistance into the number one.

For example, the reciprocal of 2 is calculated by dividing 2 into 1, in other words: Ω, or 0.5

Divide the resistance of each leg into one. Add the values from each leg together, and then divide that number into one, see below for example.

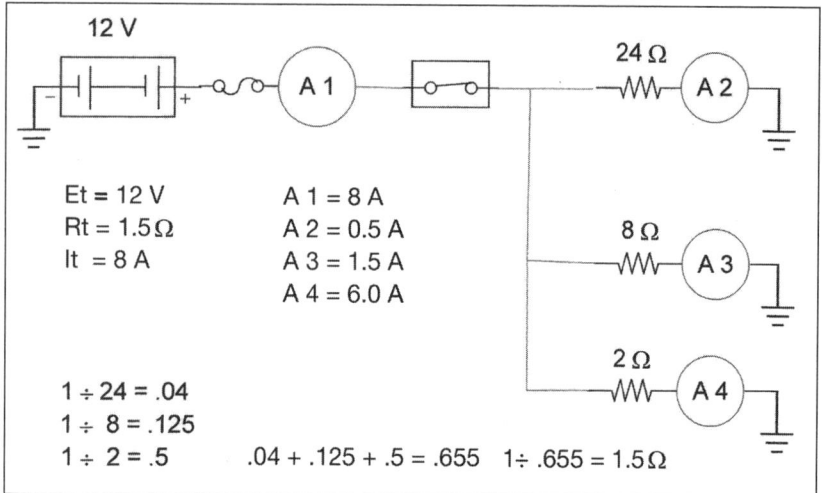
Parallel Circuit Resistance Example

If all the resistance values are the same, take the value of one resistance and divide by the total number of resistors. The image below represents a bank of fuel injectors; the resistance value for each injector is 18 ohms. There are four injectors on the circuit; divide a single injector's resistance (18 Ω) by the total number of injectors (4). This will give the total resistance value for that circuit (4.5 Ω).

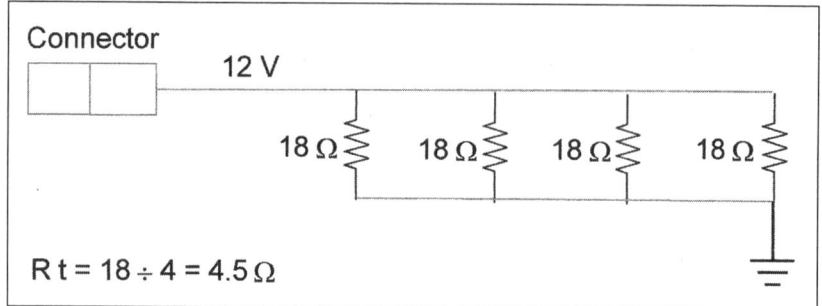
Fuel Injector Bank Resistance Values

Notes:

SECTION 2 • THE MULTIMETER & CIRCUIT DESIGNS

Series-Parallel Circuits

The image below shows that a series-parallel circuit is a combination of a series circuit and a parallel circuit. It has two or more loads in the parallel, plus an additional load or loads in the series leg. If there is a problem in the series portion of the circuit, it will affect all of the parallel legs.

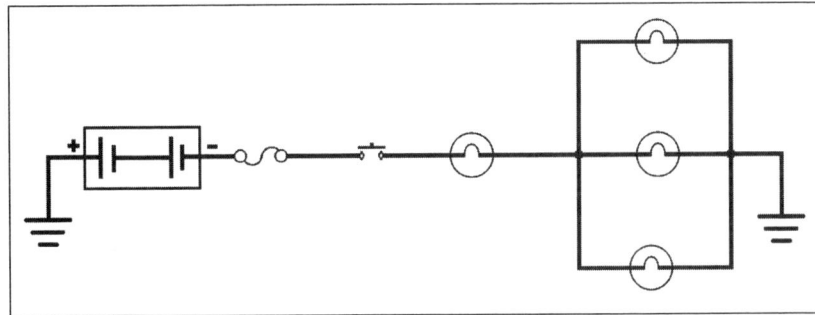

Series Parallel Circuit

To calculate total circuit resistance in a series parallel circuit, first find the resistance value for the parallel legs. The diagram below shows the value is 4 ohms. (12 x 6) divided by (12 + 6). In other words, 72 ÷ 18 = 4. Add this to the series leg resistance (10 ohms), and the total circuit resistance is 14 ohms.

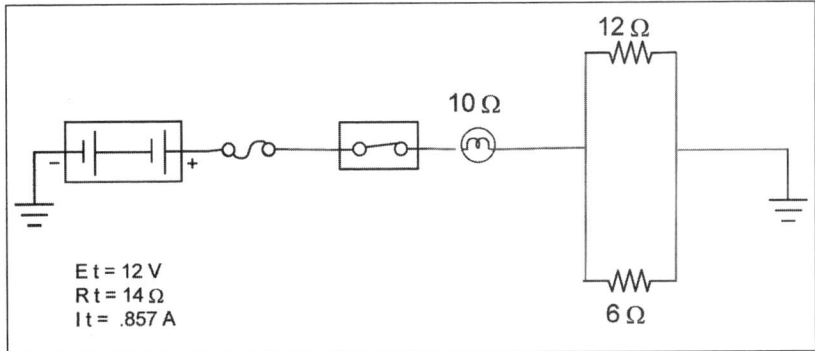

Series Parallel Circuit Example

Notes:

Circuit Faults

There are two common types of circuit faults – an open circuit or a shorted circuit.

Below is an example of an open circuit, which is where the circuit's complete path is broken. In this case, a connector has opened up, breaking the circuit. Depending on where the break occurs, the electrons cannot get from the source to the load, or they cannot get back to the source (as is the case here). Either way, no current flows and the circuit will not operate.

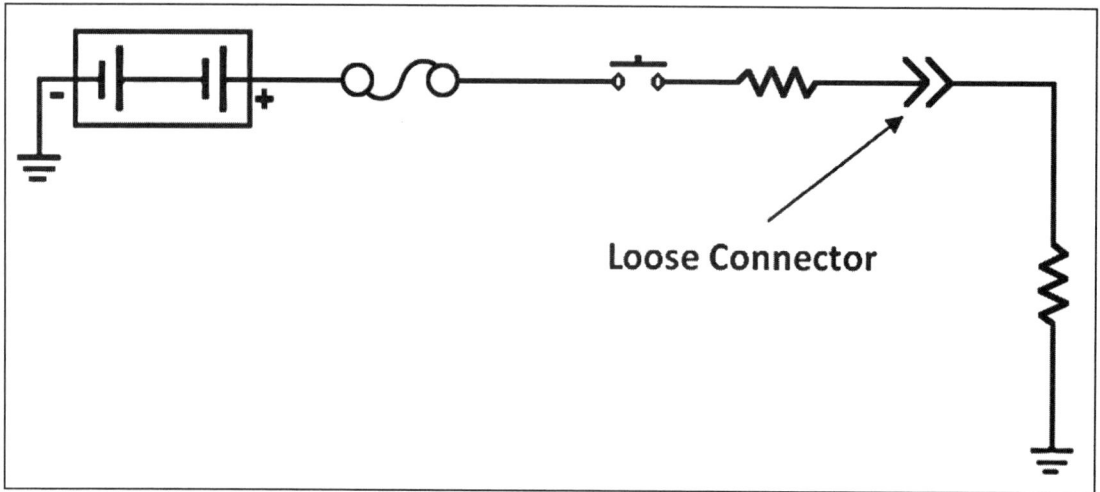

An Open Circuit - Path Broken

The image below shows a short to ground, which provides an unwanted path for the electrons to flow to ground. If the short to ground is on the battery (or power) side of the load, the circuit's fuse will blow, as there will be no load present to control the current in the circuit.

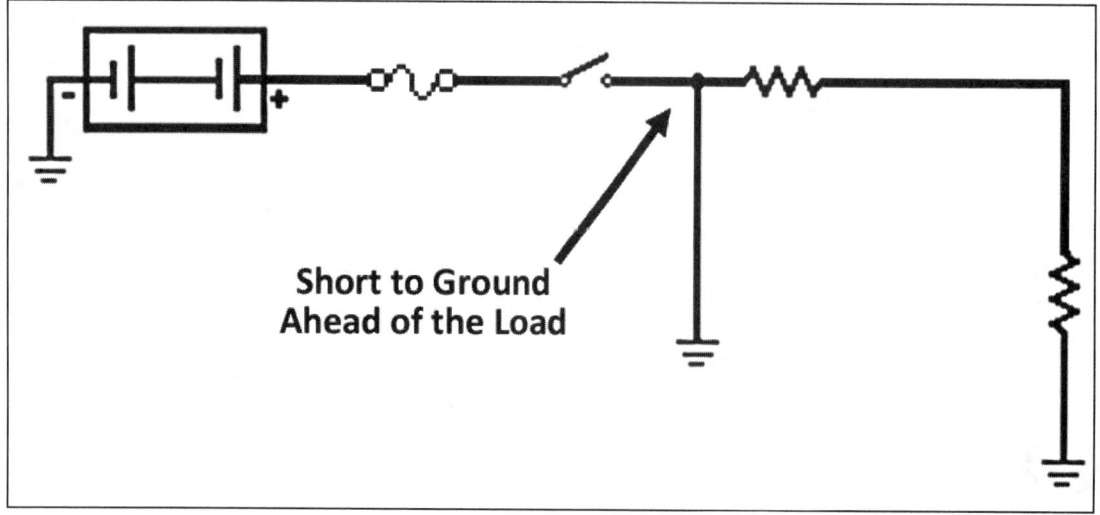

Short to Ground Ahead of the Load

The image below also shows a short to ground. In this situation, the motor will have a constant ground, resulting in the switch being ineffective and the motor running all the time.

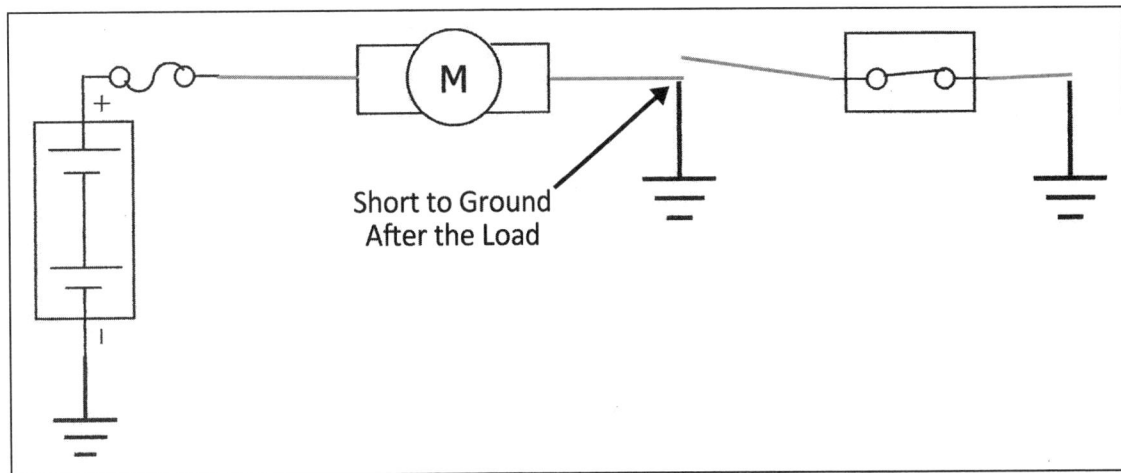

A Short Circuit to Ground After the Load, but Before the Switch

Another situation can be a short to power. This can be caused when the insulation on a wire is damaged and voltage from one circuit feeds into another circuit. This may result in a switch controlling more than just the intended circuit, or voltage feedback, causing the circuits to do abnormal things. One example of a short to voltage is when the parking light filament in a tail lamp bulb shorts across to the stop light filament. When the headlamps are turned on, the turn signal indicator in the instrument cluster will illuminate.

Notes:

Testing for Voltage Drop

There are various ways to perform a voltage drop test, depending on what the interest is. The A/C clutch circuit is a series circuit with only one load. In the image below, the voltage drop across the A/C compressor clutch is being checked.

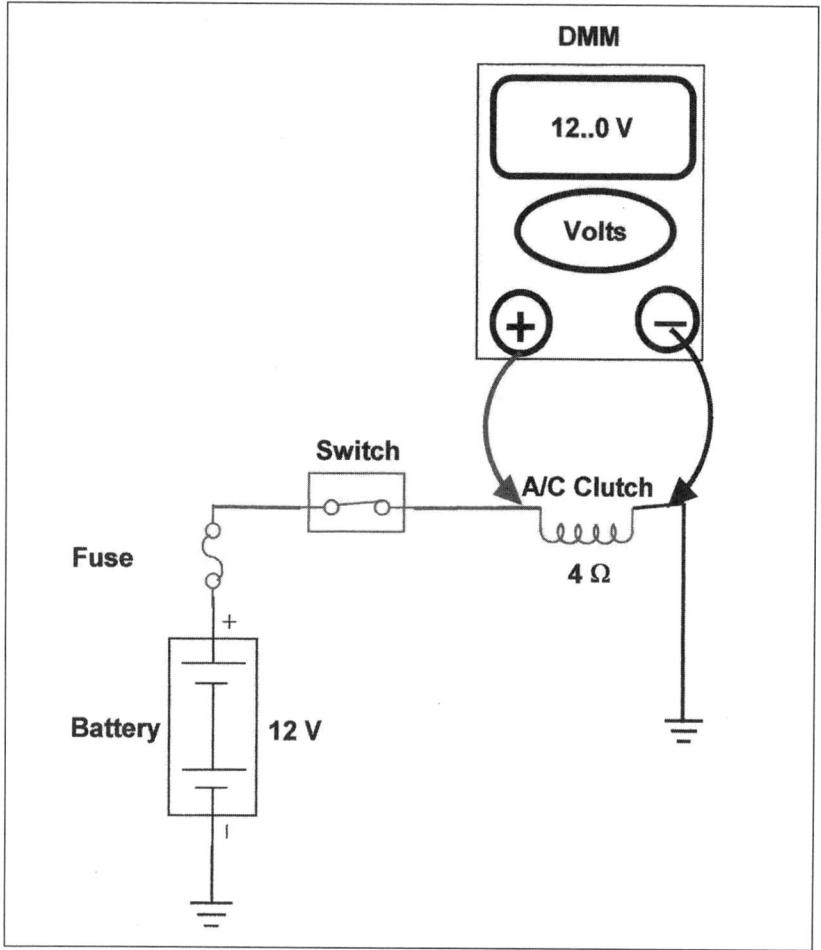

Voltage Drop Test - A/C Compressor Clutch

Notes:

SECTION 2 • THE MULTIMETER & CIRCUIT DESIGNS

Check the circuit as follows:

1. Connect the positive lead of the voltmeter to the battery feed terminal of the A/C clutch coil.
2. Connect the negative voltmeter lead to the ground terminal of the A/C clutch coil.
3. Operate the A/C clutch.
4. The voltmeter will display the difference in the voltage between the two terminals.

The voltage across the A/C clutch coil will be very close to source voltage if the circuit is operating properly.

If the voltage across the clutch coil is below source voltage, there may be a problem reducing the voltage available to the clutch.

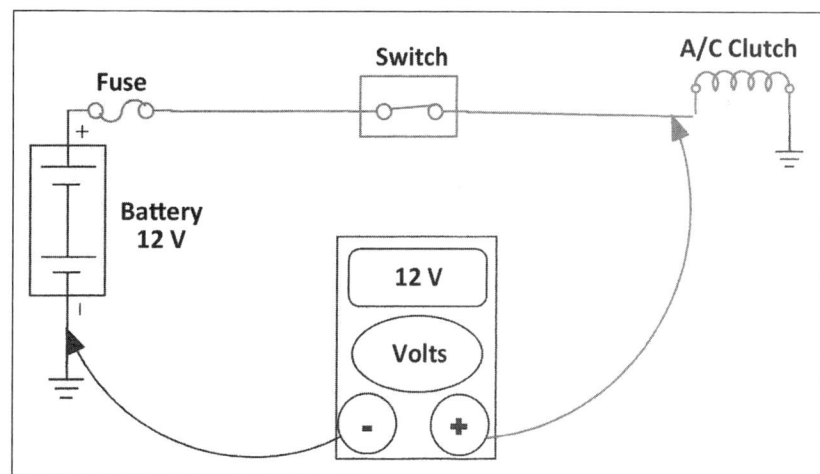

Voltage Available to Clutch Coil

To check for this, connect the voltmeter as shown below:

1. Connect the positive lead of the voltmeter to the battery feed terminal of the A/C clutch coil.
2. Connect the negative voltmeter lead to the negative battery terminal.
3. Operate the A/C clutch.
4. The voltmeter will display the voltage available to the clutch coil.

The voltage available to the clutch coil should be very close to source voltage. If it is not, it is likely that voltage is being lost somewhere between the battery and the clutch coil positive terminal, possibly due to corrosion at a connection.

Another possible problem is an unwanted voltage drop on the ground side of the clutch. As shown below, voltage drop is being measured on a circuit that has unwanted resistance on the ground side. The voltmeter shows 8.57 volts when checked from the clutch coil's positive terminal to its negative terminal. Since this is a series circuit, the sum of the voltage drops must equal source voltage. This reading indicates that there is unwanted resistance in the A/C clutch coil circuit. Again, corroded connectors are a common cause of this. The image illustrates that the unwanted resistance is shown in the ground circuit.

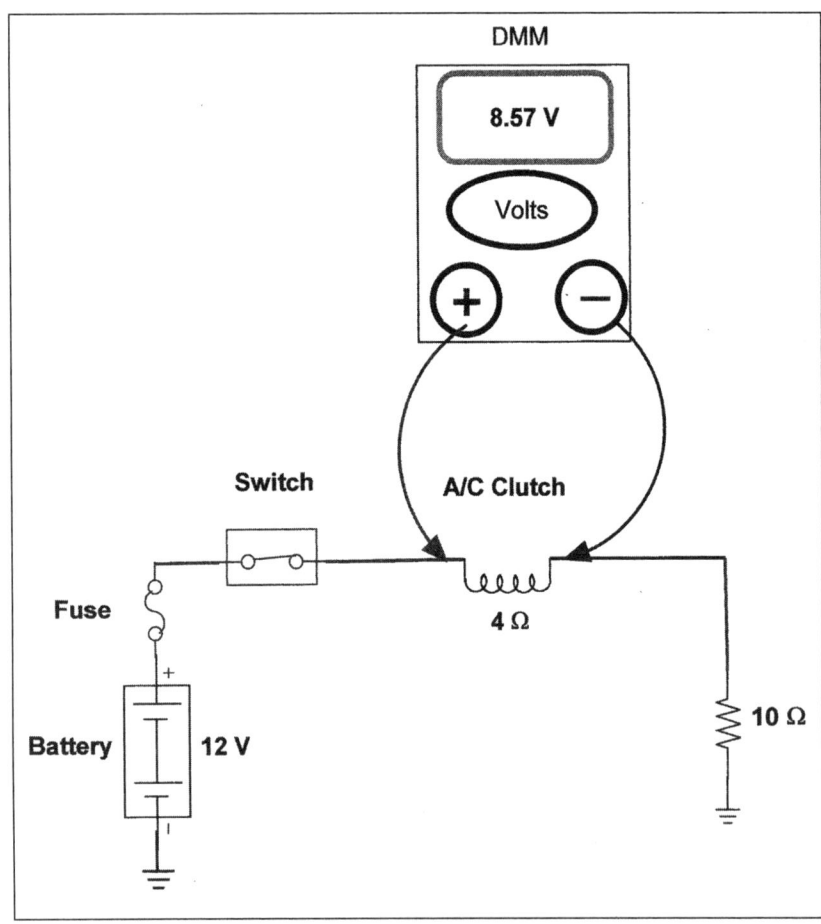

Clutch Ground-Side Voltage Drop

To find the excessive resistance, move the DMM negative lead to the negative battery post, and using the positive lead, work connector by connector through the circuit, until the meter reading drops to a normal voltage drop value (0.2 volt per connection or 0.5 volt or less over an entire circuit). The excessive resistance is located between that point and the point prior to it.

This same process also could be used to locate an unwanted voltage drop somewhere between the battery and the clutch coil if the clutch available voltage is low.

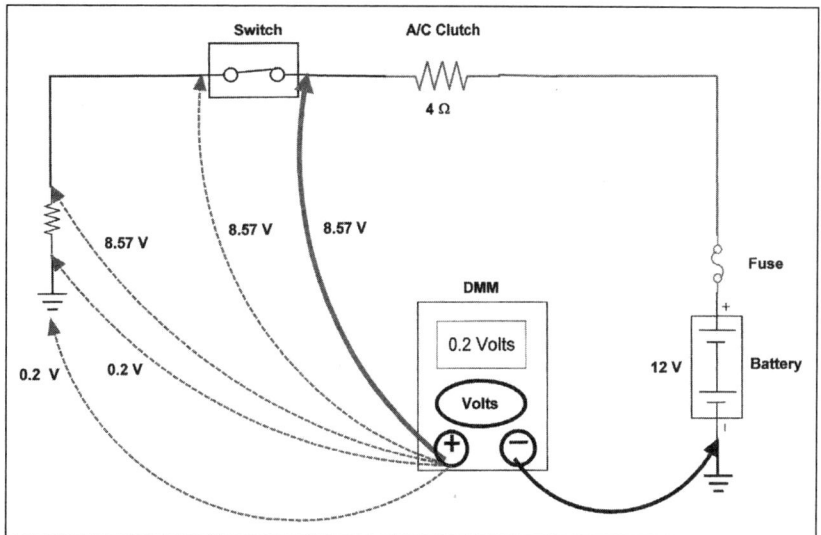

Voltage Drop Between Battery and Clutch

The image below shows a voltage drop across two loads in a series circuit. Both of the bulbs have the same resistance value, so the voltage drop across each bulb will be 1/2 the total circuit voltage. In a series circuit, the total voltage drop must equal the source voltage.

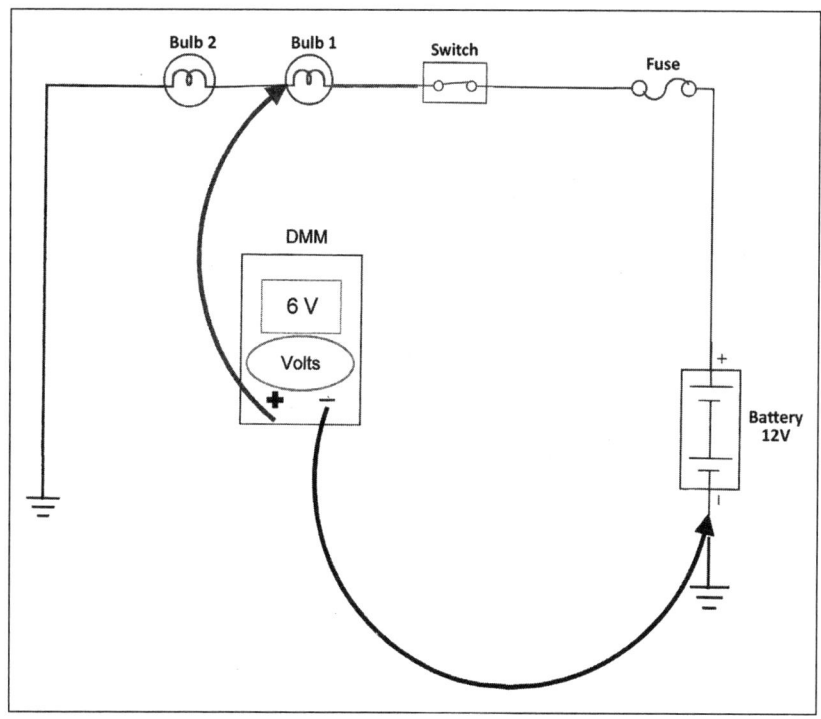

Voltage Drop Across Bulb 1

THE MULTIMETER & CIRCUIT DESIGNS • SECTION 2

The image below shows a DMM being used to measure current flow.

1. The DMM must be placed in series with the circuit. Find a convenient point in the circuit to connect the DMM. This can be at the switch, the fuse panel, or a connector.

2. Place the meter leads in the correct jacks; the maximum current rating of the meter must not be exceeded, or the meter fuse will blow.

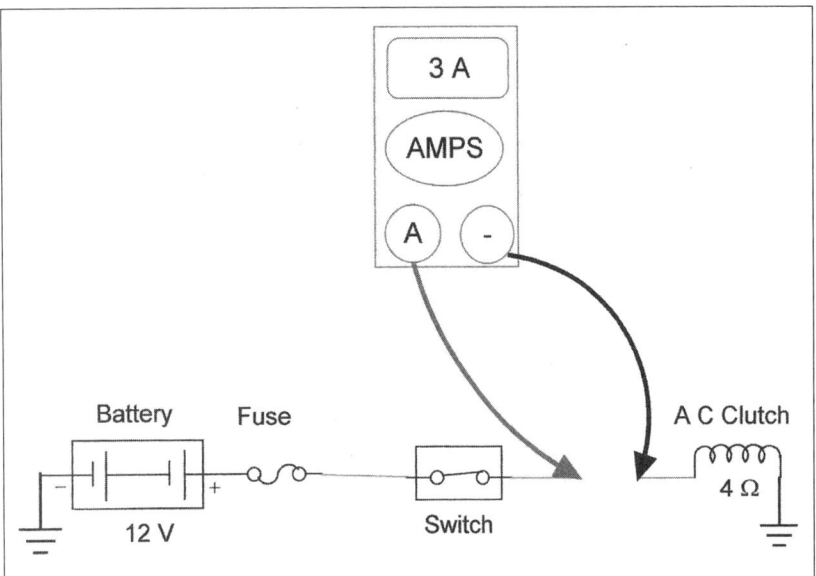

DMM Used to Measure Current Flow

3. Operate the circuit and read the value on the meter.

   If the ampere reading is:

   a. Zero – The circuit is open or not powered up.

   b. Higher than specifications – There could be a short circuit to ground or the circuit is bypassing the load.

   c. Lower than specifications – Too much resistance in the circuit or low available voltage.

The DMM can also be used with an inductive amp clamp to check current flow without opening the circuit.

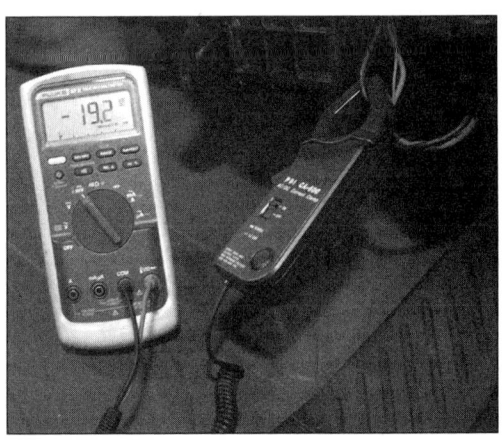

DMM with Inductive Amp Clamp

SECTION 2 • THE MULTIMETER & CIRCUIT DESIGNS

The image below shows a DMM being used to measure resistance, specifically that of a compressor clutch coil.

1. Disconnect the load to be tested from the circuit and other loads.
2. The ohmmeter has its own voltage supply, never connect an ohmmeter to a live circuit.
3. Touch the leads to the load terminals; polarity does not have to be observed.
4. Be sure the meter is on the correct scale (Ω).

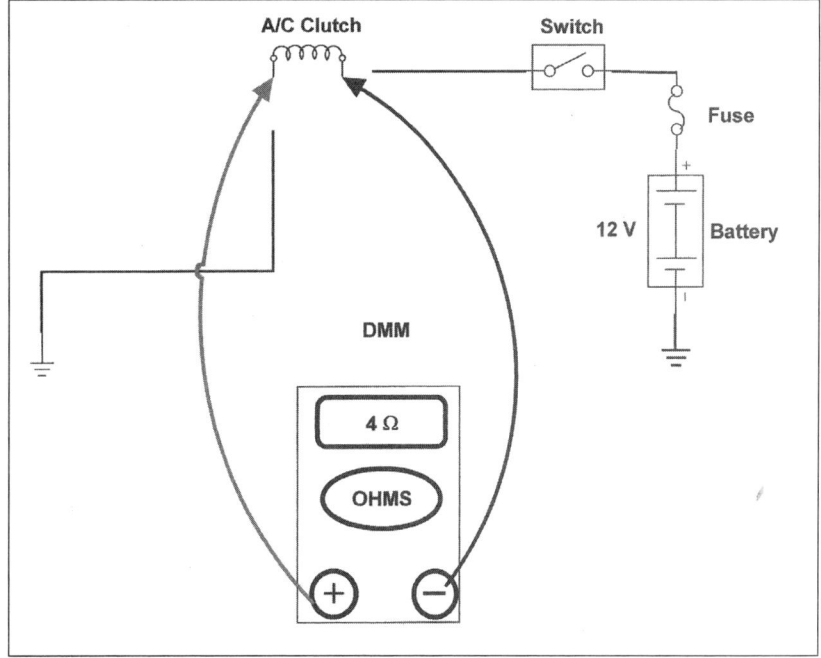

Compress Clutch Coil Resistance Being Measured with the DMM

To measure resistance to ground, touch one lead to the terminal and the other to ground.

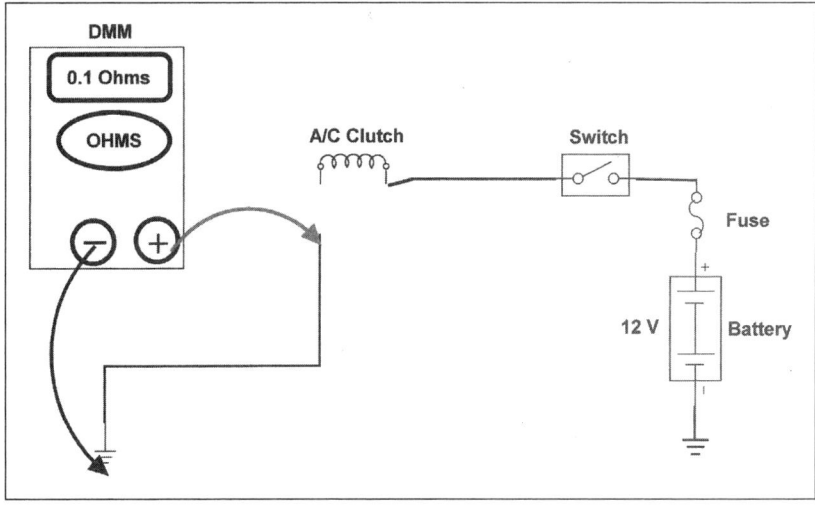

How to Measure Ground Resistance using DMM

Digital Multimeter Tips

1. Always check to be sure that your meter is working properly. Leads in the wrong jacks, low batteries, damaged leads, or a blown meter fuse can add unwanted time to a repair.
2. Measuring for voltage drop in a live circuit will provide more information about the condition of the circuit than performing resistance testing. Voltage drop testing will find unwanted resistance before a load.
3. In the ohms setting, the meter provides the voltage needed to measure the component's resistance.
4. In the amps mode, circuit current flows through the meter. Be sure that the test leads are in the correct jacks, and that the current flow does not exceed the rated value of the meter. If the current to be measured exceeds the meter's capability, use an inductive amp clamp. If the meter will not function in the ammeter setting, check the meter's fuses.
5. Be sure to place the leads in the proper jacks when switching meter modes.
6. Be cautious of 0.00 ohms readings. Nearly all circuits have a small amount of resistance that can be measured.

Notes:

Clean test connection
testing diodes make sure diode symbol is on screen

SECTION 2 • THE MULTIMETER & CIRCUIT DESIGNS

Worksheet 1 – Section 2

Task: Measure A/C Clutch Available Voltage and Circuit Voltage Drops

Tools and Materials Needed:

- MACS HVAC Systems, Volume 2 - Electrical and Electronic Systems Operation Manual
- Late model vehicle
- Digital multimeter

Vehicle to be used:

Year _____ Make _____ Mode _____

VIN _____

Engine Type _____ Displacement _____

Procedure:

Using an available vehicle and Section 2 of the MACS HVAC Systems, Volume 2 - Electrical and Electronic Systems Operation Manual as a reference, perform the following A/C Clutch-related voltage measurements:

1. Available voltage

2. Voltage across the clutch coil

3. Ground circuit voltage drop

Record the results below:

Available voltage: Desired: _____ volts   Actual: _____ volts

Across the clutch coil: Desired: _____ volts   Actual: _____ volts

Ground circuit voltage drop: Desired: _____ volts   Actual: _____ volts

Is the circuit operating correctly? _____

_____

_____

Are the voltages that were found acceptable? _____

_____

_____

Section 2 Review – The Multimeter and Circuit Designs

1. True or False: A digital multimeter has a very low input impedance.
    - A. True
    - B. False

2. Technician A says when measuring resistance, the circuit must be powered up. Technician B says when measuring current, the meter must be placed in series with the circuit. Who is correct?
    - A. Technician A
    - B. Technician B
    - C. Both Technician A and Technician B
    - D. Neither Technician A nor Technician B

3. The resistance 6,300,000Ω might also be written as:
    - A. 630 KΩ
    - B. 630 MΩ
    - C. 6.3 MΩ
    - D. 63 MΩ

4. In a series circuit:
    A. The total current flow is equal to the sum of the current flows through the individual branches of the circuit.
    B. The source voltage is equal to the sum of the individual voltage drops across the circuit components.
    Which is/are correct?
    - A. Statement A is correct
    - B. Statement B is correct
    - C. Both statements are correct
    - D. Neither statement is correct

5. Technician A says low available voltage can cause a circuit to not operate properly. Technician B says high resistance in the ground side of a circuit is OK as long as the voltage drop does not exceed 50% of available voltage. Who is correct?
    - A. Technician A
    - B. Technician B
    - C. Both Technician A and Technician B
    - D. Neither Technician A nor Technician B

Notes:

Section 3: Wiring Diagrams and Service Information

Successful electrical troubleshooting and diagnosis not only requires hand tools, a multimeter and other specialty tools, but service information is also very critical. Service information includes wiring diagrams, component locators, connector diagrams, harness routing views and circuit operation descriptions. The OEMs and many aftermarket suppliers offer this information.

WIRING DIAGRAMS

Like street maps of a city, wiring diagrams provide detailed information about the electrical circuits found on a vehicle. It is important to note that the wiring diagrams in this section are strictly intended to illustrate the typical features found in diagrams and do not represent a specific vehicle or vehicle circuit and are not drawings of real circuits.

Notes:

34 WIRING DIAGRAMS & SERVICE INFORMATION • SECTION 3

Most vehicle wiring diagrams today are arranged with the power side of the circuit near the top of the page and the ground side of the circuit near the bottom of the page. All switches and components are shown in the rest position with the doors closed and the ignition off.

The various callouts describe the details of the diagram shown below.

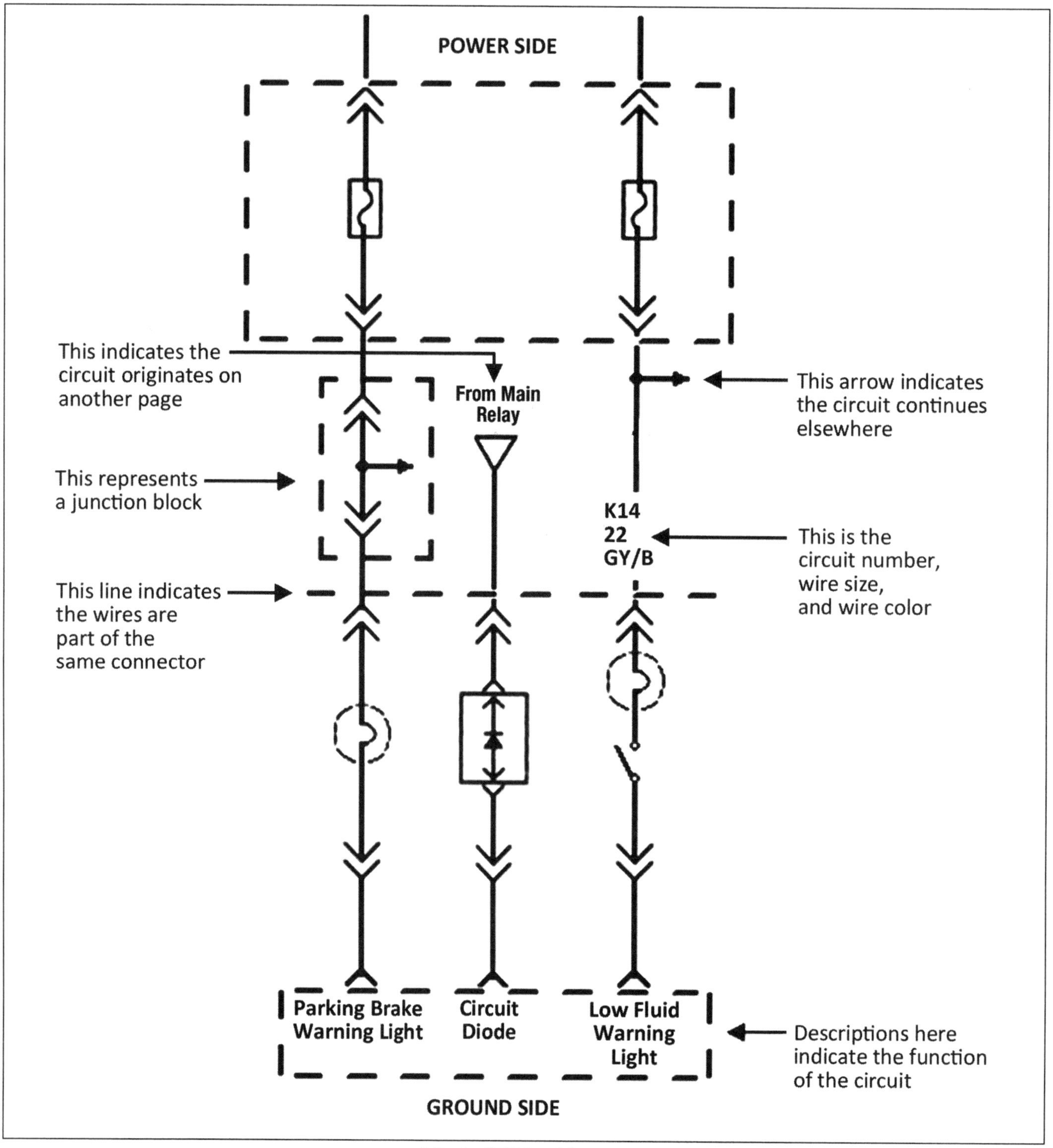

A Typical Wiring Diagram

Modern Automotive HVAC: Electrical and Electronic Systems   © 2012 Mobile Air Conditioning Society

SECTION 3 • WIRING DIAGRAMS & SERVICE INFORMATION

Components are shown either with a solid line indicating a complete part, or with dashed lines indicating that the component is part of another module or unit. Incomplete components have a reference number to indicate where the complete component can be found. Wiring and components on the diagrams do not represent how they appear on the vehicle. The length of a line in a wiring diagram does not indicate the length of the wire. Components are shown as simply as possible.

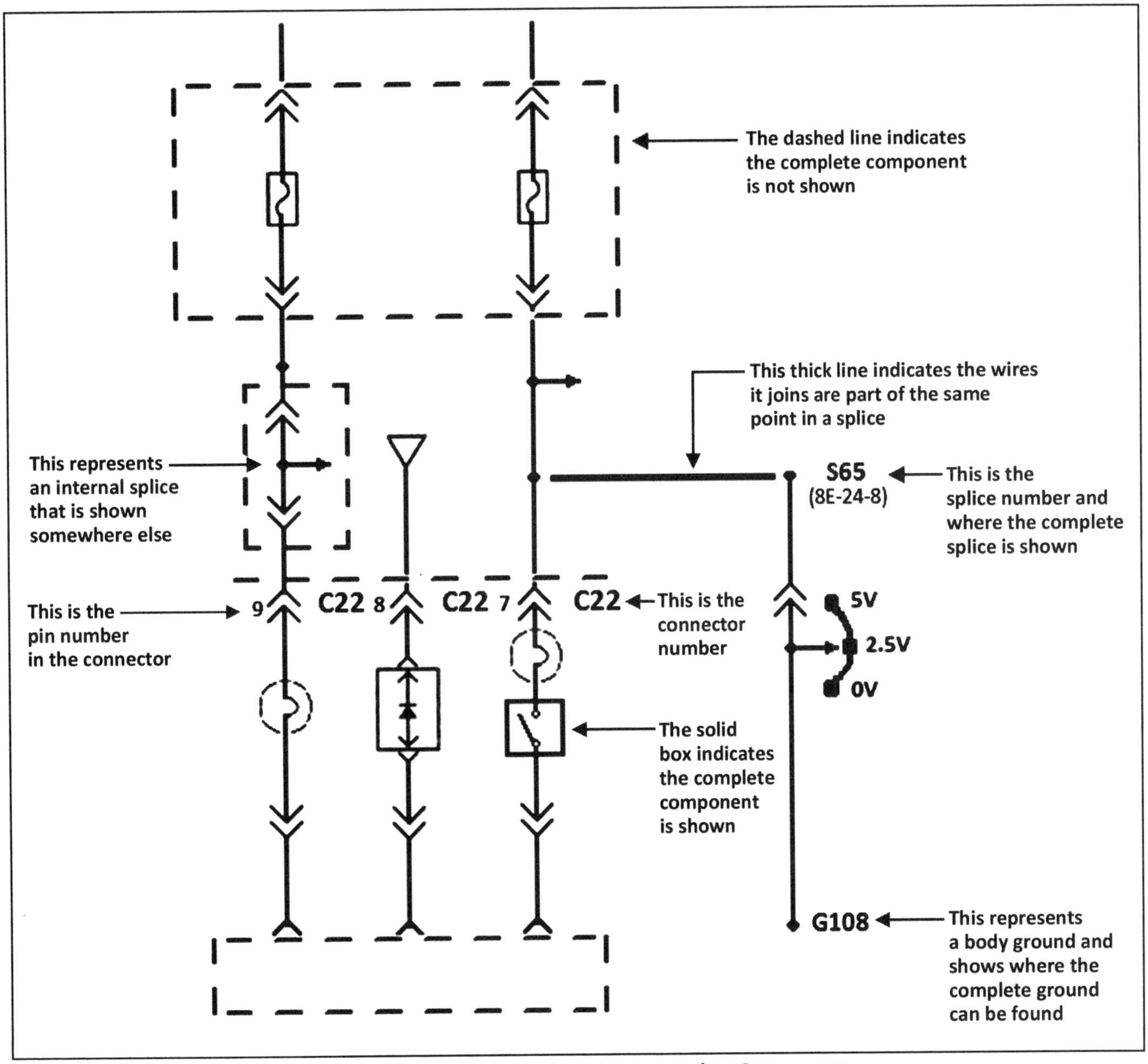

A Typical Wiring Diagram Showing Incomplete Components

Notes:

WIRING DIAGRAMS & SERVICE INFORMATION • SECTION 3

Wiring diagrams often use international symbols which are consistent with those being used worldwide. The image below shows examples of commonly used symbols.

Typical Wiring Diagram Symbols				
Battery	Fuse	Circuit Breaker	Fusible Link	Diode
Resistor	Variable Resistor	Potentiometer	NPN Transistor	PNP Transistor
Open Switch	Closed Switch	Motor	Reference to Drawing Page (16W-32-18)	Stator
In-Line Connector	Male Connector	Female Connector	Ground	Bulb
Wire Coil	Capacitor	Heater Element	Crossing Wires Not Connected	Splice
Transformer or Ignition Coil	Relay (Variations)		Relay Pin Callout	Solenoid

Commonly Used International Wiring Diagram Symbols

Notes:

SECTION 3 • WIRING DIAGRAMS & SERVICE INFORMATION

Using Wiring Diagrams to Trace a Circuit

Often, a problem in an electrical circuit is straightforward; a blown fuse or a faulty switch or sensor. However, there are times when it will take some investigation and review of the wiring to solve the problem.

The following diagrams are related to an HVAC circuit. Notice that there are several diagrams that contain information about the circuit. The first schematic shown below is power distribution under the hood.

Notice that the underhood wiring harness junction block has dashed lines, indicating that the two ignition switch feed circuit fuses are located in the junction block. The connection ID is listed, and in this case, the connector is C4, a blue connector. The power distribution diagram also shows fusible links, battery cable routing and which circuits are hot at all times.

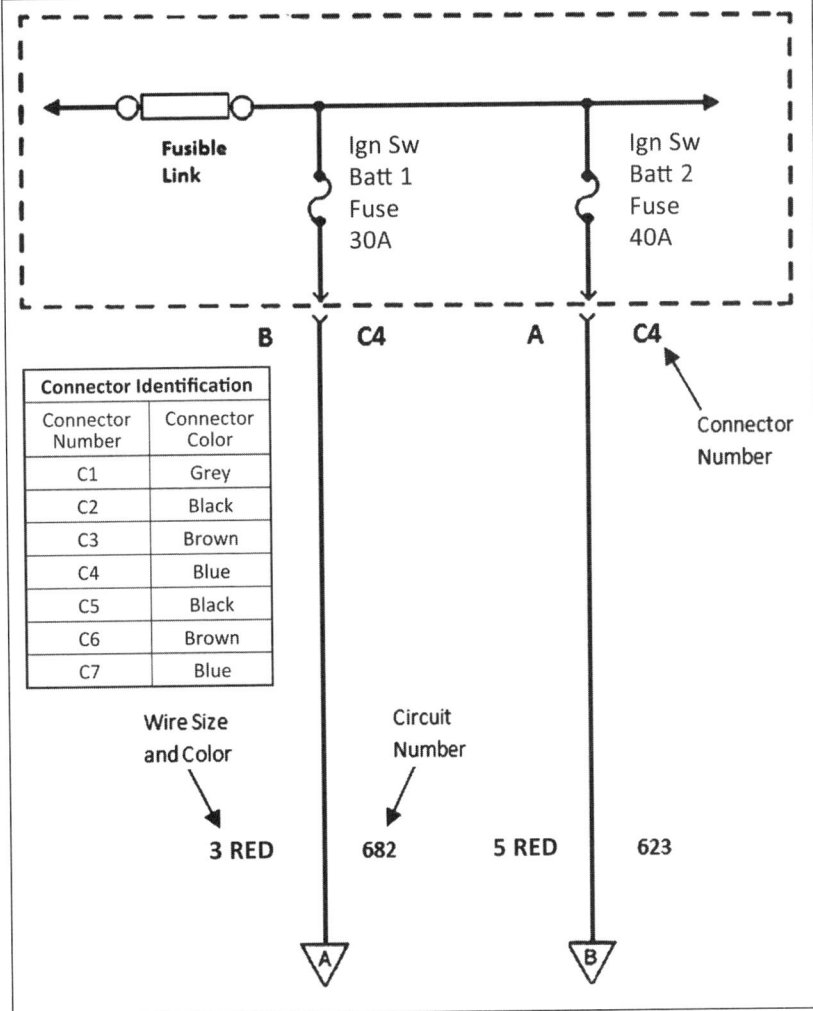

Underhood Wiring Diagram

WIRING DIAGRAMS & SERVICE INFORMATION • SECTION 3

Looking at the diagram, the circuit number is on the right side of the wire. To the left of the circuit wire, is another number and a color. This identifies the wire size in and the wire color.

When connector C4 is viewed in the component locator section of the manual, the diagram shows the two circuits that feed the ignition switch (682 and 623); this corresponds with the vehicle's option package. If the other connectors are viewed, the wire circuit numbers will be different. The connectors are labeled with the component they are connected to, or the connector number. In addition, the color of the connector, the connector family or series name is also provided.

Connector Information: 2-Way – Color: Blue				
Pin	Wire Color	Circuit #	Purpose
A	Red	682	Battery Fuse Output
B	Red	623	Battery Fuse Output

Connector C4 Component Locator

Looking at the underhood power distribution center, the two fuses identified in the image below (30A and 40A), protect circuits 623 and 682.

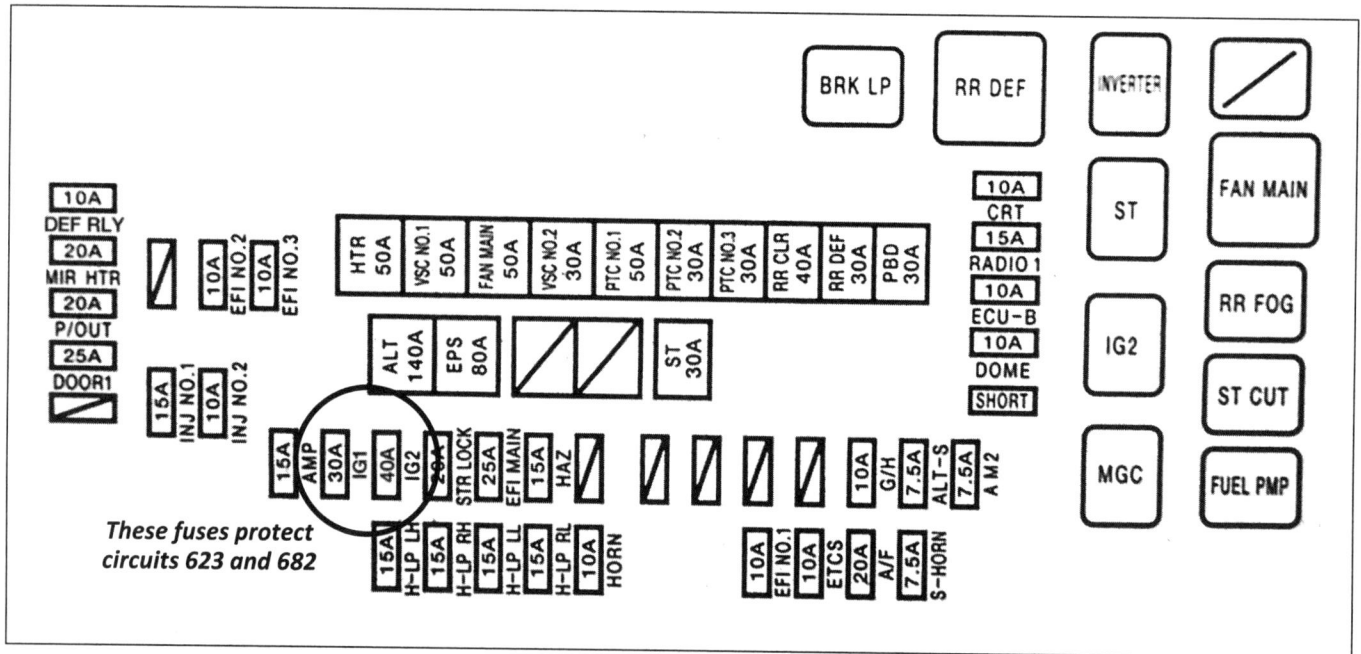

Underhood Power Distribution Diagram

Notes:

SECTION 3 • WIRING DIAGRAMS & SERVICE INFORMATION

Notes:

The next diagram shows circuit E entering the underhood wiring harness junction box at connector C3, pin A6. Note that only the applicable section of the junction box is shown. This is circuit 300, the wire size is 3 mm^2 and the wire color is orange. Circuit 300 is protected by a 10 amp fuse, number 46. The voltage leaves through pin A11 in connector C3. It is now circuit 41, the wire size is 0.35 mm^2 and the wire color is brown.

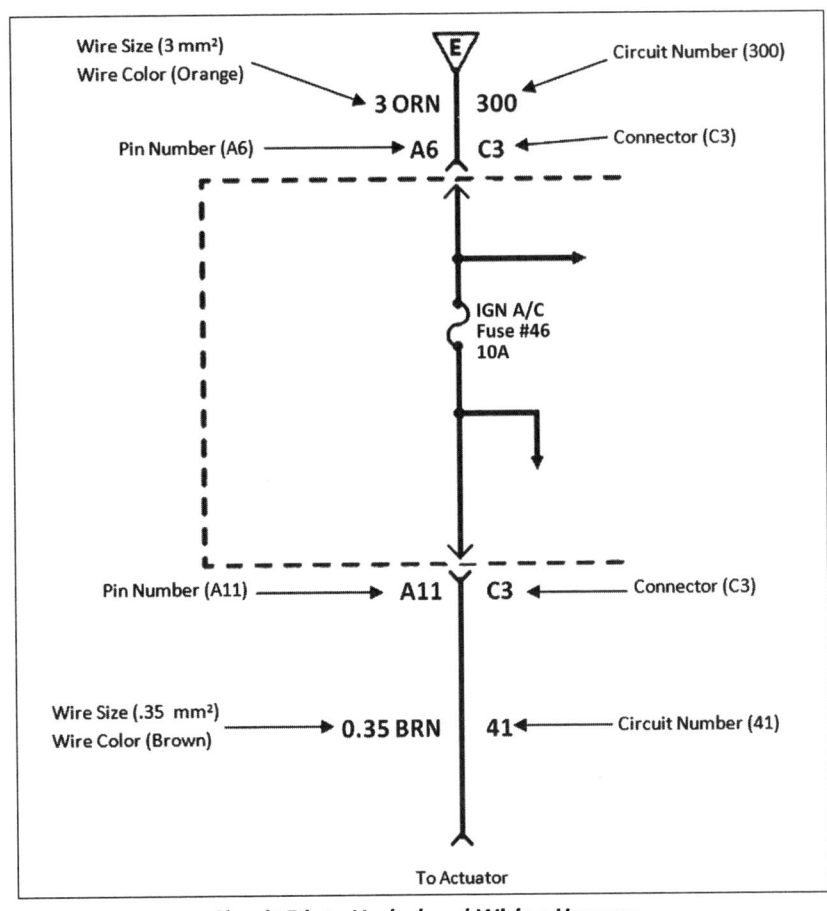

Circuit E into Underhood Wiring Harness

Metric Wire Size (mm^2)	American Wire Gauge (AWG)
0.22	24
0.35	22
0.5	20
0.8	18
1.0	16
2.0	14
3.0	12
5.0	10
8.0	8
13.0	6
19.0	4
32.0	2

Metric to American Wire Gauges

In the previous examples, metric wire sizes were shown. Most manuals will provide a conversion chart to American Wire Gauge (AWG) sizes as shown at left.

40 WIRING DIAGRAMS & SERVICE INFORMATION • SECTION 3

The diagram below shows the HVAC control head, and contains a lot of information. At top left, the heater/AC ignition 10 amp fuse feeds pin B8 in the C8 connector. Connector C8, circuit 12, enters the Control head at connector C4 terminal C.

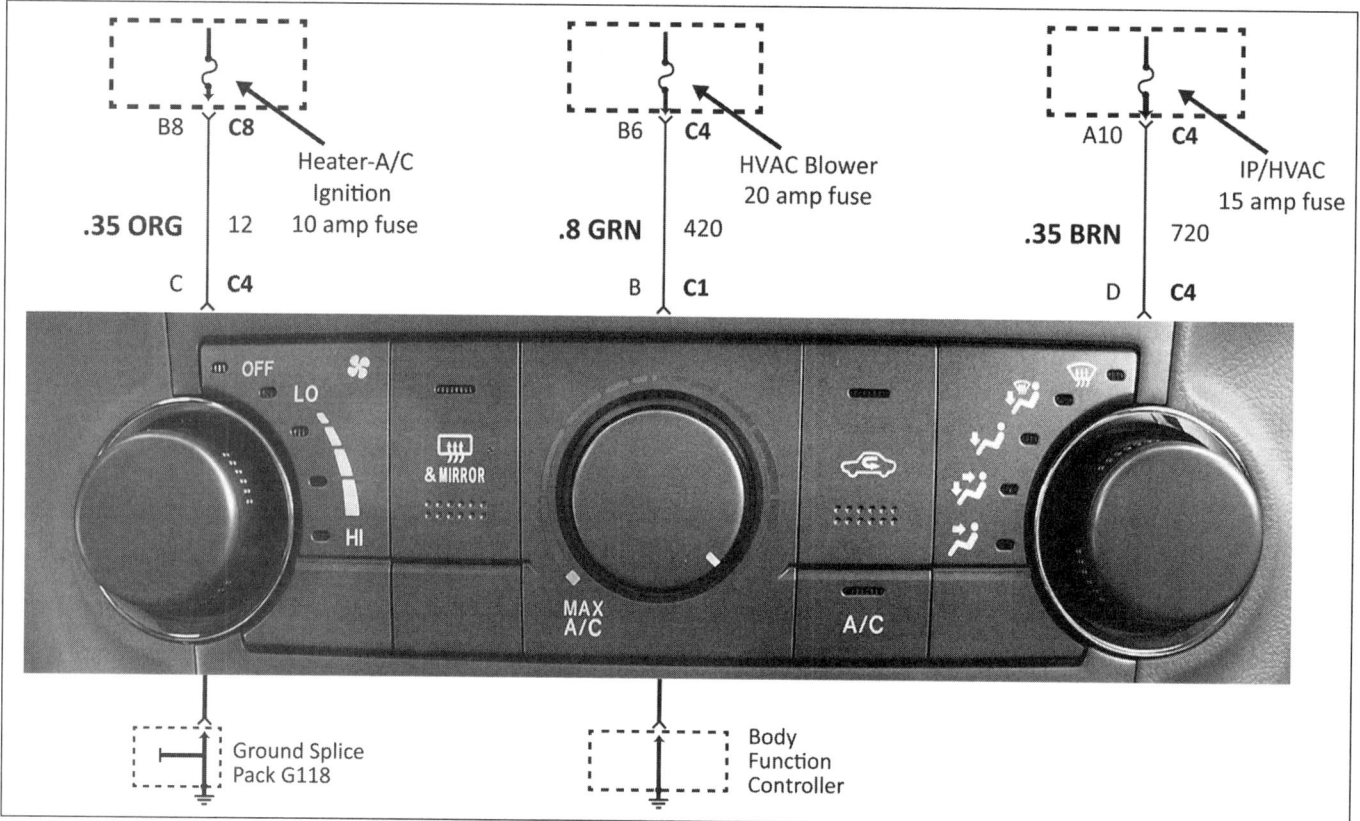

HVAC Control Head Wiring Diagram

In the center top, the HVAC blower 20-amp fuse feeds pin B6 in connector C4. This is circuit 420, the wire size is 0.8 mm² and the wire color is green.

The connector on the top right is fed by the IP/HVAC 15-amp fuse through pin A10 in connector C4. This becomes circuit 720, the wire size is 0.35 mm² and the wire color is brown.

The bottom of the diagram shows the controller sends an input signal to the body function controller. It also shows that the HVAC control head is grounded at ground splice pack G118.

Not shown is that two of the three power feeds come from junction boxes on each side of the instrument panel. If the proper wiring diagrams are not used, these power sources may be overlooked if there is limited operation of the HVAC system, but the fuse in the underhood junction block is good.

SECTION 3 • WIRING DIAGRAMS & SERVICE INFORMATION

The image below shows the junction block that is on the passenger's side of the instrument panel. Fuse C is the IP/HVAC 15 amp fuse.

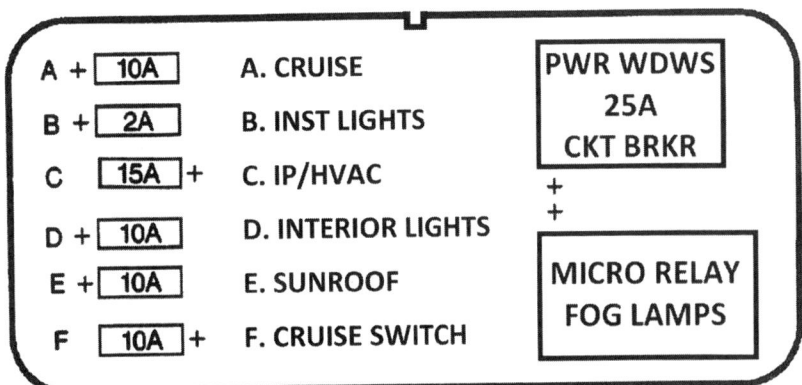

Passenger's Side Junction Box Panel

The junction block in the image below is on the driver's side of the vehicle. Note Fuse E, the 20 amp HVAC Blower fuse.

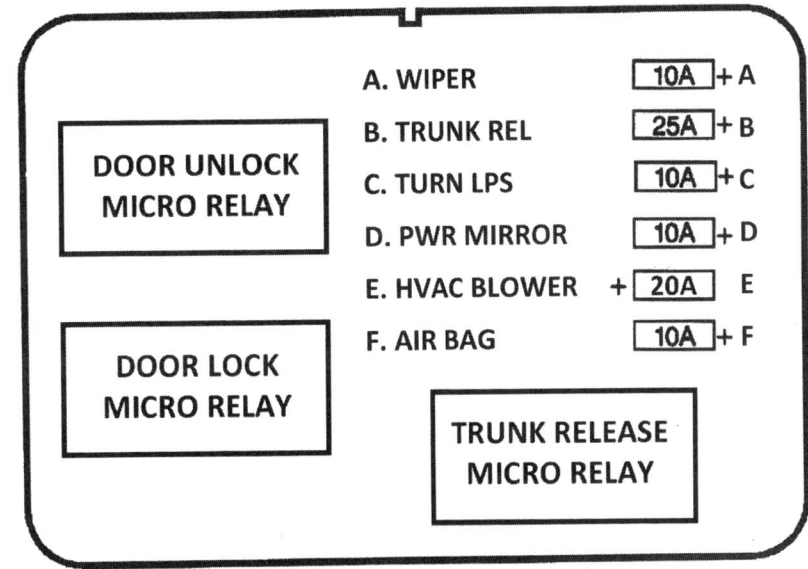

Driver's Side Junction Box Panel

Notes:

WIRING DIAGRAMS & SERVICE INFORMATION • SECTION 3

Ground circuit diagrams are also helpful for electrical troubleshooting.

Refer to the image below – if the blower motor will not operate at any speed, but testing shows that source voltage is available at the motor, ground splice G114, directly below the blower motor, could be at fault.

Driver's Side Junction Box Panel

Many vehicles use ground splice connections, as at left. Several ground terminals will connect to a common fastener that is mounted to a bracket or to a body panel.

Notes:

Ground Splice Connection

SECTION 3 • WIRING DIAGRAMS & SERVICE INFORMATION

In the following ground schematic, all of the components that share this ground are shown. If the blower motor will not operate, and there is power to the blower motor, a quick check of the ground circuit will show if any other components share the ground. If the other components are also not functioning, it's very likely that the ground terminal may be at fault. If the other components on the circuit are working, the problem is strictly in the blower motor circuit.

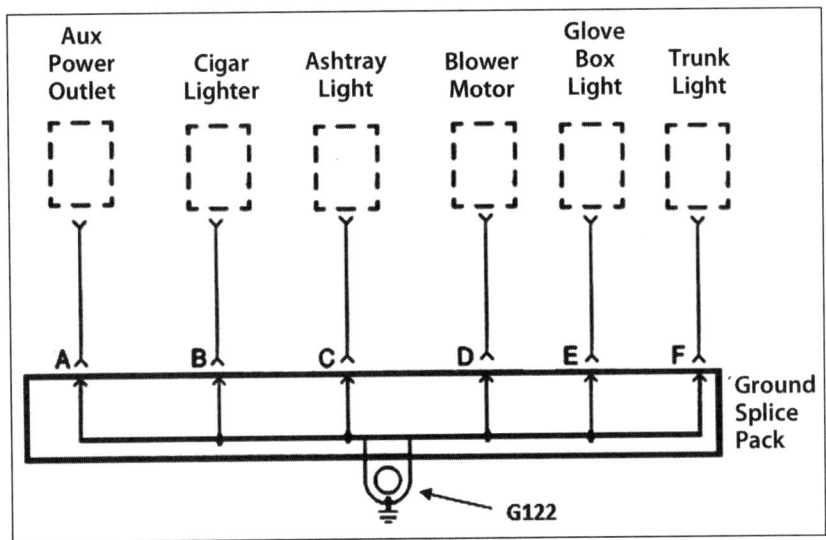

Ground Schematic

Once the ground splice is identified, where is it? The component locator section of the service information will show.

Notes:

Circuit Troubleshooting Procedures Tips

This chart provides a step by step process to help find an electrical circuit problem.

1. Confirm the vehicle owner's concern. Remember that this may require a road test, perhaps with the customer present.
2. Obtain a wiring diagram of the circuit to be diagnosed.
3. Decide on the test points in the circuit where measurements will be taken. These should be points that will provide the maximum information possible.
4. Predict what the measured values should be at those points.
5. Perform the measurements.
6. Based on these measurements, determine whether the problem is on the power side of the circuit or the ground side of the circuit:
   a. If the source voltage is low, the problem is "upstream" of the test point.
   b. If the source voltage is OK (within 0.4 volt of battery voltage), the problem is not "upstream."
   c. Next measure the voltage drop on the ground side of the circuit. If it exceeds 0.4 volt, the problem is "downstream" from the test point.
7. If the source voltage and the ground side voltage drop are both acceptable, the component itself is faulty.
8. If the problems is with source voltage or the ground side voltage drop, repeat steps three through six on the part of the circuit where the problem is, and work thought the circuit point by point until the cause is pinpointed.

Notes:

Notes:

WIRING DIAGRAMS & SERVICE INFORMATION • SECTION 3

Worksheet 2 – Section 3 • Page 1

Task: Use Wiring Diagrams and Information Systems

Tools and Materials Needed:

- MACS HVAC Systems, Volume 2 - Electrical and Electronic Systems Operation Manual
- Late model vehicle
- Vehicle service information

Vehicle to be used:

Year _____ Make _____ Model _____

VIN _____

Engine Type _____ Displacement _____

Procedure:

Using an available vehicle, Section 3 of the MACS HVAC Systems, Volume 2 - Electrical and Electronic Systems Operation Manual as a reference, and vehicle service information, perform the following:

1. Using the wiring diagrams for the vehicle's A/C system, identify the following (if available):

    a. Wire gauges

    b. Wire colors

    c. Circuit numbers

    d. Connector and pin numbers

2. Identify those same items on the actual vehicle.

3. Using the component locator section, determine the location(s) of the following:

    a. All fuses and relays relating to the vehicle's A/C system

    b. Cycling clutch switch (if applicable)

    c. A/C pressure sensor (if applicable)

    d. Data link connector (DLC)

4. Identify these same items on the actual vehicle.

5. Using the wiring diagrams or component locator as needed, locate the ground points (splices) relating to the vehicle's A/C system

Record the results on next page.

SECTION 3 • WIRING DIAGRAMS & SERVICE INFORMATION

Worksheet 2 – Section 3 • Page 2

Step 1:

Circuit Number _____ Connector Number _____ Pin Number _____ Wire Color _____ Wire Gauge _____

Circuit Number _____ Connector Number _____ Pin Number _____ Wire Color _____ Wire Gauge _____

Circuit Number _____ Connector Number _____ Pin Number _____ Wire Color _____ Wire Gauge _____

Circuit Number _____ Connector Number _____ Pin Number _____ Wire Color _____ Wire Gauge _____

Step 2:

HVAC Fuses:

    Circuit this fuse protects _____ Where the fuse is located _____

    Amperage rating of this fuse _____

    Circuit this fuse protects _____ Where the fuse is located _____

    Amperage rating of this fuse _____

    Circuit this fuse protects _____ Where the fuse is located _____

    Amperage rating of this fuse _____

Relay(s):

    Circuit controlled _____ Where located _____

    Circuit controlled _____ Where located _____

    Circuit controlled _____ Where located _____

Cycling clutch switch • A/C pressure sensor   (circle which is used)

    Where located on vehicle _____

Data link connector:

    Where located on vehicle _____

Step 3:

Ground Splices

    Where located on vehicle _____ Circuits sharing this splice _____

    Where located on vehicle _____ Circuits sharing this splice _____

    Where located on vehicle _____ Circuits sharing this splice _____

WIRING DIAGRAMS & SERVICE INFORMATION • SECTION 3

Section 3 Review -
Wiring Diagrams and Service Information

1. True or False: When viewing a wiring diagram, the power side of the circuit is usually on the left side of the page.
    - A. True
    - B. False

2. This symbol ─╲╱╲╱─ is used to represent a:
    - A. Power source
    - B. Diode
    - C. Resistor
    - D. Ground

3. Which statement below is correct regarding the wiring diagram shown on right:
    A. 0.35 is the wire size and BRN is the wire color
    B. C3 is the connector number and A11 is the pin number
    - A. Statement A is correct
    - B. Statement B is correct
    - C. Both statements A and B are correct
    - D. Neither statement A nor B is correct

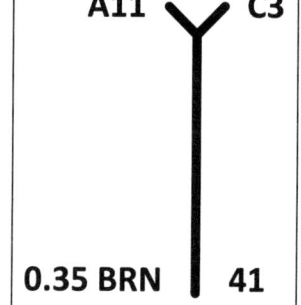

4. Technician A says the higher the american wire gauge (AWG) number is, the larger the wire diameter is. Technician B says metric wire size is measured in mm². Who is correct?
    - A. Technician A
    - B. Technician B
    - C. Both Technician A and Technician B
    - D. Neither Technician A nor Technician B

5. Which of these statements is/are correct?
    A. If power is available to a blower motor but it does not operate, the voltage drop on the circuit ground size might be excessive.
    B. If the resistance at a ground splice is excessive, it may affect more than one circuit.
    - A. Statement A is correct
    - B. Statement B is correct
    - C. Both Statements A and B are correct
    - D. Neither Statement A nor B is correct

Notes:

SECTION 4 • BASIC COMPUTER OPERATION & FUNCTION

Section 4: Basic Computer Operation & Function

The first sections of this book provided an overview on electrical fundamentals, meter usage and using wiring diagrams. This section covers computer basics and system controls, including sensors and input-output functions that can affect A/C operation.

The purpose of any electronic device is to control or direct the flow of electricity, and components may relate to the generation, distribution, switching and storage of energy as well as converting it to other forms of energy. The most common electronic devices are diodes, transistors and integrated circuits.

Some electronic or "solid state" components can act as switches, and still others allow very weak electrical signals to be amplified and used elsewhere in a circuit

CONTROLLING MODERN HVAC SYSTEMS

For many years, the air conditioning compressor was controlled directly from the dashboard; when the A/C button was pushed, voltage would typically travel from the control head through the evaporator switch, the protection switch and through the compressor clutch to ground.

But that changed with the advent of on-board control computers, and since the 1990s, the compressor clutch on most passenger vehicles has been controlled by or through the engine computer. Technology continues to become more complex and today HVAC controls are being integrated into the vehicle's total electrical system.

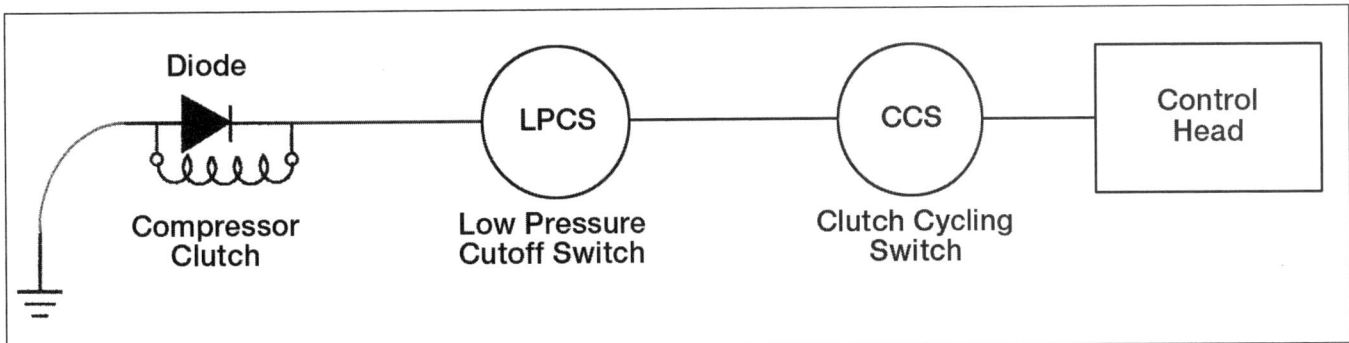

Typical Manual A/C Compressor Control Circuit

Notes:

In modern control circuits, engaging the dash button only sends a request signal to at least one electronic control module, not directly to the compressor clutch. When the request signal is received, the control module will check a number of data values (coolant temperature, engine rpm and several others) to determine if the compressor clutch should be enabled. If all the conditions are correct, the control module will ground the A/C control circuit relay which energizes the compressor clutch.

The A/C request signal will be a voltage reference; either high (12 volts) or low (0 volts) depending on system design and vehicle manufacturer.

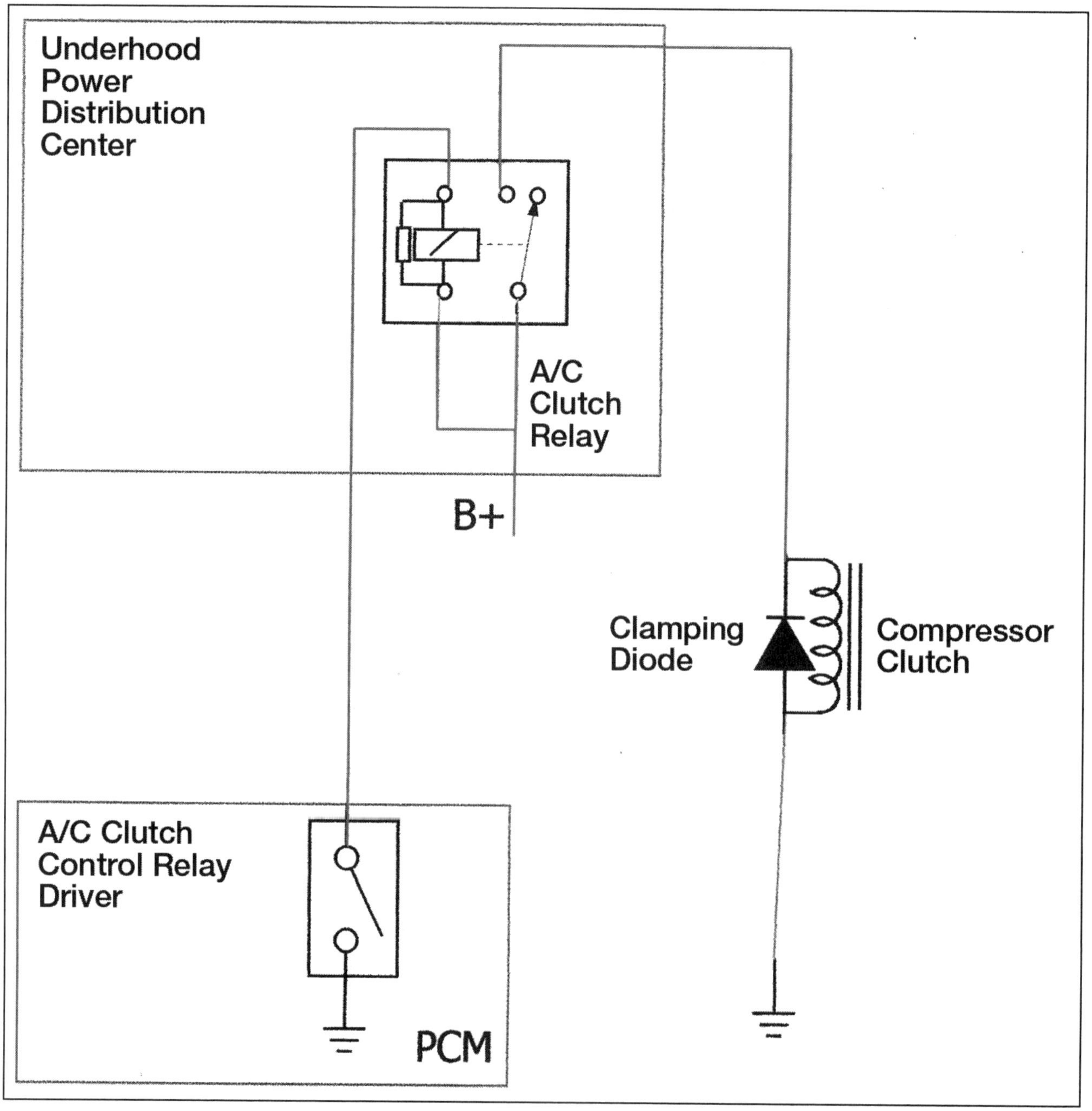

Example of a PCM Controlled Compressor Clutch Circuit

SECTION 4 • BASIC COMPUTER OPERATION & FUNCTION

COMPUTER COMMUNICATION

Any computer, including those in vehicles, is simply a device designed to process information it receives. The information is received and transmitted at different voltages and in two different manners: analog and digital.

Analog and Digital Voltage Signals

Analog signals are continuously variable and may be sent at any value within their operating range. These voltages are used to relay information about values that change continuously such as temperatures, airflow, or speed.

Digital signals may also vary, but not continuously. A digital signal is limited to only two levels; they are often termed "high or low," "on or off," "yes or no." Such signals are commonly used to indicate a switch position or that a pressure is within (or outside) a predetermined range.

A system with only two options is called binary; it uses only zeroes and ones as counting values. On vehicles with negative ground electrical systems, the one indicates positive voltage and zero indicates no voltage. Each one or zero is called a bit, and messages are sent over the control network in packages or 8-, 16-, 32- or 64-bits. A higher bit rate allows more information to be transmitted more quickly, and different communication rates will be found in different systems.

In the early days of computer control, one central computer unit could handle all the management responsibilities for the vehicle. But as new systems were developed the workload overwhelmed the single computer.

Engineers and designers began to assign certain system management functions to dedicated, smaller computers – often termed control modules – to oversee functions such as HVAC, ABS, traction control, or electrical body functions including cruise control and security. While each of the smaller computers oversees its own domain, it is quite common for them to communicate with the main engine or powertrain computer to receive or transmit information.

A computer is programmed or mapped to react to the information it receives. In the most basic description, it is making "if-then" decisions according to the permanent programming. Some of the programming is very sophisticated—the "if" list may be very long and require data from many sensors and inputs before any output occurs.

A program designed to turn on the compressor clutch may consist of dozens of steps, and both input and output components must communicate with the computer before any operation is permitted.

COMPUTER COMPONENTS

Regardless of size or function, any computer or control module will have some of the same components. The microprocessor, also called the central processing unit (CPU) is the brain of the computer. It performs calculations and makes decisions. The remaining components support the CPU's operation. Microprocessors require a stored set of instructions (a program) in order to operate. Computers must have storage devices. These devices are called memories.

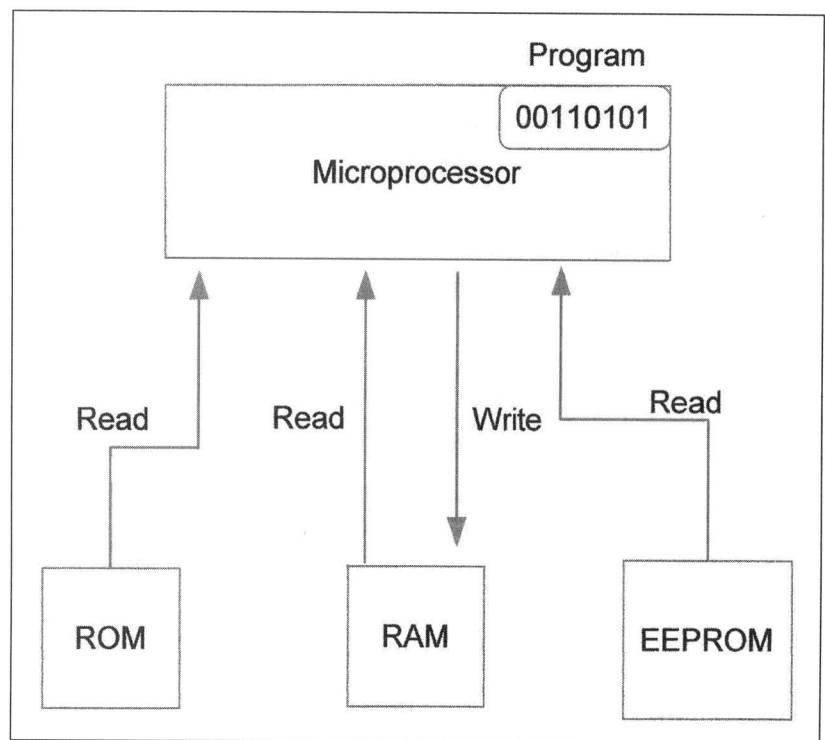

Standard Computer Architecture

SECTION 4 • BASIC COMPUTER OPERATION & FUNCTION

The three types of memory are:

Read-only memory (ROM): when a computer is assembled, the programs which control the CPU operation are stored here. The CPU can only read instructions from ROM; it cannot write information to the ROM.

Random access memory (RAM): is used for temporary storage. For example, the microprocessor will write a value to RAM, and then read it each time it is needed. The RAM can be connected directly to the battery, so that it still has power when the ignition is off. This is called "keep-alive" RAM. However, if the battery cables are disconnected or the battery goes dead, the stored information may be erased.

The electrically erasable programmable read-only memory (EEPROM) is a chip that can be erased electronically. This chip will be used to store information such as the vehicle identification number (VIN), vehicle options, and mileage driven.

The clock generator drives the microprocessor, each of the memories, and its digital interface devices. It keeps each component in time and operating at the same speed. The clock generator provides a steady and constant stream of pulses.

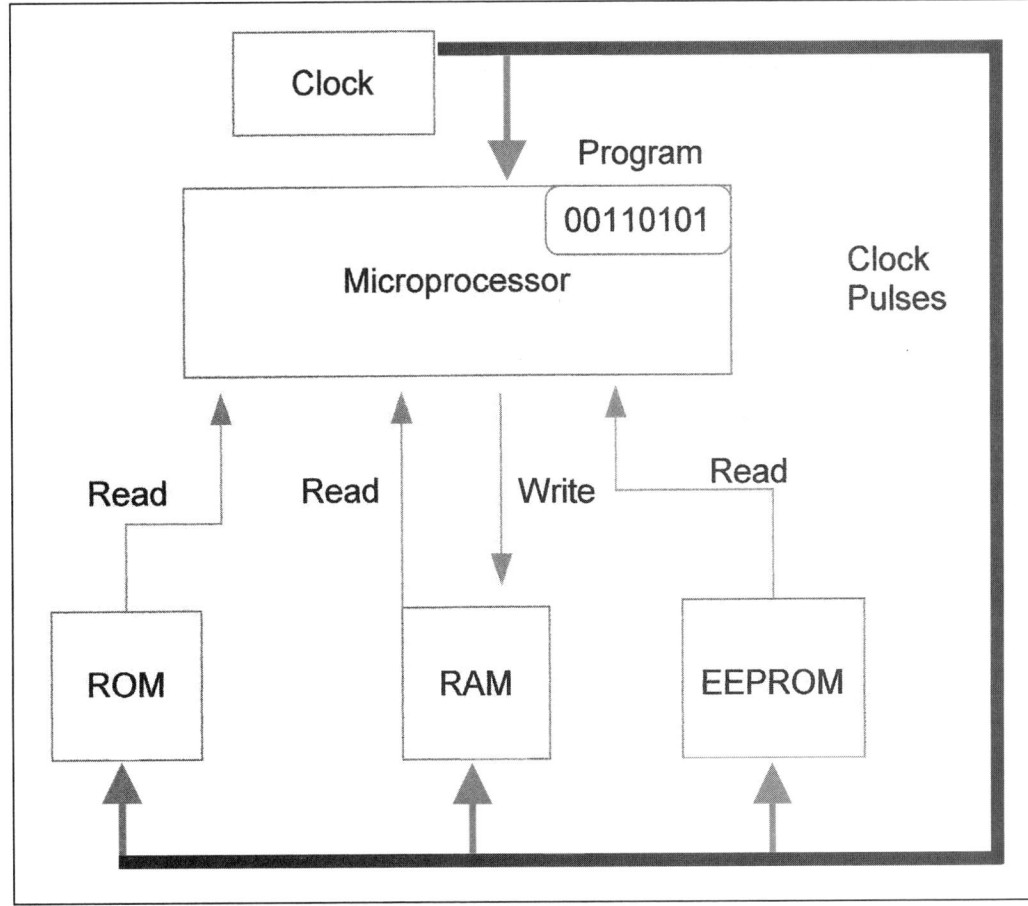

Clock Generator Diagram

Computer Interfaces

The information coming in and the results going out are what make the computer useful. The computer needs interfaces to handle the incoming and outgoing information. The interfaces protect the electronics in the CPU from high voltage in the electrical circuits. They also translate the input and output signals.

When the computer receives an analog signal, the input interface converts it to binary code. If the computer must operate an analog device, the output interface changes the digital signal to an analog signal. The image below shows the relationship between the computer and its inputs and outputs.

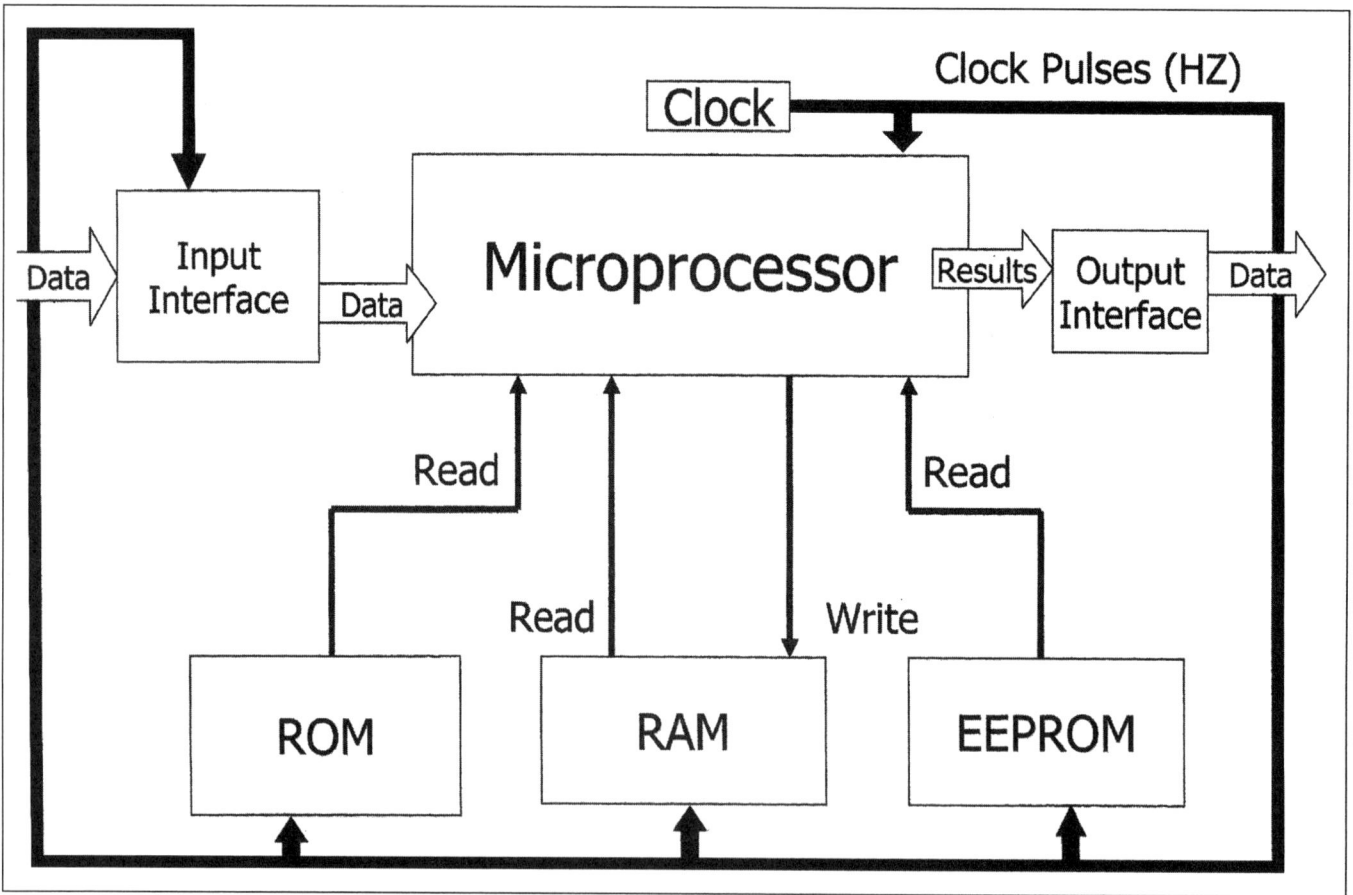

Computer/Component Relationship

Notes:

SECTION 4 • BASIC COMPUTER OPERATION & FUNCTION

Communications

Computers have to receive and send many kinds of signals, both in analog and digital form. Each signal represents different kinds of information. Analog signals provide variable information; sensors, potentiometers, and rheostats are examples of components that produce an analog signal. Computers send and receive digital signals through data lines.

Automotive computer systems use several electronic units that communicate over data lines; engine control modules, body control modules, and powertrain control modules are some examples. As shown in the image below, some data lines are unidirectional (communicate in only one direction) and only from one device to another, while others are bidirectional (two way), communicating back and forth between modules.

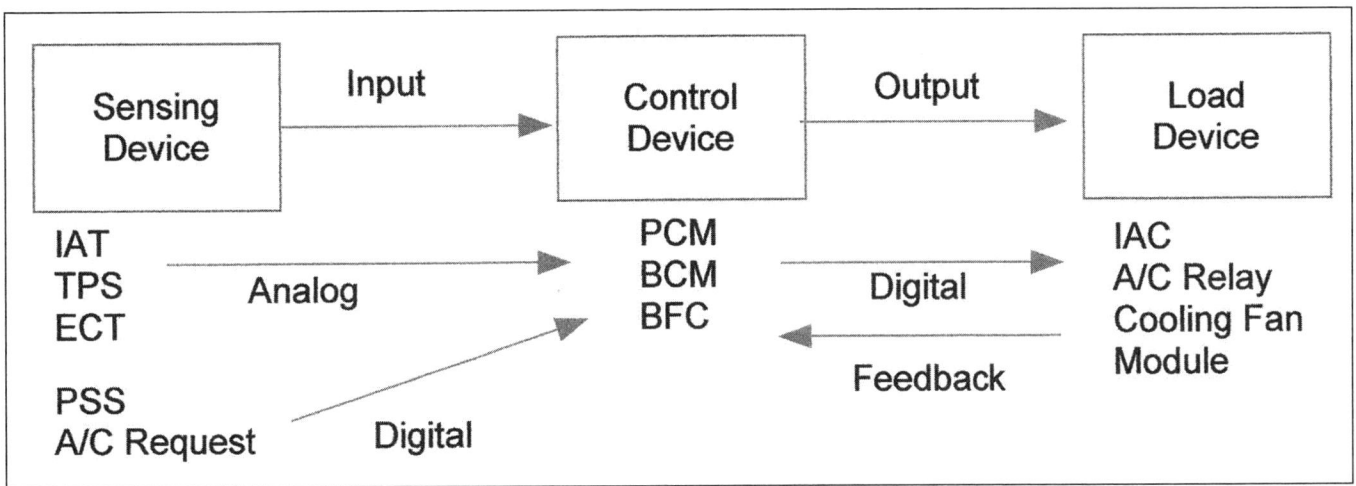

Bidirectional Communication

Computers also receive data from driver-operated controls and send data to electronic displays, such as the instrument cluster and the HVAC controls. This information often goes directly to and from the computer, and may not use data lines. A signal from a switch is an example of this type of digital input.

In summary, a computer has a microprocessor that communicates with various memories, using binary code. Strings of zeros and ones pulse from one section of the computer to another. A clock generator keeps all the data flowing smoothly from each component and will distinguish binary numbers so the correct data is sent. The output interface translates the binary code into an analog signal when needed for operating output devices.

ELECTRICAL/ELECTRONIC COMPONENTS THAT AFFECT SYSTEM OPERATION

Modern HVAC systems network with many other systems on the vehicle. This makes diagnostics more complicated than it was when the HVAC system was a standalone design.

Often when the A/C compressor clutch will not engage, even with the proper refrigerant charge in the system, the problem may be caused by a signal or input from a device that seems unrelated to the A/C system. There are various input and output devices connected with the engine management modules that can affect the operation of the A/C compressor clutch.

Engine Management Modules

The operation of any computer or control module can be broken down into three basic elements of organization: sense, decide, and act. These main processing units receive a number of input signals. The unit takes these signals and compares them with information stored in memory. From that information it makes a decision. The computer then commands outputs as a result of this comparison.

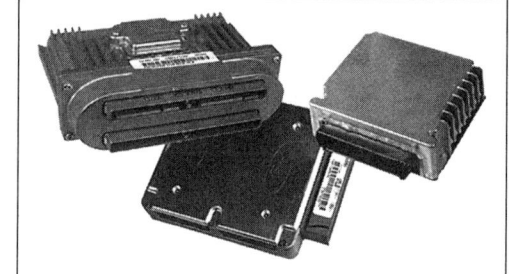

Typical Engine Management Modules

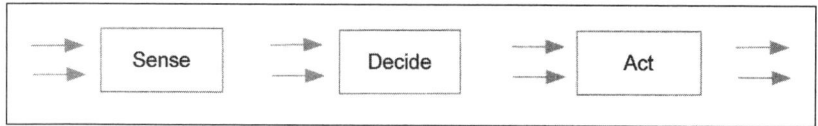

Computer "Reasoning"

The flow of information is shown by the arrows in the chart above – for example, an A/C request is sensed by the computer, and it decides if the conditions are correct for the A/C compressor clutch to engage. In the act stage, the information becomes the desired action, which can either be work or information – in this case, the compressor clutch engaging.

Notes:

SECTION 4 • BASIC COMPUTER OPERATION & FUNCTION

In an HVAC control system, we have input information (sense), the flow of information internally, inside the control unit (decide), and the resulting actions (act). HVAC and engine management systems use this strategy to control operation of the engine fans, the compressor clutch, blower fans, and actuator motors. Specific monitoring devices are used to protect the HVAC system from major failures. The image below shows compressor clutch activation strategy based on specific inputs and outputs to and from the HVAC control and powertrain control modules.

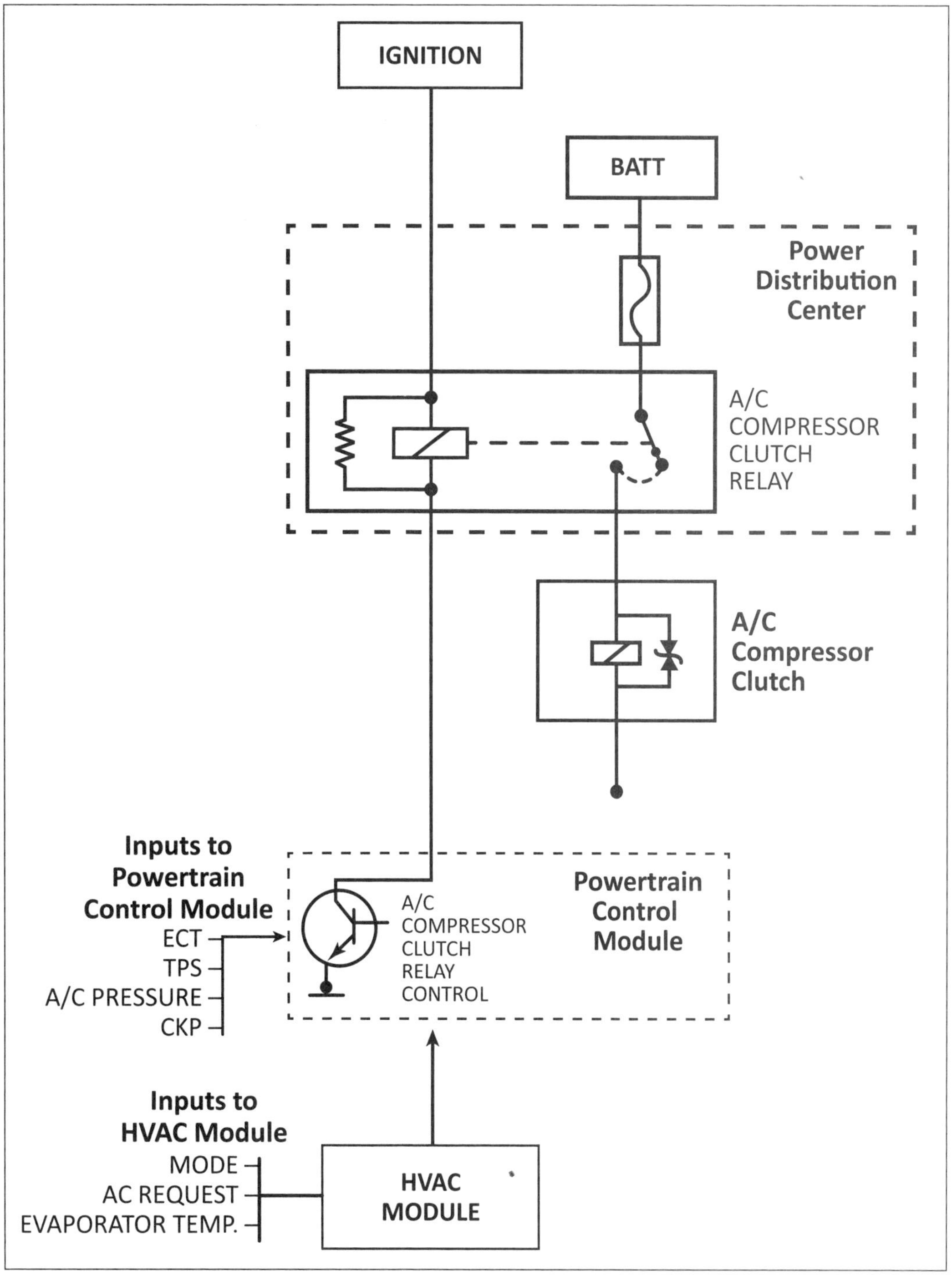

Typical HVAC Control System Inputs and Outputs

HVAC MODULE DEFINITIONS

HVAC Control Head

The HVAC control head is used for operator input. It may be an electronic module that contains a microprocessor, or simply contain switches and knobs.

Two Examples of HVAC Control Head Panels

The control head A/C request signal may be sent to the body control module (BCM) and then to the powertrain control module (PCM) to activate the A/C clutch.

Body Control Module (BCM)

The BCM is a separate computer which handles the operation of in-vehicle controls. The BCM may be called by different names depending on the manufacturer or year and model of a vehicle. For example, Ford Motor Company will call the BCM a front electronic module (FEM), and on a minivan such as the Windstar, will use an additional unit called a rear electronic module (REM) to control the front and rear HVAC systems. All these BCM modules can identify circuit faults and set a diagnostic trouble code (DTC). A scan tool will be needed to retrieve the codes.

Notes:

Powertrain Control Module (PCM)

The PCM is the computer that usually controls the compressor clutch. It will override the A/C request during certain engine operating conditions. For example, if the engine is overheating, or if the throttle is wide open, the A/C clutch will not be allowed to engage or remain engaged.

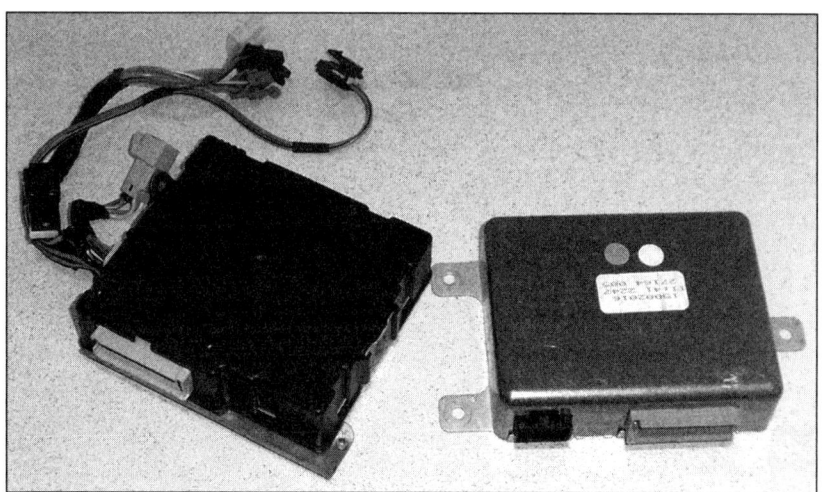

Powertrain Control Modules

A/C COMPRESSOR CLUTCH ENGAGEMENT

When the operator selects A/C on the control panel, an A/C request is sent to the PCM. If the pressure in the A/C system is within specifications, and the engine operating conditions are within the programmed parameters, the PCM will allow the compressor clutch to engage. The clutch will be controlled by a relay or a field effect transistor (FET).

Notes:

The PCM will constantly monitor inputs from various engine sensors, including coolant temperature, throttle position, intake air temperature, and power steering system pressure, but is not limited to these only.

The PCM will also monitor A/C system pressure using various sensors and switches. These inputs will determine if system pressure is in the correct range to allow the compressor clutch to engage, and if the cooling fans should be operating.

In most cases, the PCM will control compressor clutch engagement through a relay. The control side of the relay is activated by a circuit in the PCM. When the control side is closed, the contacts in the relay close, and voltage is fed to the clutch.

Relays are remote-controlled electrical switches. They are used to connect source voltage to an electrical load when the control circuit in the relay is energized.

Typical Relays

Notes:

SECTION 4 • BASIC COMPUTER OPERATION & FUNCTION 61

When the control circuit is completed, an electromagnet pulls the movable contacts of the load circuit closed. When the control circuit is open, a spring opens the contacts on the load side.

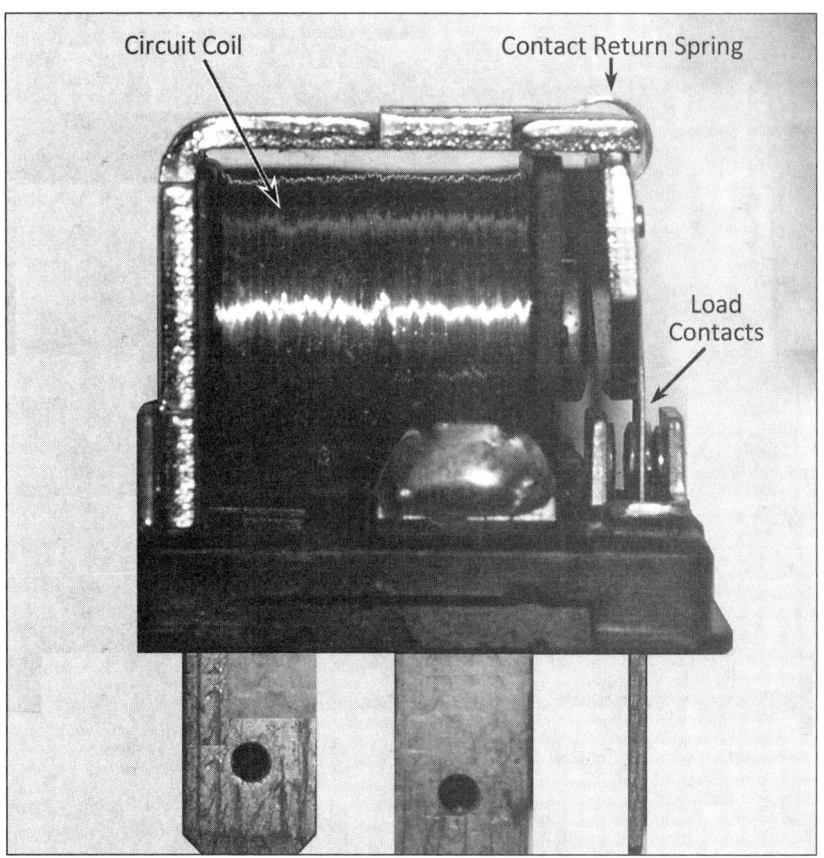

Internal View of a Typical Relay

Relays are necessary on computer controlled systems. Computers are not designed to carry large current loads; the control circuit in the relay uses low current to close the load contacts. This small current flow allows the systems to use smaller gauge wires, and micro switches that do not have to carry large amounts of current. This saves weight and helps to reduce tailpipe emissions, as well as improving fuel economy.

Notes:

ENGINE MANAGEMENT OPERATION

In order for the computer to perform control functions, it requires specific inputs about the vehicle's conditions.

The computer can also use these inputs to verify its output commands

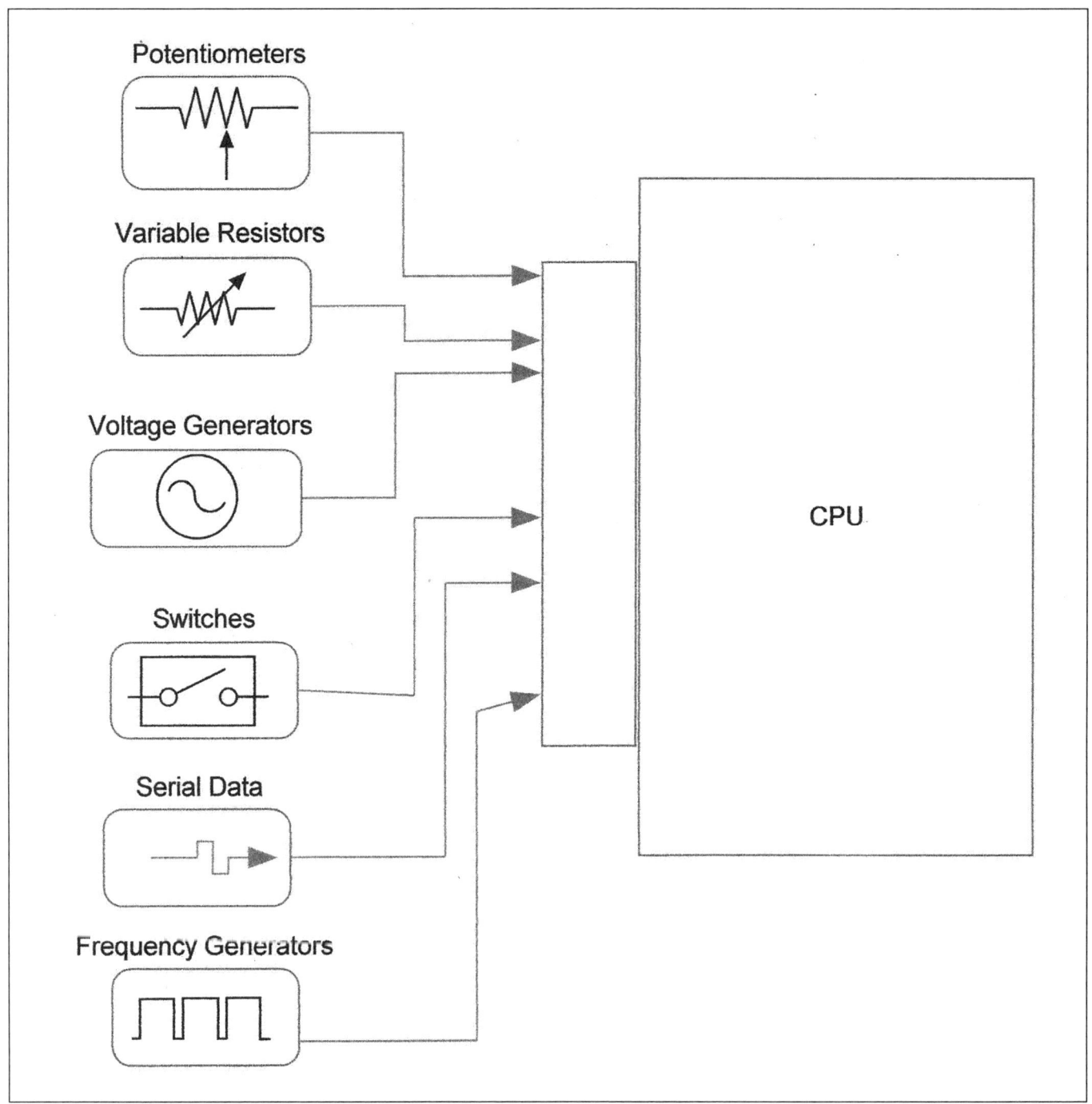

Input Devices

SECTION 4 • BASIC COMPUTER OPERATION & FUNCTION

Computer Inputs

Inputs that the computer uses to determine if the compressor clutch may engage are:

POTENTIOMETERS

Potentiometers are devices that vary resistance based on mechanical changes; a throttle position sensor is an example of a potentiometer.

The PCM supplies a 5-volt reference signal and a ground to the sensor. The throttle position (TP) sensor sends a voltage signal back to the PCM relative to throttle plate position.

Throttle Position (TP) Sensors

The manifold absolute pressure (MAP) sensor sends a voltage signal back to the PCM relative to intake manifold pressure.

The PCM can detect if the TP sensor or the MAP sensor is out of range by comparing the two values to engine speed.

Manifold Absolute Pressure (MAP) Sensor

VARIABLE RESISTORS

Variable resistors change their resistance based on ambient conditions. Examples of variable resistors are engine coolant temperature sensors or intake air temperature sensors.

These sensors are called thermistors. A thermistor is a resistor that changes value with temperature change. The PCM supplies a voltage signal to these sensors. As temperatures increases, the thermistor's resistance value decreases. The change in resistance will change the voltage reading sent back to the PCM. Based on this voltage value, the PCM will adjust fuel delivery, idle speed, and cooling fan operation.

Engine Coolant and Intake Air Temperature Sensors

Notes:

VOLTAGE GENERATORS

Voltage generators are examples of input devices that produce their own voltage signals. Some voltage generators are of a permanent magnet design. These sensors produce an alternating current (AC) voltage signal as a toothed wheel rotates past them. This is because the toothed wheel has an effect on the strength of the sensor's magnetic field, and this generates the AC signal. Other voltage generating sensors are semiconductors which use pressure or vibration to cause a voltage change. Examples of voltage generators are crankshaft and camshaft position sensors and vehicle speed sensors.

Camshaft Position Sensor

FREQUENCY GENERATORS

Frequency generators are sensors that generate variable frequency signals. The computer receives this signal and interprets changes in the frequency to determine changes in engine RPM or vehicle speed. Examples of frequency generators are mass airflow sensors and a knock sensors.

A typical mass airflow sensor input to a PCM is a signal which varies in frequency from 3000 Hz at idle to 7000 Hz at full throttle. This signal is converted to grams per second by the PCM. This indicates the amount of air entering the engine.

Mass Airflow Sensor

Notes:

SECTION 4 • BASIC COMPUTER OPERATION & FUNCTION 65

Knock Sensor

A knock sensor detects engine detonation, and produces an AC voltage signal. The amplitude and frequency of the voltage is dependent upon the level of the knock being detected. If a knock is detected, the PCM will retard spark timing based on the signal from the knock sensor.

VARIABLE PRESSURE SENSOR (TRANSDUCER)

The A/C pressure sensor (ACP) is mounted in the high pressure side of the system. The sensor's output is a variable voltage signal between 0.5 and 4.7 volts. The voltage value increases with an increase in A/C system pressure. If the pressure is too high or too low, the compressor clutch is disengaged by the PCM.

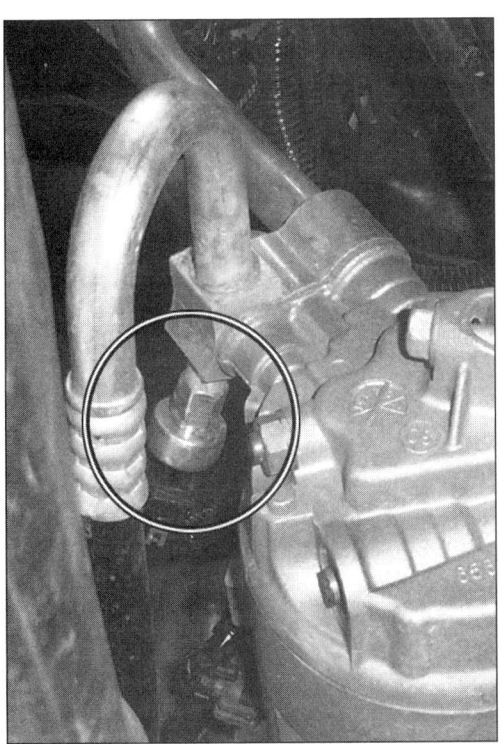

A/C Pressure Sensor

Notes:

SWITCHES

Switch inputs are on/off signals to the computer, that provide information about the state of a component or system operation. Examples are the A/C button on the control head, power steering pressure, or a transmission range switch.

Pressure Switches

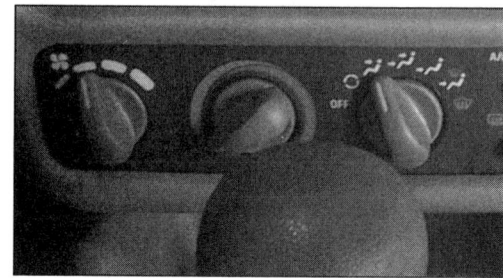
Switches on Dashboard

SWITCH CIRCUITS

The computer uses one of two switch circuit designs to read the switch position; pull-up or pull-down.

In a pull-up circuit, an external voltage runs through the switch to the computer.

When the switch closes it completes the circuit and the computer sees the voltage. When the switch opens, the voltage reads 0 at the computer.

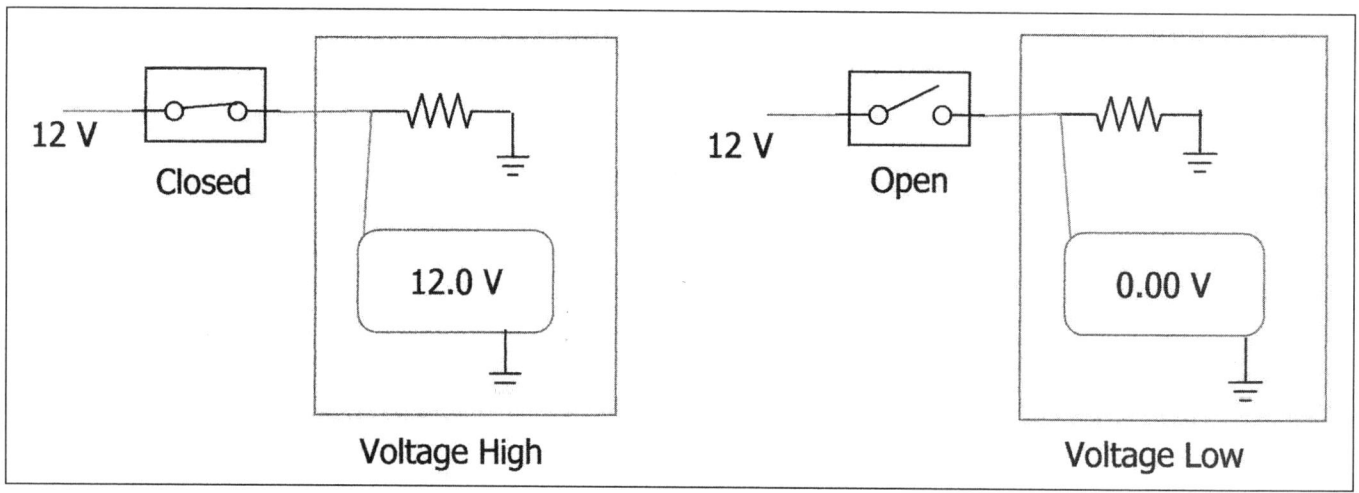
Pull-up Switch Circuit

Notes:

SECTION 4 • BASIC COMPUTER OPERATION & FUNCTION 67

In a pull-down circuit, the computer sends a voltage through an internal resistor.

When the input switch opens, the computer will see the voltage. When the switch closes, the voltage will go to ground and the computer will see no voltage.

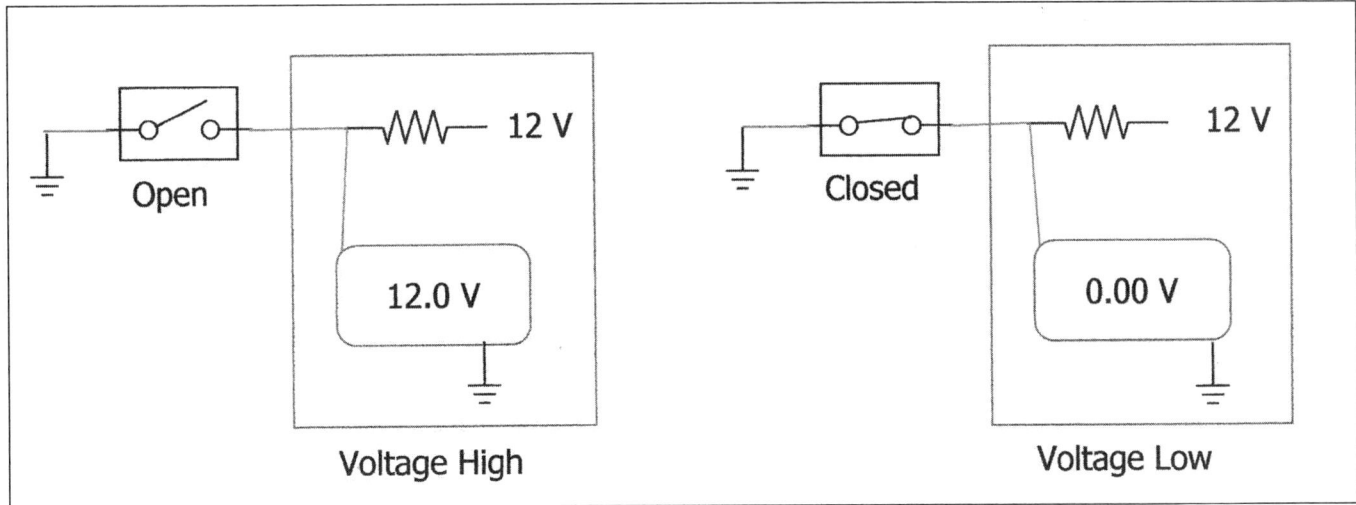

Pull-down Switch Circuit

Serial Data

Serial Data

Serial data can be an input or an output. The computer uses serial data to send information to various modules on the vehicle, as well as to a scan tool.

However, serial data can also be an input. For example, the PCM receives an A/C request signal from the control head. This request arrives over the serial data line. When A/C is requested, the PCM will ground the compressor clutch relay if conditions permit.

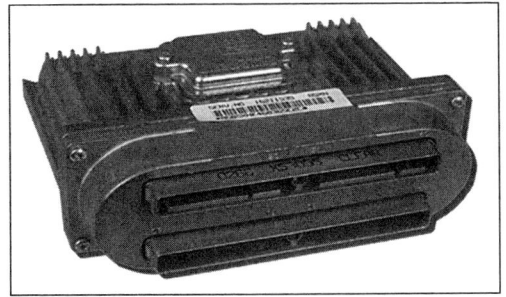

Powertrain Control Module (PCM)

A main computer module, often the powertrain control module, receives readings directly from the various inputs. It will send the readings to other computer modules that require the data.

COMPUTER OUTPUTS & OUTPUT DEVICES

After input data is processed by the computer modules, there are several output circuit configurations that are designed to perform specific tasks.

Outputs fall into one of the following six groups:
1. Relays
2. Solenoids
3. Motors
4. Controllers
5. Diagnostics
6. Serial Data

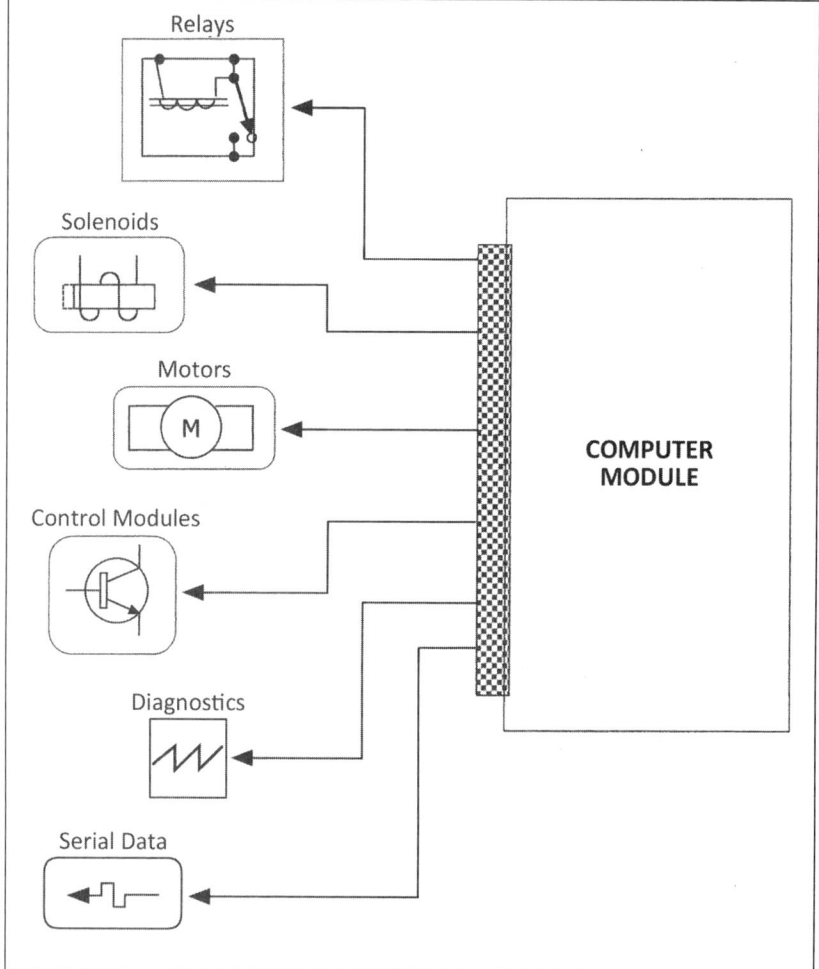

Six Output Groups

Computer output circuits are designed to perform specific tasks. Work that is directed or performed by the computer module is achieved by applying ground to an electrical circuit, applying power to an electrical device, or providing both power and ground to an electrical circuit.

Notes:

SECTION 4 • BASIC COMPUTER OPERATION & FUNCTION

Relays

Relays allow the computer to operate components that require more current than the computer is capable of handling. A relay is an electromagnetic switching device using low current to open or close a high-current circuit.

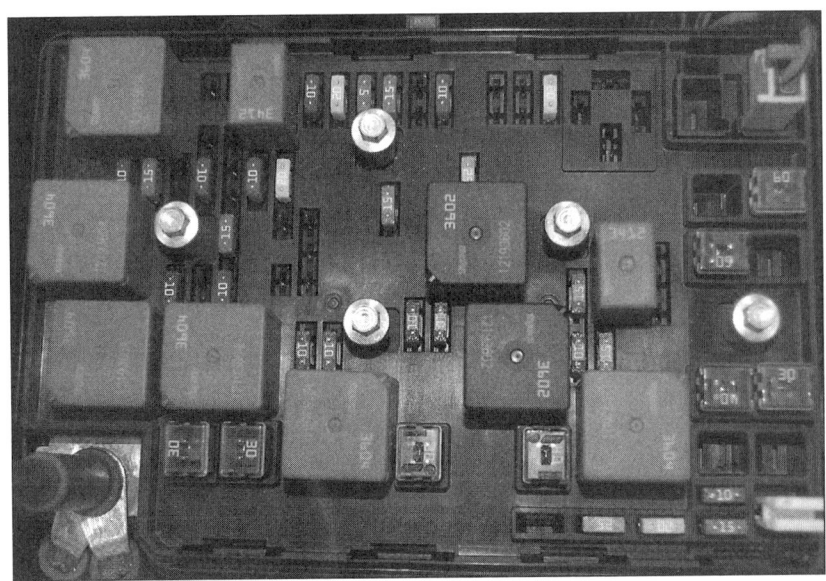
Relay Box

Relays may either be power or ground controlled. Power controlled relays receive power from the computer to turn on the relay. Ground controlled relays (the most common type) are grounded by the computer to energize the relay.

Blower motors, compressor clutches, and cooling fan motors are controlled with relays.

Most relays are voltage-spike protected. They will have a diode or a resistor that dissipates electrical spikes to protect switches, transistors, or computers.

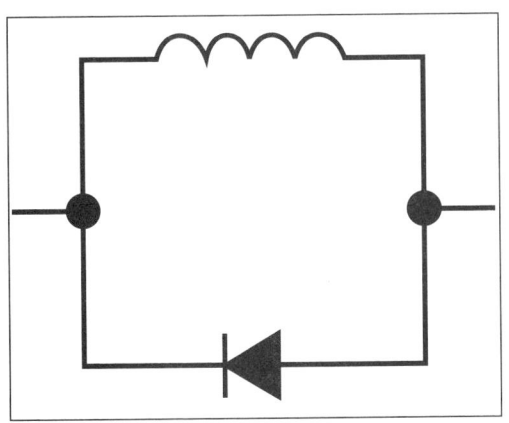
Voltage Spike Resistor Diagram

Notes:

Solenoids

The computer uses solenoids as actuators to perform tasks. The image below shows a simple solenoid. A solenoid is a device that converts electrical energy to mechanical movement. It may switch a component on and off, move a valve to control hydraulic pressure or fuel pressure, or engage a device such as a starter motor.

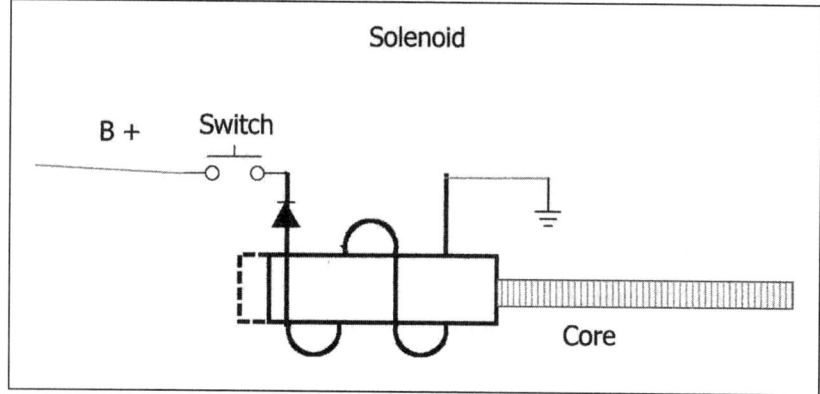

Diagram of Simple Solenoid

Solenoids may either be power or ground controlled. Most automotive solenoids are ground controlled.

A solenoid has a wire coil with a movable core which changes position by means of electromagnetism when current flows through the coil. Many solenoids are voltage-spike protected and will have a diode, resistor or capacitor to dissipate high voltage spikes when the circuit is opened.

If the windings inside the solenoid short together, excessive current will pass through the computer circuit that is controlling the solenoid, and damage to the computer will occur.

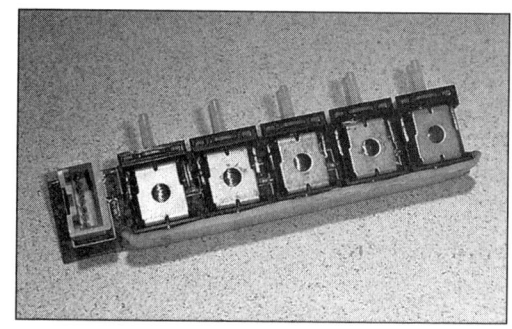

Solenoid Bank

Notes:

SECTION 4 • BASIC COMPUTER OPERATION & FUNCTION

Motors

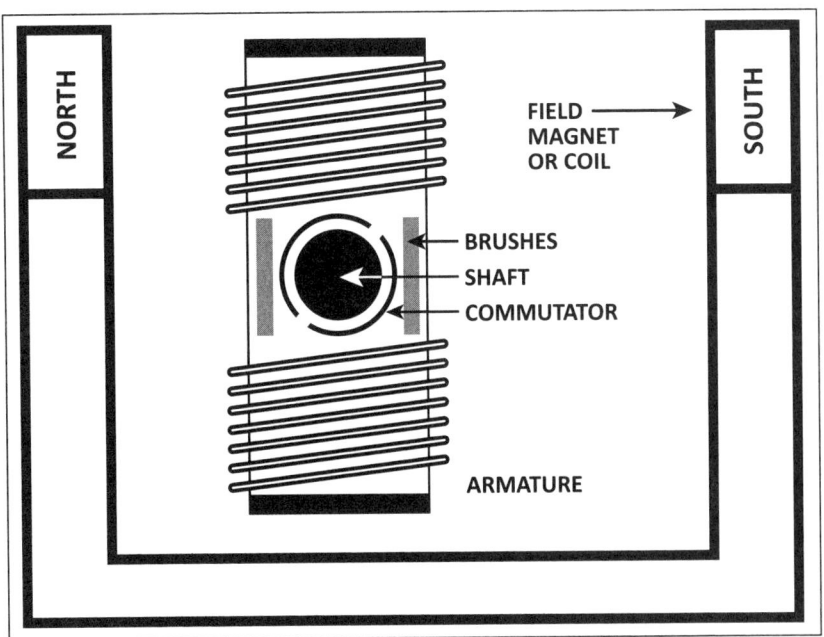

A Typical Motor

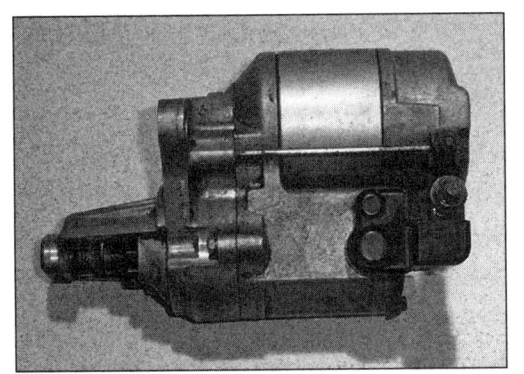

Hi-Torque Starter Motor

There are many different motors found on a modern vehicle. A motor is another device that converts electrical energy into mechanical movement. Motors come in various designs, one of which is series-wound. A series-wound motor has the field coils connected in series with the armature. A high-torque starter motor might be of this design.

Shunt-wound Blower Motor

A shunt-wound motor has the field coils in parallel with the armature. Shunt winding gives the motor a constant maximum speed at a given voltage. An HVAC blower motor is an example of a shunt wound motor.

COOLING FAN MOTORS

The computer may control the cooling fan motor(s) through a relay. The computer will use inputs from the engine coolant sensor, intake air temperature sensor, A/C mode selector, A/C pressure sensor and the vehicle speed sensor to determine when the fan(s) should operate.

The air conditioning pressure sensor will send the A/C system pressure as a voltage to signal the computer to turn on the cooling fans, or the engine coolant temperature sensor will input the engine coolant temperature and signal the PCM when the coolant is approximately 225° F.

The computer will activate the control circuit in the cooling fan relay(s) and the cooling fans will turn on with a power supply from the battery.

Electric Cooling Fans in Vehicle

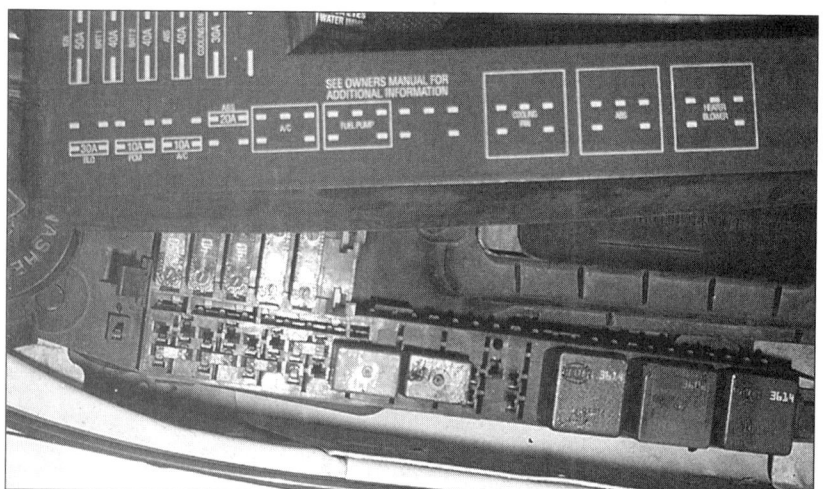
Cooling Fan Control Circuit Relay

ACTUATOR MOTORS

The computer can control low-current motors such as an A/C blend door motor and air delivery motors. The computer controls motor direction by controlling the voltage polarity to the motor. By switching the polarity of the voltage signal, the motor can turn in either direction. This is how the computer switches the blend door to control whether hot air or cold air is delivered from the HVAC vents. If the motor is bidirectional, the computer will supply both power and ground.

Actuators

Notes:

SECTION 4 • BASIC COMPUTER OPERATION & FUNCTION

Cooling Fan Module

Controller Modules

Controller modules allow a computer to operate high amperage devices. The computer sends a low amperage signal to the controller, and the controller operates the high amperage device. Control modules can operate on the power or ground side of a circuit. Examples of controller modules are integrated control modules used to control cooling fans and blower motors.

Cooling fan modules are solid state devices that use pulse width modulation to control cooling fan operation. The module sends 12 volts to the PCM. The PCM then pulses the module ground circuit to control fan speed.

Warning Light on Control Knob

Diagnostics

Computers on many vehicles contain built in diagnostics that will alert the operator if a malfunction has occurred. A diagnostic indicator may be a warning lamp, flashing LED, or a buzzer. When these warning indicators are activated, the next step is to use scan tools, a multimeter and service information to pinpoint the problem.

Warning Light on Dash

Notes:

SERIAL DATA OUTPUTS

Computers can send large amounts of serial data through various networks to scan tools and other computers and controllers. In the case of the controller area network (CAN) bus on a late model vehicle, the speed can be as high as a half million bits per second (bps).

Controller Area Network (CAN)

Modern vehicles offer state of the art features such as adaptive cruise control, vehicle stability control, occupant classification system, and displacement on demand. Some of these advances were brought to reality through an advanced on-board networking system termed controller area network (CAN). The fast CAN systems deliver information in real time so modules can react almost instantaneously.

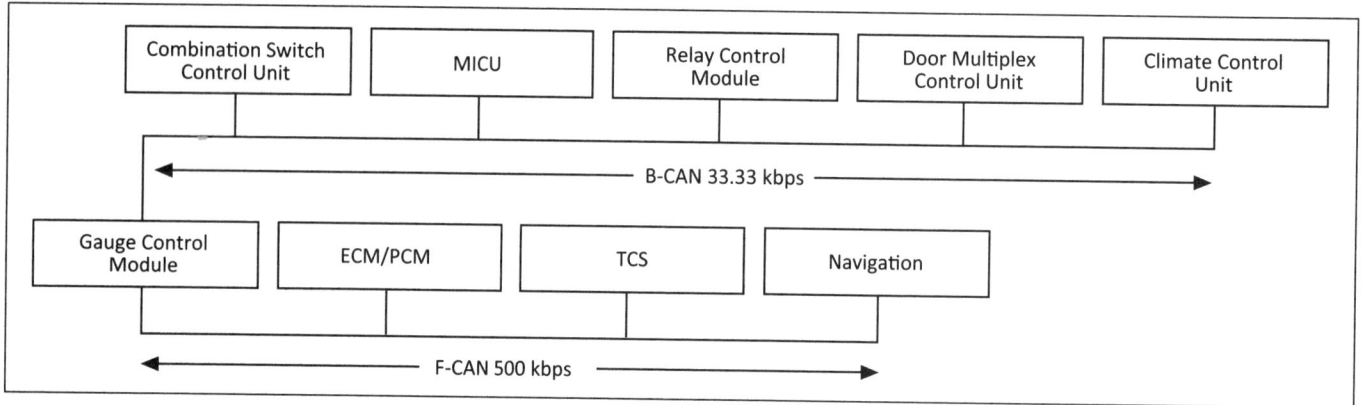

CAN Network

CAN systems vary greatly from one manufacturer to another. The CAN protocol dictates the design of the message structure. The physical layer of the CAN system determines how the messages will be sent, including voltage, current, frequency, and the number of wires.

Some busses will be a twisted pairs of wires or may be a single wire depending on manufacturer or system being controlled.

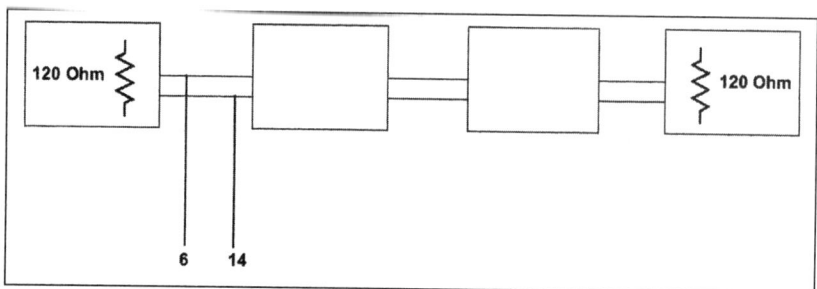

Twisted Pair CAN bus Network

SECTION 4 • BASIC COMPUTER OPERATION & FUNCTION

CAN bus system modules broadcast messages almost simultaneously over the data bus.

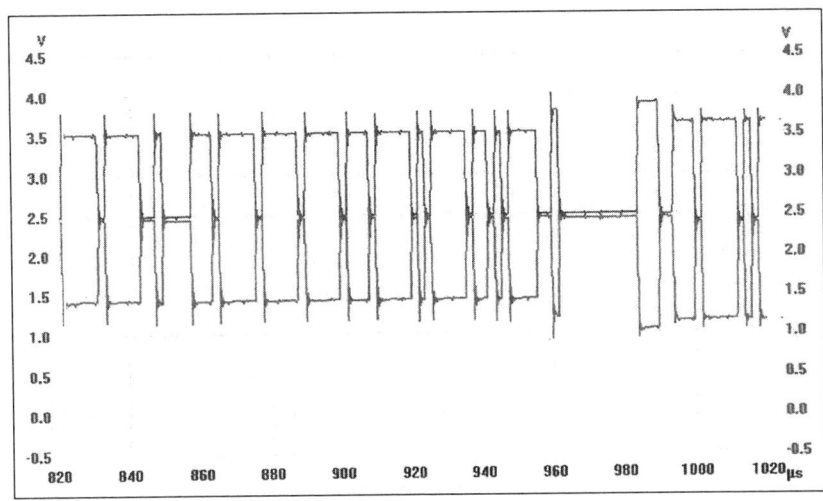

CAN Transmission Rate Diagram

A body CAN transmission rate may be as high as 83,300 bits per second. Body and convenience modules that do not require real time communications use this protocol. CAN for body functions supports single wire mode for many fault problems. If a problem occurs on either wire of the twisted pair, this network can move to the remaining wire for messaging. CAN body also uses sleep and wake-up functionality to lower ignition off draw (IOD), which otherwise could produce parasitic draw and drain the battery.

The chassis-CAN (C-CAN) transmission rate is at 500,000 bits per second. Systems such as PCM, electronic stability control, and a supplemental inflator module require real-time data, so will use C-CAN networks. C-CAN operates in the key on position and has no wake-up or sleep function.

Notes:

A high-speed scan tool and lab scope are required to work on CAN systems. Using wiring diagrams and the scan tool, retrieve DTCs from the control modules on the bus. The DTC may point to a single module or circuit as the problem.

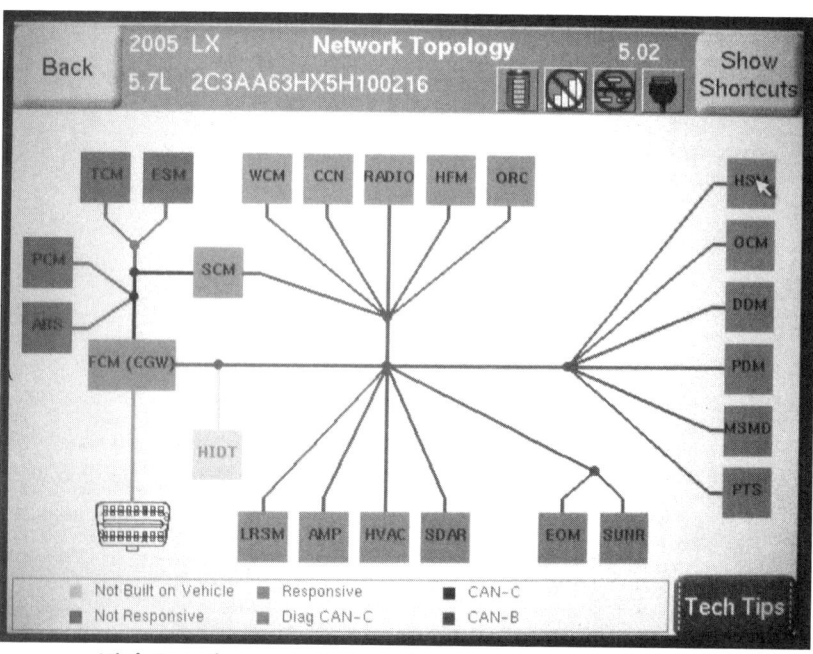

High Speed Scan Tool Displaying Modules on the CAN bus

If a scan tool test shows more than one module stating that another specific module is not communicating, that particular module should be looked at first.

Bus Communication Error Messages

SECTION 4 • BASIC COMPUTER OPERATION & FUNCTION

If a bus is shorted to a ground, battery voltage, or to a 5-volt circuit, the bus will shut down. In the case of a complete bus failure, start by disconnecting individual modules. If the bus becomes active when a module is disconnected, that may be the one at fault. If all the modules except one are disconnected, the bus wiring is probably at fault. The image on the preceding page indicates three individual bus communication failures.

The computers process information at a very fast rate. Using a multimeter is not a practical way to collect data. A scan tool is the most effective way to communicate with, and peer into, computers, and to display data. CAN operating systems require a scan tool that is capable of reading the high speed data lines.

Newer systems will require using a laptop with a special interface to read the growing number of super-fast data lines on vehicles.

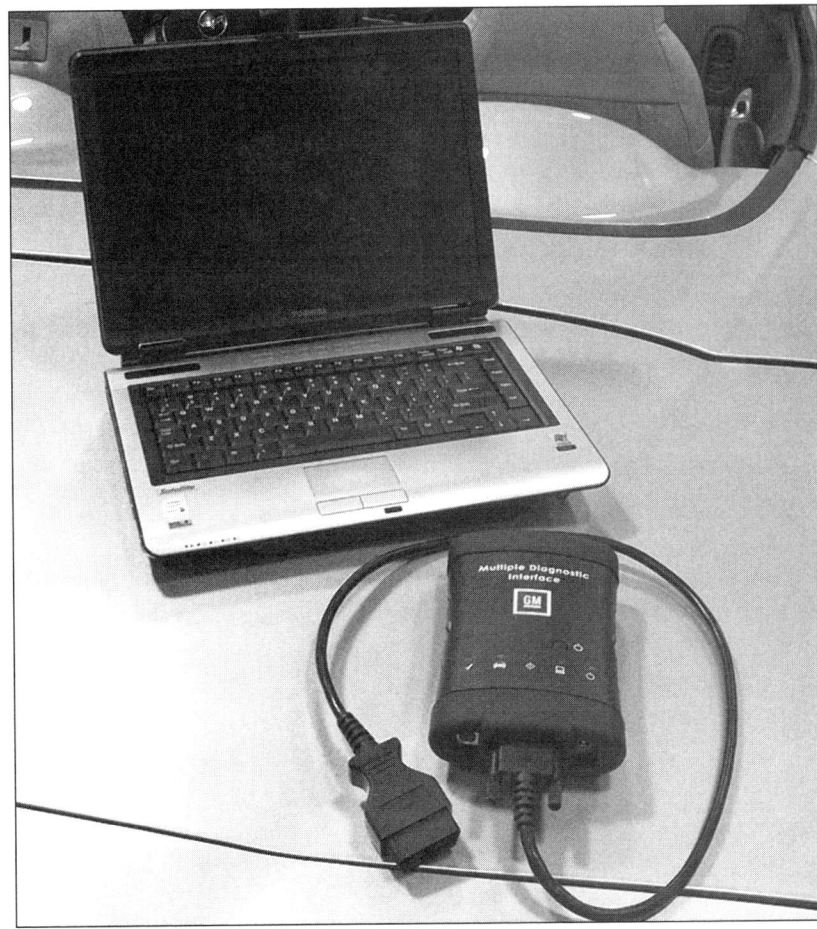

Newer Diagnostic Tool with Laptop

SEMICONDUCTORS

Throughout this section, the terms diodes, transistors, and thermistors have been used. The term semiconductor is linked to the diode. A semiconductor is literally a half conductor. A conductor generally provides a very low resistance in either direction, but semiconductor materials have higher resistance to electron flow or conduction in one direction.

Diodes

Diodes are the basic building block of electronic components, electronic switches that may be used for rectification, voltage regulation or voltage suppression, depending how one is used in a circuit. The semiconductor materials are joined in a special way so that when the correct polarity voltage is applied, electrons flow through both materials across the junction.

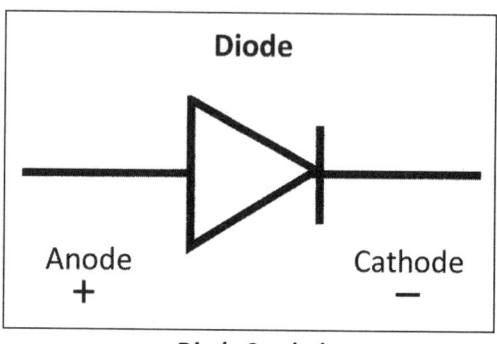
Diode Symbol

A diode uses two types of materials that pass electrons freely in one direction, but oppose electron flow in the opposite direction. Unlike a resistor or capacitor, which can be placed in a circuit without regard to electron flow, the diode must be installed facing the proper direction. A diode has a positive and a negative side. The negative side of the diode must be placed on the positive leg of the circuit or the diode will be destroyed. The image to the right shows the symbol used in a wiring diagram that is used to represent a diode.

As discussed in the section on magnetism, a voltage spike is developed when a coil field collapses; this "clamping diode" will force the voltage spike to ground.

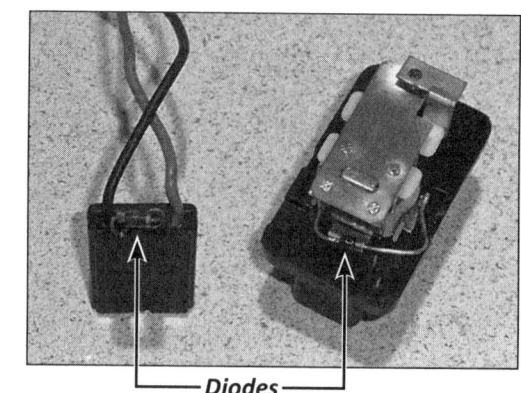

Notes:

SECTION 4 • BASIC COMPUTER OPERATION & FUNCTION

Two other types of diodes that are commonly found on vehicles are Zener diodes and light emitting diodes (LED).

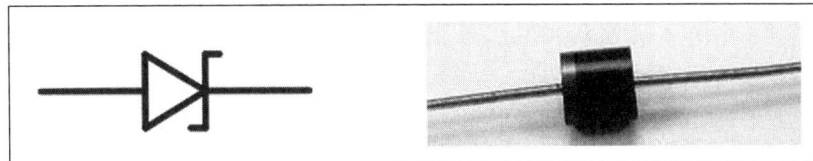

Zener Diode and Symbol

A Zener diode can conduct in the opposite direction after a certain voltage is reached. This voltage is called breakdown voltage; the Zener diode is designed to tolerate this voltage that would destroy an ordinary diode. A Zener diode is often used to control the maximum voltage level in a low current computer circuit, or to maintain the value of a reference voltage.

Light emitting diodes (LEDs) are made with materials that are translucent. When current flows through an LED, light is emitted. The image to the left shows the symbol used to represent a light emitting diode.

LEDs are used as indicator lamps and are increasingly being used for vehicle lighting.

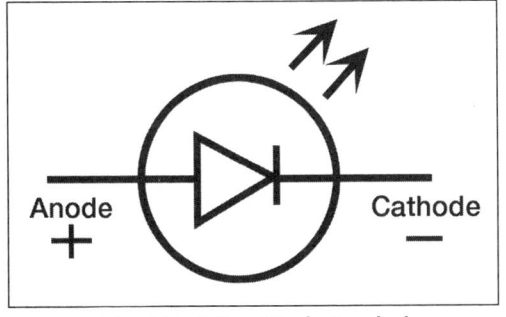

Light Emitting Diode Symbol

Resistors

Resistors are used to drop voltage. Most resistors have a fixed value.

Resistors have replaced diodes in some spike suppression applications, such as inside relays. The advantage of a resistor is that it is not polarity sensitive.

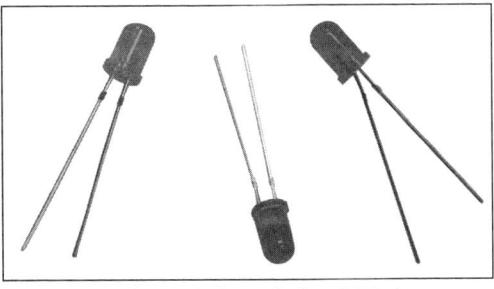

Light Emitting Diodes (LEDs)

Notes:

Devices like the A/C pressure sensor (ACP) and the throttle position sensor (TPS), discussed earlier, are variable resistors. Called potentiometers, variable resistors have a movable contact and a fixed contact. As position or pressure changes, voltage passing through the potentiometer will increase or decrease.

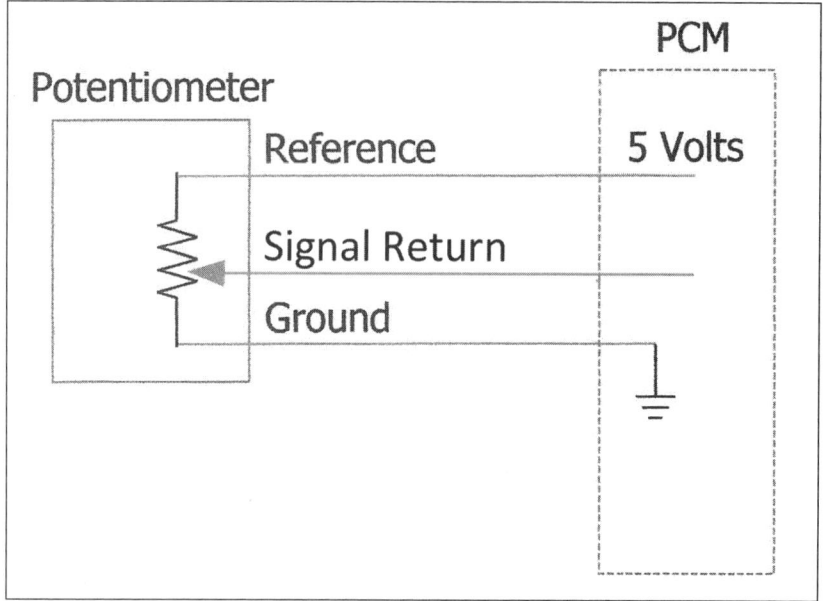

Potentiometer to PCM Diagram

THERMISTORS

Thermistors are a type of resistor designed to do the opposite of what a "normal" resistor would do; as the temperature of a thermistor increases, the resistance value decreases. Thermistors are used for various engine sensors such as engine coolant temperature (ECT) and intake air temperature (IAT).

The HVAC system will use thermistors for outside and in vehicle temperature sensors and for evaporator temperature sensors, to prevent evaporator freeze up. A multimeter can be used to measure a thermistor's resistance.

Thermistors

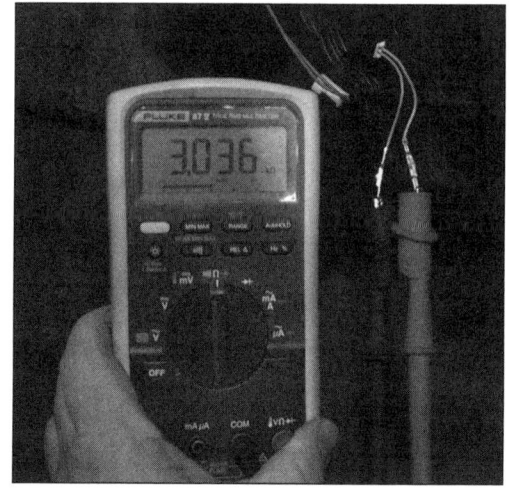

DVM Measuring Thermistor Resistance

SECTION 4 • BASIC COMPUTER OPERATION & FUNCTION

Capacitors

Capacitors act as electrical storage tanks.

They are useful for keeping circuits alive for a specific amount of time after a circuit is turned off. Supplemental Restraint Systems rely on capacitors for "emergency" power. Capacitors are also used in electronic circuits to block the flow of DC current while still allowing AC current to flow.

Capacitors

Transistors

Transistors are semiconductor devices that have three terminals. They are made of the same types of materials as diodes. Transistors are used to control current flow, and as such, often are used as a switch or relay. Many circuits found in HVAC systems use transistors in the place of mechanical relays. The benefit of a transistor is that it will not wear out like a relay, which has mechanical contact points, movable joints and springs. The electronic relay can switch faster than a mechanical design, which is necessary in fast operating computer circuits.

There are two basic types of transistors: NPN and PNP. The operation of both types of transistors is the same except for the polarities of the connections used. The center letter indicates if the base is positive (P) or negative (N). The three transistor legs and their purpose are:

- Base – The base is the center layer of material in the transistor. Voltage applied to the base controls the amount of current that is allowed to flow through the other two layers. The base is represented by the straight line connected to the middle terminal.

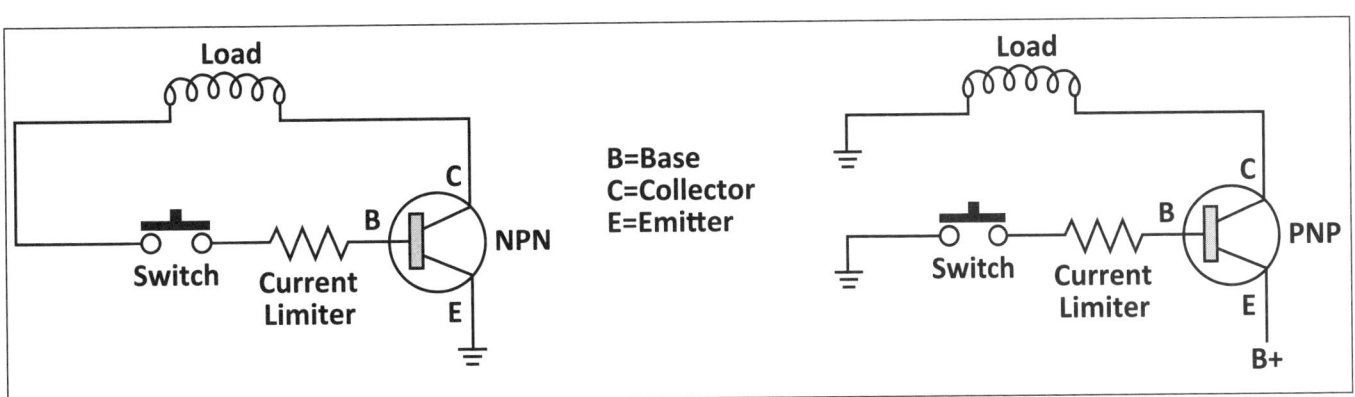
NPN and PNP Transistors Diagram

- Emitter – One of the outside layers of material, it gives off electrons when the base has voltage applied to it. The emitter is represented by the diagonal line with the arrow.
- Collector – The other outside layer of material, it collects the electrons given off by the emitter. The collector is represented in the symbol as a diagonal line.

INTEGRATED CIRCUITS

Integrated circuits (IC) contain a number of diodes, transistors, resistors and capacitors.

ICs provide the ability for designers to create complex circuits and systems that can be packaged in small spaces for less cost.

Integrated Circuit (IC) Board

Many HVAC control heads contain ICs and have the ability to make decisions and send output signals.

HVAC Control Head showing Internal Integrated Circuits

Notes:

SECTION 4 • BASIC COMPUTER OPERATION & FUNCTION

Worksheet 3 – Section 4

Task: Read Available CAN Bus Data Using a Scan Tool

Tools and Materials Needed:

- MACS HVAC Systems, Volume 2 - Electrical and Electronic Systems Operation Manual
- Late model vehicle
- Vehicle service information
- An OE or aftermarket scan tool

Vehicle to be used:

Year _____ Make _____ Model _____

VIN _____

Engine Type _____ Displacement _____

Procedure:

Using an available vehicle, Section 4 of the MACS HVAC Systems, Volume 2 - Electrical and Electronic Systems Operation Manual as a reference, vehicle service information, and a scan tool, perform the following:

1. Identify the DLC pins that are used by the CAN bus(es).
2. Identify those same DLC pins on the actual vehicle.
3. Using a scan tool, read all information/data available pertaining to the bus(es).
4. Record the results below.

How many bus circuits does this vehicle use? _____

What are the DLC pin numbers used by the CAN bus circuits? _____

Describe the data available using the scan tool:

_____

_____

_____

_____

_____

_____

_____

Section 4 Review –
Introduction to Electronics and System Controls

1. Technician A says there are two types of signals: analog and digital. Technician B says computers prefer an analog signal. Who is correct?
   - A. Technician A
   - B. Technician B
   - C. Both Technician A and Technician B
   - D. Neither Technician A nor Technician B

2. Which of these statements is/are correct?
   - A. On many late model vehicles, the powertrain control module (PCM) controls the A/C system.
   - B. An incorrect signal from the crankshaft position sensor may affect A/C operation.
       - A. Statement A is correct
       - B. Statement B is correct
       - C. Both Statements A and B are correct
       - D. Neither Statement A nor B is correct

3. True or False: The use of a relay allows a large current from a computer circuit to control a small current to a component.
   - A. True
   - B. False

4. Clamping diodes are being discussed. Technician A says the compressor clutch coil and a solenoid may use one. Technician B says a clamping diode is used to eliminate voltage spikes. Who is correct?
   - A. Technician A
   - B. Technician B
   - C. Both Technician A and Technician B
   - D. Neither Technician A nor Technician B

5. Which of these statements is/are correct?
   - A. The CAN bus on a late model vehicle is a network that carries data to and from multiple systems.
   - B. A scan tool, a lab scope or perhaps a laptop computer may be used to read data from the CAN bus.
       - A. Statement A is correct
       - B. Statement B is correct
       - C. Both statements A and B are correct
       - D. Neither statement A nor B is correct

Notes:

Section 5: Electrical/Electronic Troubleshooting and Diagnostics

TYPES OF CIRCUIT FAILURES

The type of circuit failure will dictate what must be done to repair the problem. Failures can be categorized in the following way:

- Opens – An open is a physical break in the path of current flow. In a series circuit, the entire circuit will stop operating. In parallel circuits, the open branch will stop operating, but the other branches will continue to work.
- Short to ground – A short to ground occurs when a circuit wire is grounded due to insulation failure. If it is on the feed side of the circuit, it will cause the fuse to blow, or the fusible link to open. If there is no circuit protection, the circuit may burn and could cause a fire. If the short happens after the load, the load may operate regardless of switch position.
- Short to voltage – A short to voltage occurs when a wire in a circuit makes contact with a source from the positive side of the battery. Isolation, by removing fuses, will often help find the circuit(s) that are involved.
- High resistance – High resistance is caused by loose, dirty or corroded terminals and poor connections. Circuit current flow will be lower than it should be and the circuit or a load may not operate.

ELECTRICAL/ELECTRONIC TEST EQUIPMENT

Electrical troubleshooting and diagnostics requires the use of various types of test equipment. See examples on the next page.

- **Test light** – A test light is useful to check for the voltage and in some cases is used to add a load to a circuit during a test procedure. **ATTENTION: Never use a test light on circuits that contain solid-state components; the test light will damage them! Never use a test light during a circuit or component test process unless directed by service information!**
- **Digital multimeter (DMM)** – This is a tool of choice. The DMM will indicate how much voltage is present. **ATTENTION: Be sure that the DMM has a minimum of 10-Megohm or higher impedance to prevent component damage!**

- **Jumper wires** – Jumper wires are helpful to find opens in circuits or to power a circuit. Be sure that the jumper wire has an in line fuse so that circuit protection is present while testing. **ATTENTION: Never use a jumper wire to bypass a load!**

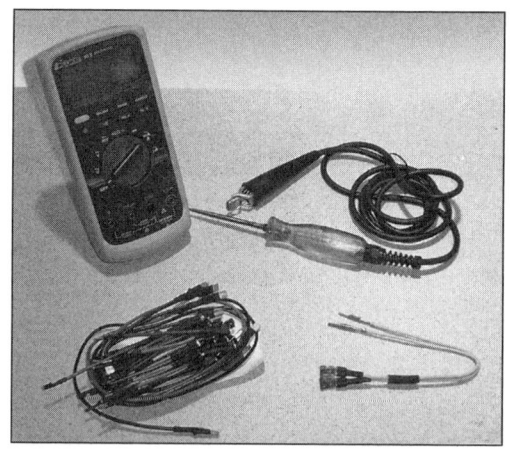

Digital Multimeter, Test Light, and Two Types of Jumper Wires

- **Scan tools** – A scan tool is a hand held diagnostic computer designed to diagnose electronic systems on vehicles. Scan tools connect to the vehicle's computers through the data link connector (DLC) and can check for communication between modules, read trouble codes, view input and output data, and perform tests of the various component controls and modules. Scan tools are available in OEM or aftermarket models. Many aftermarket models will not perform in-depth testing, or have the ability to connect with all modules on a particular vehicle.

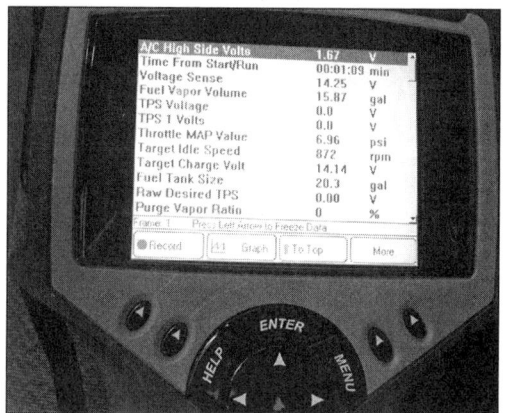

Scan Tool

Data Link Connector

- **Oscilloscopes** – Oscilloscopes, although not a required diagnostic tool, are an asset when working with CAN systems. The oscilloscope provides a visual scale of voltage and time.
An oscilloscope is useful for diagnosing suspect circuits that have intermittent problems. It will also show the pulse width modulation (PWM) on circuits such as blower motors that are powered by a module instead of through a fixed resistor.

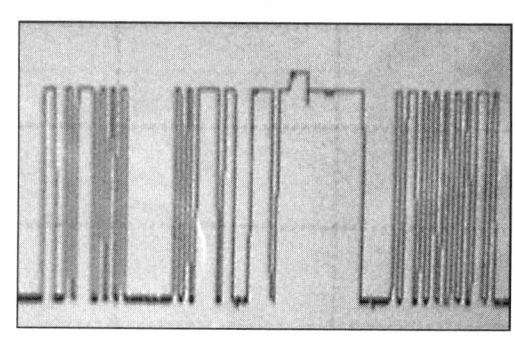

Oscilloscope Reading

SECTION 5 • ELECTRICAL/ELECTRONIC TROUBLESHOOTING & DIAG.

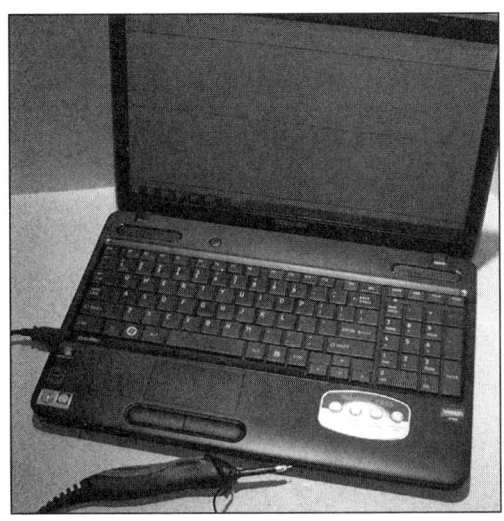

Laptop Used for Diagnosis

In some instances a laptop computer may be used as an alternative to an oscilloscope, requiring special hardware and software to adapt it.

Diagnostic Procedures

With any repair process, following a strategy helps to get the vehicle fixed right the first time:

- Interview the customer. Record their concern accurately.
- If needed, road test the vehicle.
- Verify the concern.
- Perform a visual inspection.
- Complete preliminary checks.

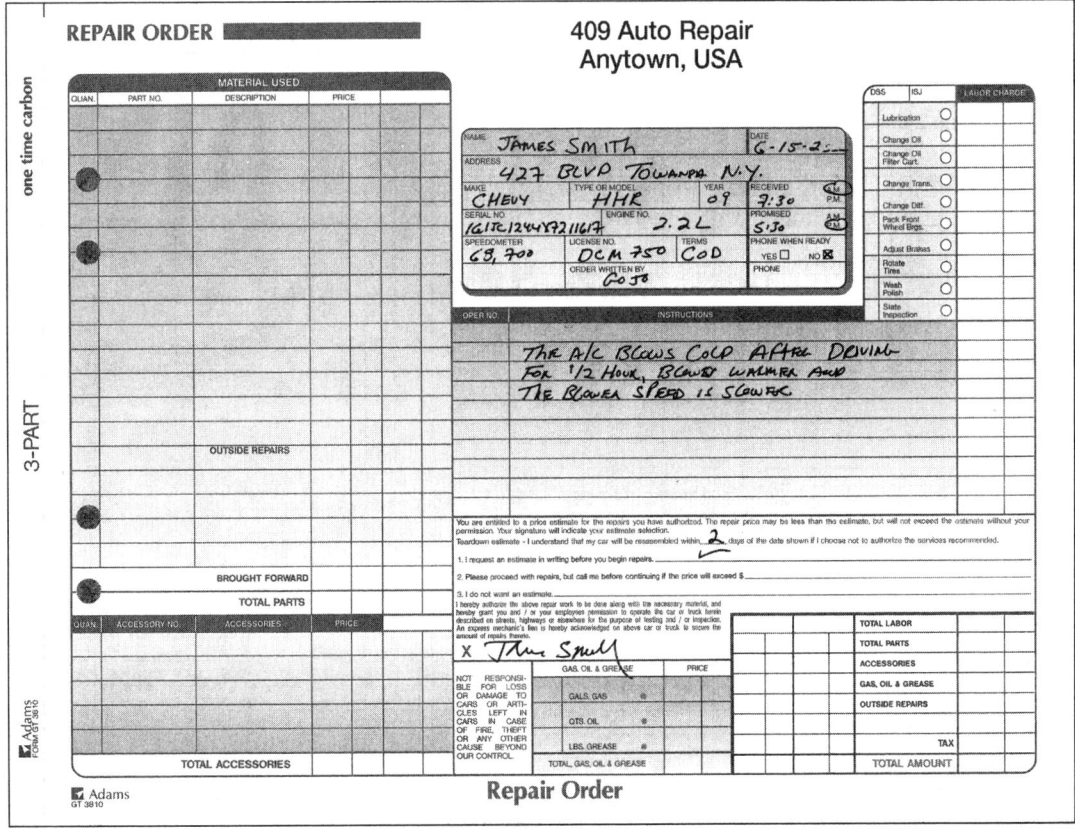

Repair Order

88 ELECTRICAL/ELECTRONIC TROUBLESHOOTING & DIAG. • SECTION 5

- Perform battery and charging system checks.
- Check for TSBs possibly showing updates and recalibrations.
- Check for DTCs.
- Review the circuit wiring diagram and circuit operation.
- Analyze the circuit and component operation.
- Find the cause and repair it.
- Verify the repair.

An accurate description of the customer's concern is important; there may not be an actual problem; the system may be functioning normally.

For example, a vehicle's HVAC system may be designed to switch into recirculation when high side pressure reaches a certain level, or to switch the HVAC system from recirculation back to normal position after a specific amount of time.

Visual Inspection is important. A visual inspection may reveal some obvious things that are causing electrical issues on a vehicle. For example, If a battery cable is not routed correctly, it can lead to voltage drop and components will not function or may be damaged.

Improperly Routed Battery Cable

Loose or missing body grounds can cause the current returning to the battery to seek alternate paths.

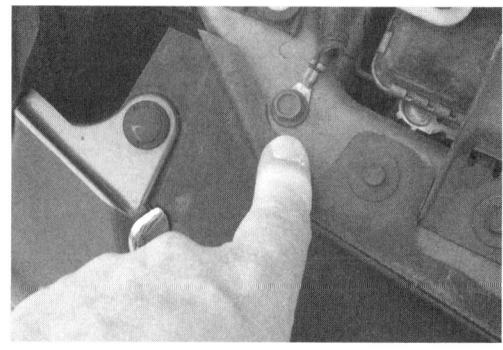
Body Ground

Notes:

SECTION 5 • ELECTRICAL/ELECTRONIC TROUBLESHOOTING & DIAG.

Corroded Battery Terminal

Corroded or loose battery terminal clamps will cause voltage drop and will affect component operation.

A voltage drop test performed between the battery terminal and the cable clamp with loads activated will confirm the voltage loss.

Drive Belt Tensioner

Check belt condition and tension; if a belt is worn or loose, the generator will not be able to keep up with the electrical loads.

Electrical problems that result in low generator output could cause a vehicle to begin "load shedding" to keep the engine running. The A/C system may be one of the first ones shut down, to maintain available voltage to critical systems. Battery voltage must be between 12 and 14 volts for many modules to successfully operate.

Preliminary Diagnosis

Preliminary diagnostic tests can help pinpoint problems in computer circuits or the computer itself. Some vehicle on-board diagnostics may flash a warning lamp, sound a buzzer, or turn on an LED to alert the operator that the vehicle has a malfunction. In some applications, this warning will result in the PCM entering diagnostic mode. The purpose of diagnostic mode is to make sure the check engine lamp is working and to see if the computer is functioning and can recognize a fault.

If the scan tool reads "No Data," check the data line. The problem may also be the scan tool itself. For a quick check, use a multimeter to check the OBD II data link connector (DLC).

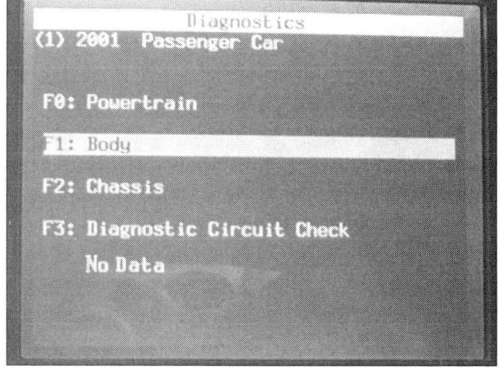
Scan Tool Reading "No Data"

Connect a multimeter from the scan tool chassis ground pin to the scan tool power pin; there should be source voltage present. See the image on the right. In our example, Pin 16 is the power pin and Pin 4 is the scan tool ground pin. Although the configuration of the DLC was standardized in 1996, it is very important to note that pin assignments are not necessarily the same from one vehicle to another.

If voltage is not present, the DLC circuit problem will have to be traced and repaired.

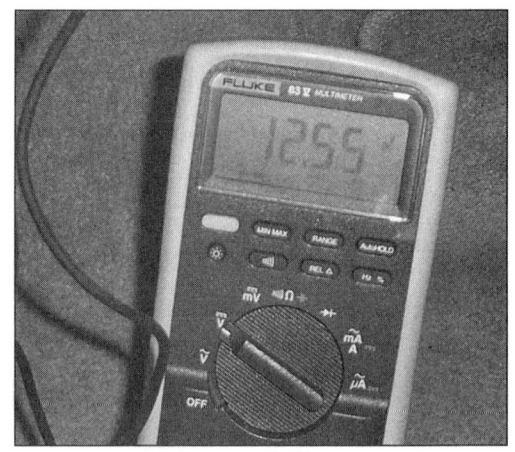
Multimeter Checking DLC

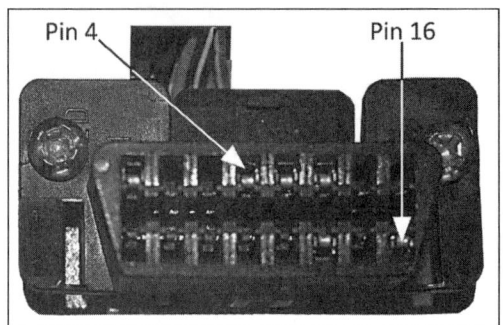
Data Link Connector Pins 4 and 16

Check the bus circuit by connecting a multimeter to the serial data pin and the serial data ground pin. See the image on the right. In our example, Pin 7 is the serial data pin and Pin 5 is the serial data ground pin. There should be pulsed voltage if the serial data line is working.

If the data line and power and ground circuits are working properly, the "no data" problem very likely lies with the scan tool itself.

Once these checks (if necessary) have been completed, and the scan tool and data lines are communicating, the next step is to perform charging system checks.

Multimeter Checking DLC

Data Link Connector Pins 5 and 7

SECTION 5 • ELECTRICAL/ELECTRONIC TROUBLESHOOTING & DIAG.

Battery and Charging System Testers

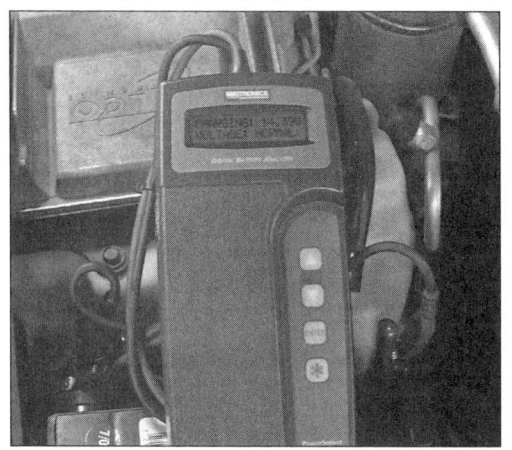

Charging System Tests

Modern vehicles may contain as many as 50 computers and if the charging system is weak, it will have a direct effect on the performance of all systems. Also, the battery must be the right size, and must be able to pass a load test. The images to the left show typical testers.

Many voltage regulator circuits are now controlled by the PCM or BCM and battery temperature is monitored. DTCs are available for the regulator and battery temperature sensor.

Do not overlook voltage drop tests between the generator and the battery, as well as testing from the engine block back to the negative battery post.

Charging System Voltage Drop Tests

Voltage drop test the positive side of the charging system by connecting one DMM lead to the generator output terminal. Connect the other DMM lead to the positive battery post.

The maximum drop should not exceed 0.4 volt.

Voltage Drop Test, Positive Side

To check the ground side, connect one DMM lead to the generator case, and the other to the negative battery post. See images on right.

The maximum voltage drop, with the charging system under some load, should not exceed 0.4 volt.

DMM Lead to Generator Case

DMM Lead to Negative Battery Post

Check for voltage drop between the negative battery post and the negative battery cable clamp. The reading should not exceed 0.1 volt.

Ground circuits are critical; most electrical failures occur on the ground sides of circuits.

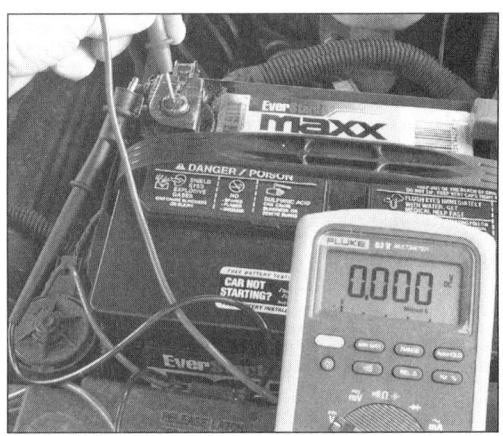
Negative Battery Post to Negative Battery Clamp

Notes:

SECTION 5 • ELECTRICAL/ELECTRONIC TROUBLESHOOTING & DIAG.

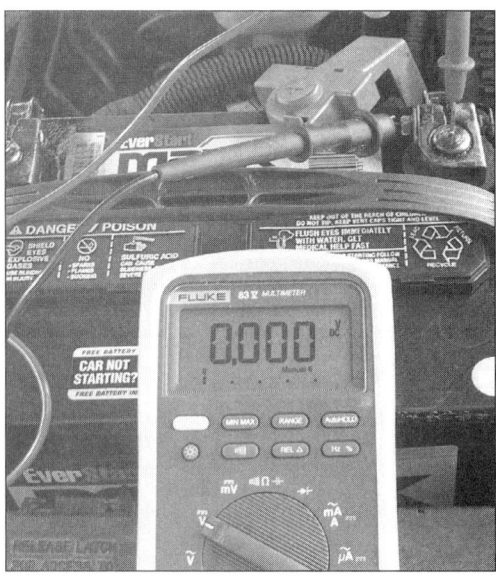
Voltage Drop Test - Positive Side

Also check for voltage drop between the positive battery post and the positive cable clamp.

The voltage drop should not exceed 0.1 volt.

Analytic Steps

Early into the analytic phase, check for updated service information. Check TSBs to see if computer reprogramming may be available to correct certain problems.

The internet is an excellent source to look for service information. A good website to obtain URLs for OEM service information sites is: www.oem1stop.com

Notes:

Scan Tool Checks

Scan tools are a necessity for diagnosing many concerns on today's A/C systems. Most A/C compressors are controlled by the PCM. The PCM will only activate the compressor clutch when the inputs received indicate that it is OK to do so. With the advent of OBD II and CAN data lines, there is a lot more data available to help pinpoint problems, particularly if a problem is intermittent.

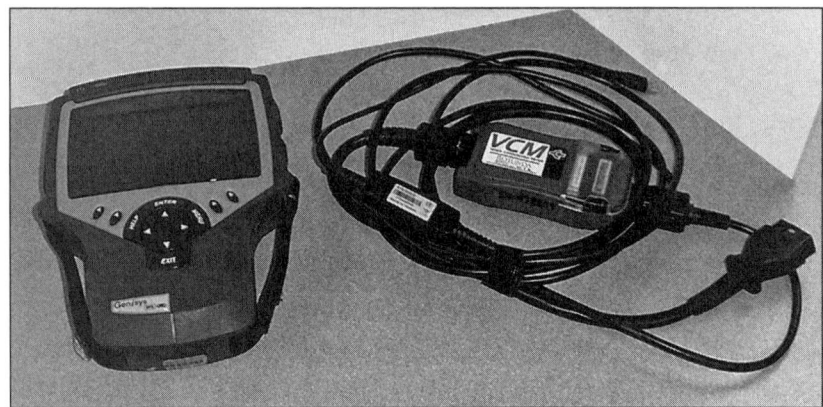
Scan Tools

Scan tools will check for the presence of DTCs. Diagnostic trouble codes are broken into four broad categories: B = Body; C= Chassis; P = Powertrain; and U = Network.

Refer to the image at right for the breakdown of a typical OBD II DTC definition. There are literally thousands of diagnostic trouble codes for today's vehicles. Always refer to the latest vehicle-specific service information for code definitions and explanations.

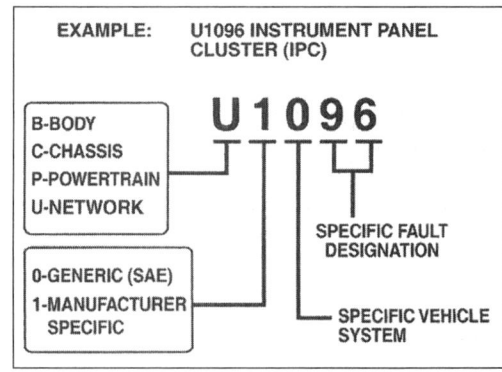
Sample Diagnostic Trouble Code (DTC)

Notes:

SECTION 5 • ELECTRICAL/ELECTRONIC TROUBLESHOOTING & DIAG.

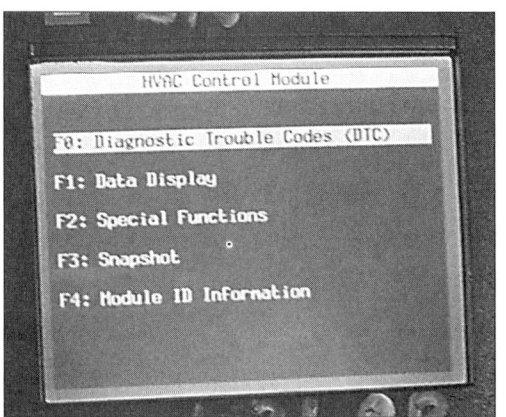

Checking an HVAC Control Module for Stored DTCs

To begin diagnosis, check for the presence of DTCs, including history and blind codes. History codes are set during the first event if an emission related malfunction occurs and requests for illumination of the MIL. For non-emission related systems, the fault will set a history code and request a service message lamp (if equipped). The image on the left shows the initial scan tool screen for retrieving an HVAC control module code.

Blind codes will be stored in history after the first failure, but will not request illumination of the MIL.

After a problem is repaired, the next step is to clear DTCs. A scan tool can be used to clear the DTCs.

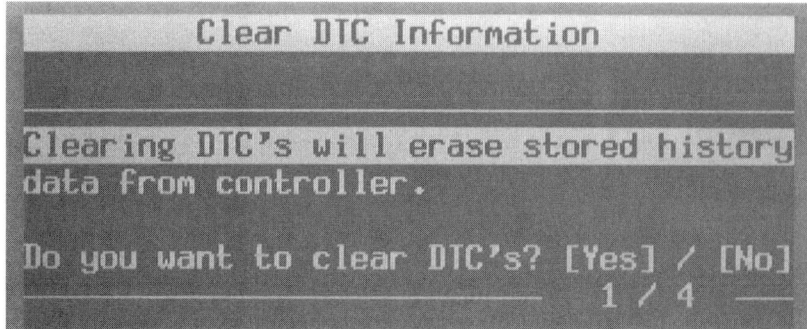

Preparing to Clear DTCs with a Scan Tool

Some scan tools can also perform recalibrations of the HVAC modules and actuators. When some actuators or HVAC control modules are removed or replaced, they must be recalibrated to work properly.

Scan Tool Being Used to Reset an HVAC Module

Notes:

96 ELECTRICAL/ELECTRONIC TROUBLESHOOTING & DIAG. • SECTION 5

Scan tools can display computer and module inputs and outputs from/to sensors and actuators. This data can be an asset when trying to determine why an A/C compressor clutch is not engaging.

Inputs that may affect A/C clutch operation include (but are not limited to):

- A/C system pressure
- Engine speed
- Throttle position
- Engine coolant temperature
- Intake air temperature
- Power steering pressure

If these sensor and switch values are either above or below the programmed operating range, the compressor clutch may not engage.

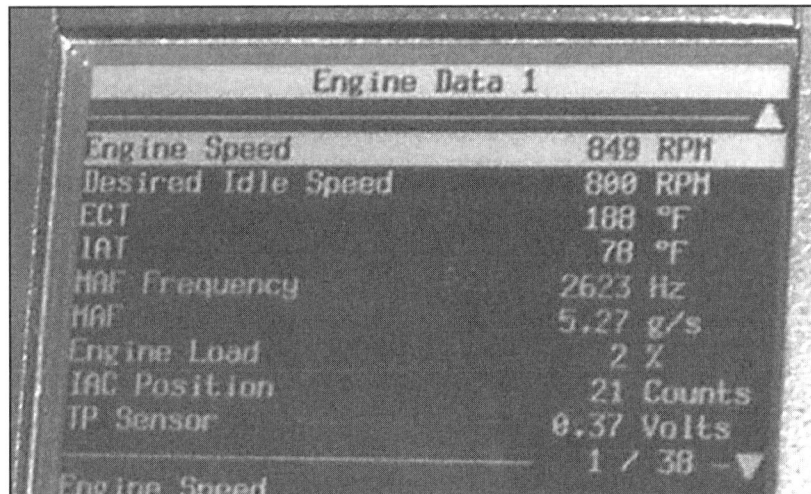
Engine Data Check

Depending on the vehicle, additional items that may effect compressor operation could include:

- A/C mode switch
- Body control module
- High and low pressure cut out switches
- Compressor clutch cycling switch
- Refrigerant pressure transducer
- Evaporator temperature sensor

The image to the right shows some of these input signals. A scan tool can also be used to check that the control head is providing an A/C request signal.

Notes:

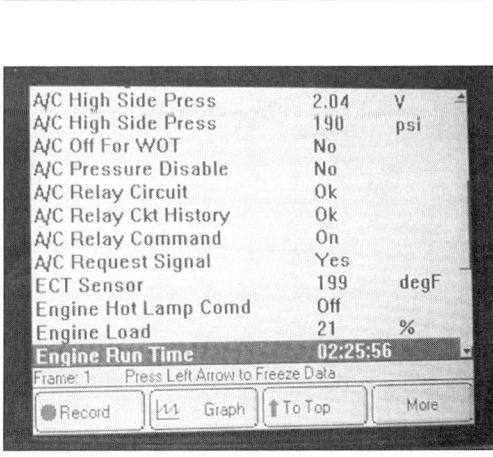
A/C System Related Input Signals

SECTION 5 • ELECTRICAL/ELECTRONIC TROUBLESHOOTING & DIAG.

The scan tool can also be used to activate relays that control the cooling fans and the A/C compressor clutch.

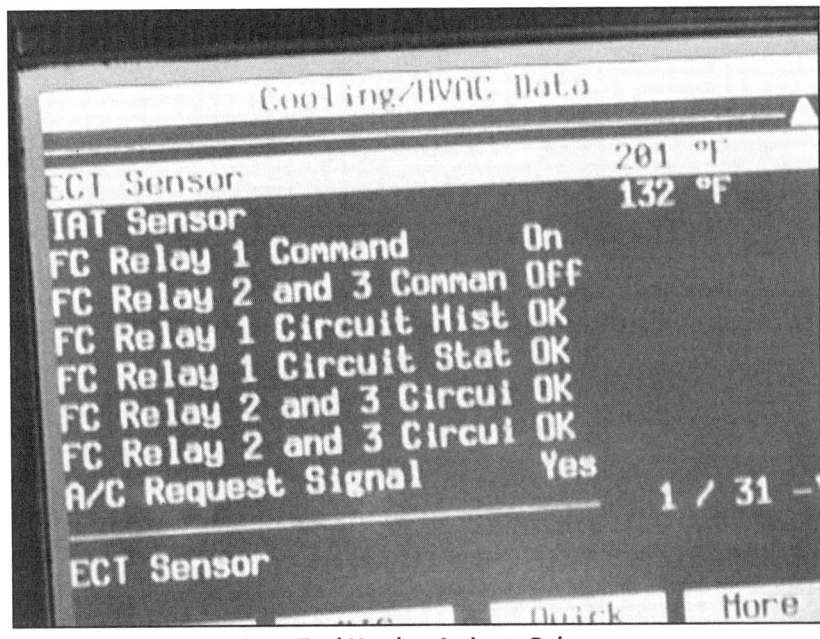
Scan Tool Used to Activate Relays

If the scan tool commands the relay to activate but a fan or clutch will not operate, then the problem is on the output side of the controller. Additional tests will be needed.

A scan tool is a versatile tester. However, a multimeter is usually required for pinpoint tests. A pinpoint test is measuring a specific voltage, current, or resistance to determine an exact cause of a problem.

Multimeter Testing

If a compressor clutch will not engage and the refrigerant charge is correct, the first step is to use a scan tool. If no DTCs are present and the scan tool cannot activate the clutch relay, the following steps should be taken:

- Perform a visual inspection; look for loose connections or obvious wiring damage.
- Using service information, review how the compressor clutch circuit is designed to operate and which switches, controls, and fuses are in the circuit.
- Using service information, locate the fuses and relays in the clutch circuit.
- Use a multimeter to measure the values of the different components to find the source of the problem.
- Make the repair and operate the circuit to be sure it is working properly.

98 ELECTRICAL/ELECTRONIC TROUBLESHOOTING & DIAG. • SECTION 5

Compressor Clutch Relay Checks

Before checking the compressor clutch relay, locate and check the fuses in the power distribution center (PDC), junction block or the fuse block.

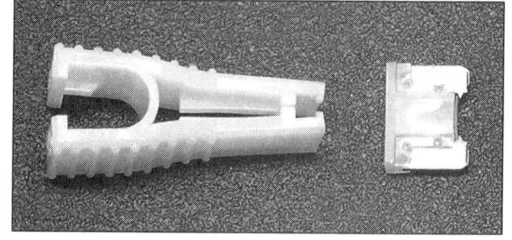
Fuse Puller and Fuse

As seen below, a fuse can be checked using the ohm setting on a multimeter. If the fuse is good, the meter will read 0 to 0.1 ohm; if the fuse is open the meter will read infinity (OL).

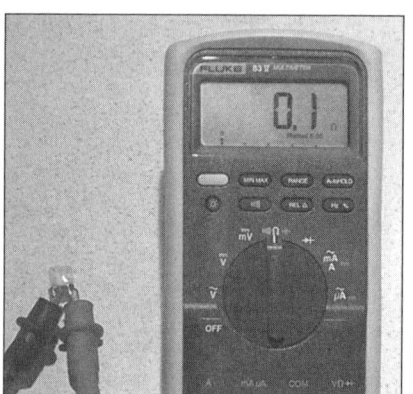 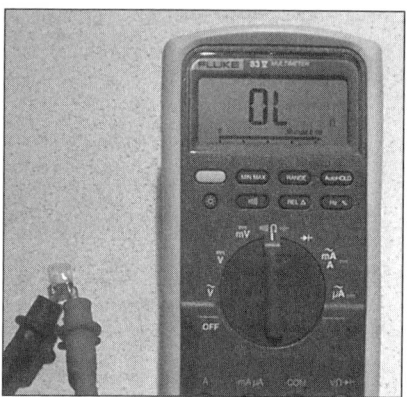
Fuse Check - Good (left) and Needs Replacing (right)

Find the compressor clutch relay in the PDC and remove the relay.

Take care when removing the relay. Avoid rocking it back and forth to prevent damage to the terminals in the PDC.

Typical Compressor Clutch Relay Location in a PDC (Power Distribution Center)

Notes:

SECTION 5 • ELECTRICAL/ELECTRONIC TROUBLESHOOTING & DIAG.

If a clutch is not engaging and the relay is suspected as the cause, a fast way to confirm it is to replace the suspect relay with a known good one. The replacement must be the correct one for the application.

The following steps outline testing a relay when necessary. The image identifies the pins on the relay.

Typical Pin Identification for Relay Test

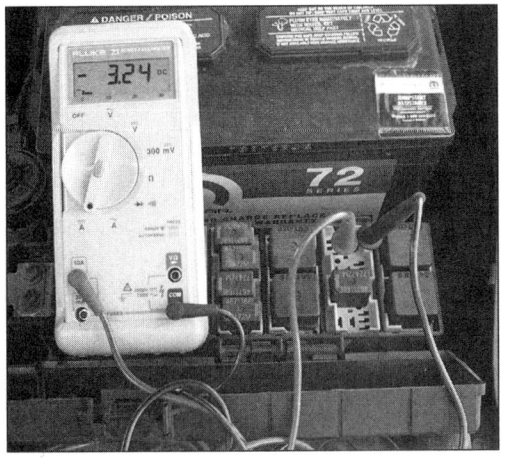

Relay Input Test

Set the multimeter to the AMPs position. Insert the red test lead into the meter's amps jack and the black lead into the meter's ground or "COM" jack.

Turn the ignition on and turn on the A/C. If the compressor clutch engages, the problem could be in the relay control circuit or the relay itself.

Continuity Check

Now, if a typical relay, check for continuity between pin 30 and pin 87A with an ohmmeter. This test should show continuity. If it does not, replace the relay.

Notes:

Now use the ohmmeter to check between pins 85 and 86. The reading should usually be between 70 and 90 ohms. If the resistance is not in this range, replace the relay.

If the meter checks shown here are within the proper range, the contact points in the relay may have excessive resistance. Replace it with a known good relay, start the vehicle and observe if the compressor clutch engages. If it does, replace the relay and perform a voltage test at the compressor clutch.

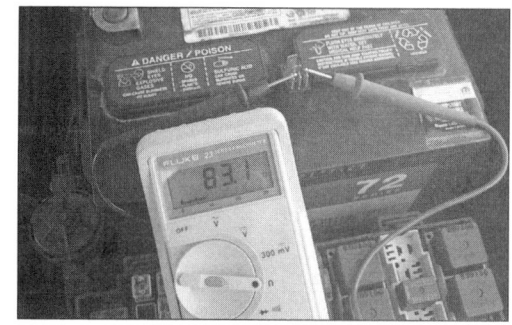

Relay Control Circuit Good

With the negative lead of the multimeter attached to the negative battery terminal, back probe the compressor clutch positive terminal with the DMM positive lead.

The voltage reading at the compressor positive terminal should be within 1.0 volt of system voltage. If the voltage is below the desired value, the circuit will have to be checked from the clutch back to the relay.

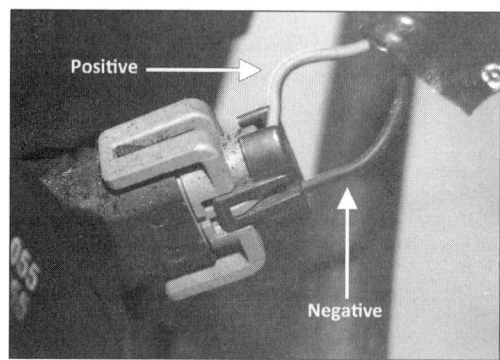

A/C Compressor Clutch Terminals

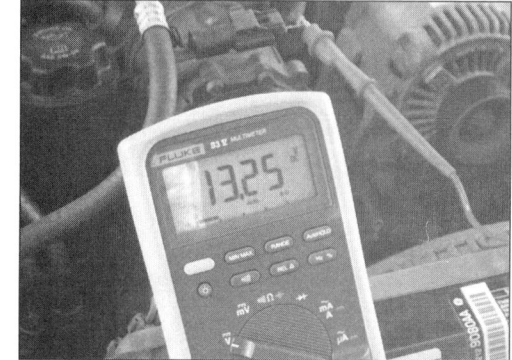

Backprobe of Compressor Clutch + Terminal Showing a Good Reading

Notes:

SECTION 5 • ELECTRICAL/ELECTRONIC TROUBLESHOOTING & DIAG.

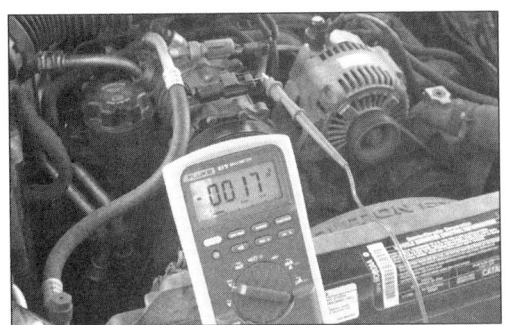

Voltage Drop Check, Ground Side of Compressor Clutch

Check the voltage drop from the negative terminal of the compressor clutch to the negative battery terminal with the multimeter on the lowest voltage setting. The reading should not exceed 0.5 volt.

If the voltage drop exceeds 0.5 volt, the circuit will have to be checked point by point from the clutch back to battery ground.

Checking Switches and Sensors with a Multimeter

This section covers using a multimeter to check typical switches found on an HVAC system. We'll start with checking a clutch cycling switch (CSS).

With the CCS closed and the circuit energized, connect the voltmeter leads across the switch terminals (backprobe). If the switch is good, there will be no voltage drop. If there is a voltage drop, replace the switch.

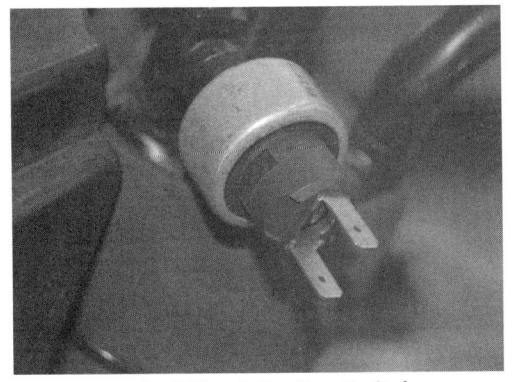

Typical Clutch Cycling Switch

Notes:

ELECTRICAL/ELECTRONIC TROUBLESHOOTING & DIAG. • SECTION 5

Another item that can be checked with a multimeter is the air conditioning pressure (ACP) sensor. Connect the meter negative lead to the negative battery terminal. Connect the positive lead to the sensor reference voltage terminal. See the image below for pin identification on our example vehicle. ALWAYS refer to vehicle specific service information to identify the correct terminal pins.

The reference voltage should be the value in the specifications for the vehicle being tested. In the example below, the reference voltage is five volts.

Pin Orientation

Pin 1:	Orange wire	Ground
Pin 2:	Red wire	Feedback (sensed voltage)
Pin 3:	Light Green wire	Reference voltage

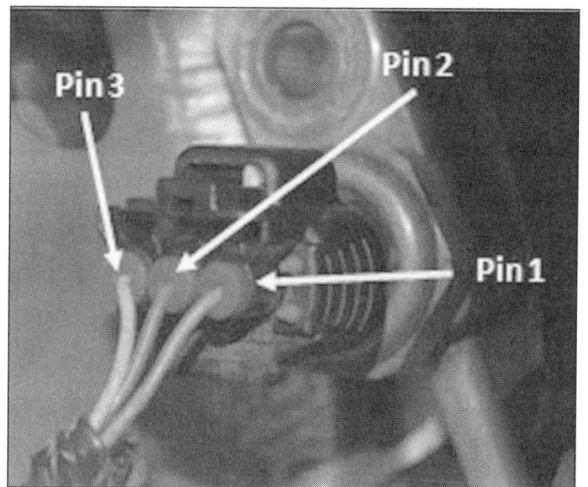
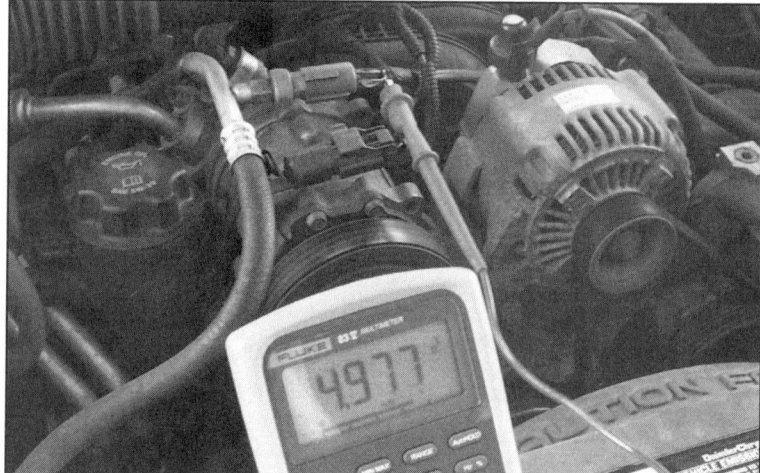

Air Conditioning Pressure Sensor (ACP) Pinout and Check

Next, check the ACP ground circuit [Pin 1 in our case] to the negative battery terminal. If the circuit is good the voltage should not exceed 0.2 volt.

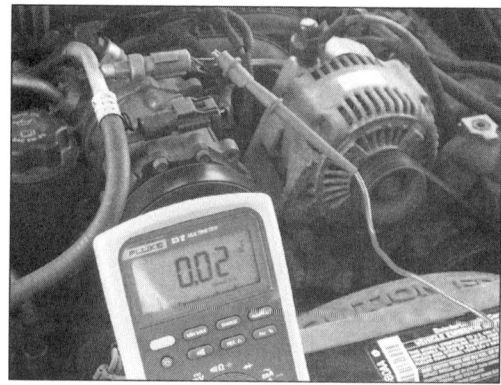

Check ACP Ground Circuit

Notes:

SECTION 5 • ELECTRICAL/ELECTRONIC TROUBLESHOOTING & DIAG. 103

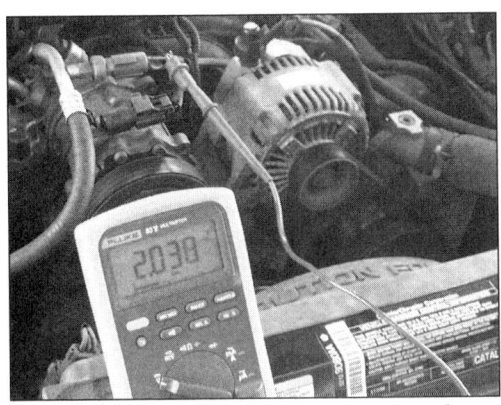
Measure Feedback (Sensed Voltage)

Finally, check the feedback or sensed voltage. Measure voltage from Pin 2 to the negative battery terminal. This reading will vary between 0.5 volt and 4.9 volts on this particular vehicle. If the voltage drops below 0.5 or exceeds 4.9, compressor clutch engagement will be denied.

Any voltage between the low and high values will allow the compressor clutch to engage.

Powertrain Control Module (PCM) Check

If all switches and components check out, the problem could be a faulty PCM. Check the wiring diagram to find which PCM connector contains the clutch relay control circuit. Remove the connector from the PCM and ground the circuit. If the relay energizes and the compressor clutch engages, the PCM may be faulty.

Helpful Troubleshooting Tips

1. When checking for available voltage anywhere in any circuit, always use a long test lead connected directly to the negative battery terminal as the ground.
2. Before measuring voltage in any circuit, start by measuring battery voltage. A fully charged battery will provide 12 – 12.7 volts.
3. Start measurements at a point in a circuit that is easy to access and that will provide the most information. That will often be right at the component that is suspected to be malfunctioning.
4. Identify all components in a circuit that are not working, and all components that are working. This will help to determine where in the circuit the problem(s) begin.
5. Do the simplest checks first – don't make the job harder than it needs to be.
6. A complete circuit will show voltage drops across components that are the result of the resistance of that component.
7. The total of the voltage drops across all non-load components in a circuit should not exceed 0.5 volt.

Notes:

ELECTRICAL/ELECTRONIC TROUBLESHOOTING & DIAG. • SECTION 5

Circuit Testing Guidelines

If the meter reading in the circuit		
on the power side of the load is	on the ground side of the load is	this indicates
Source Voltage	Less Than 0.2 VDC	The circuit is OK. The problem is the component.
Source Voltage	Source Voltage	The circuit is OPEN on the ground side.
Source Voltage	More than 0.2 VDC	The circuit has HIGH RESISTANCE on the ground side.
Less Than Source Voltage	Less than 0.2 VDC	The circuit has HIGH RESISTANCE on the power side.

Notes:

SECTION 5 • ELECTRICAL/ELECTRONIC TROUBLESHOOTING & DIAG.

Worksheet 4 – Section 5

Task: Check/Diagnose the Compressor Clutch Relay and the Cycling Clutch Switch or A/C Pressure Sensor

Tools and Materials Needed:

- MACS HVAC Systems, Volume 2 - Electrical and Electronic Systems Operation Manual
- Late model vehicle
- Vehicle service information
- Digital multimeter

Vehicle to be used:

Year _____ Make _____ Model _____

VIN _____

Engine Type_____ Displacement _____

Procedure:

Using an available vehicle, Section 5 of the MACS HVAC Systems, Volume 2 - Electrical and Electronic Systems Operation Manual as a reference, vehicle service information, and a digital multimeter, perform the following:

1. Locate the compressor clutch relay on the vehicle and test it by following the steps outlined in Section 5 in the MACS manual.

2. Determine whether the vehicle uses a cycling clutch switch or an A/C pressure sensor.

3. Using service information, locate and perform the testing procedures for the cycling clutch switch or pressure sensor.

4. Record the results below.

Outline the steps used to test the clutch relay on the vehicle _____

_____

Is the relay functioning correctly? _____

Cycling clutch switch/pressure sensor (circle which is used)

Where is it located on the vehicle? _____

Outline the steps used to test the switch or sensor_____

_____

Is the switch / sensor functioning properly? _____

_____

**Section 5 Review –
Electrical/Electronic Troubleshooting and Diagnosis**

1. Technician A says a short to ground on the feed side of a circuit will usually blow the fuse or open the fusible link. Technician B says a short to ground after the load will usually cause the load to operate regardless of the position of the switch. Who is correct?
    A. Technician A
    B. Technician B
    C. Both Technician A and Technician B
    D. Neither Technician A nor Technician B

2. True or False: A test light should not be used to diagnose a circuit containing solid state components.
    A. True
    B. False

3. Which of these statements is/are correct?
    A. The voltage drop on the source side of the compressor clutch circuit is acceptable if it does not exceed 3 volts.
    B. The voltage drop on the ground side of the compressor clutch circuit is acceptable if it is 0.1 volt.
        A. Statement A is correct
        B. Statement B is correct
        C. Both statements A and B are correct
        D. Neither statement A nor B is correct

4. Compressor clutch relays are being discussed. Technician A says a scan tool can be used to test relay operation. Technician B says a digital multimeter should not be used to test a relay. Who is correct?
    A. Technician A
    B. Technician B
    C. Both Technician A and Technician B
    D. Neither Technician A nor Technician B

5. True or False: If the voltage measured on the ground side of a circuit is equal to source voltage, the likely cause is an open on the ground side of the circuit.
    A. True
    B. False

Notes:

Section 6: HVAC Control Systems

COMPRESSOR CLUTCH CONTROLS

Introduction

COMPRESSOR CLUTCH CONTROL

When air conditioning operation is selected on the HVAC control head, that signal will usually end up at the PCM or other engine control computer.

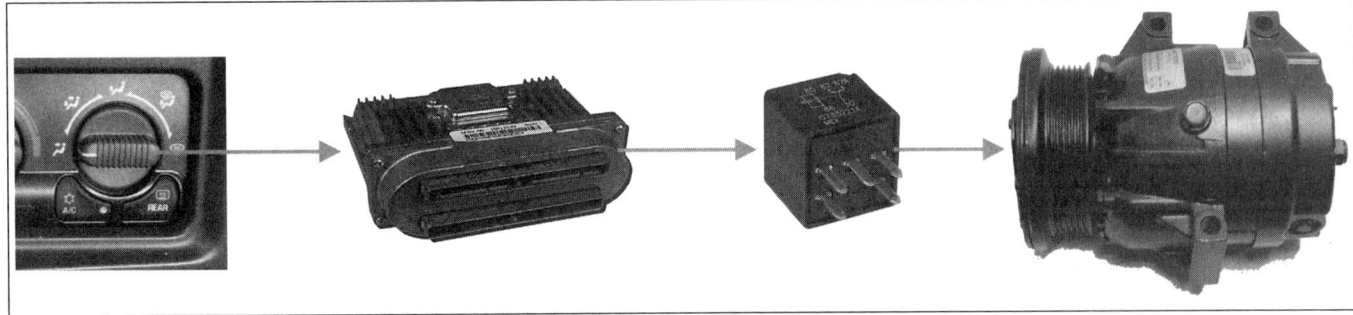

A/C Request Signal Routing

How that signal is controlled and routed will vary by vehicle makes and models.

Final control of the compressor clutch is usually through a relay controlled by the PCM.

There are two primary methods of maintaining evaporator temperature to prevent freeze-up: clutch cycling and variable displacement compressors.

The cycling clutch system will be discussed first.

Notes:

Clutch cycling systems can be divided into two sub-categories: pressure cycling and temperature sensing. The image on the right shows a pressure cycling switch and an evaporator temperature sensor, and the image below shows a typical circuit using a clutch cycling switch.

Pressure Cycling Switch and Evaporator Temperature Sensor

Clutch Cycling Designs

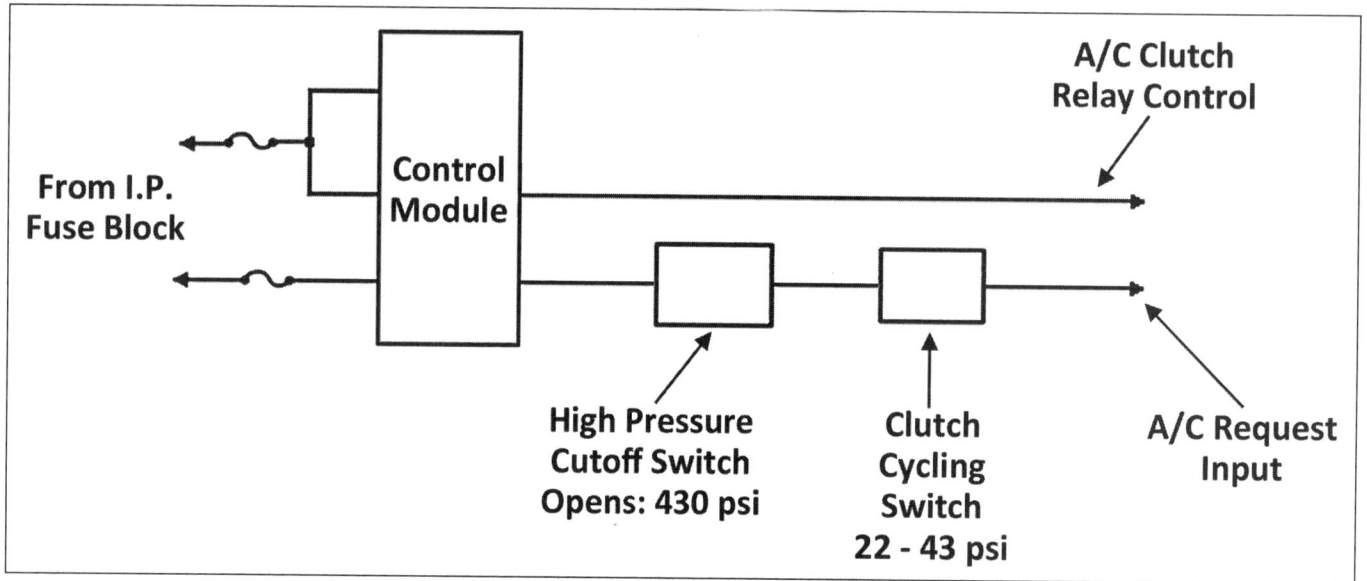

Typical Clutch Cycling Switch Circuit

The clutch pressure cycling switch will cycle the compressor off and on to maintain evaporator temperature. The pressure range is usually about 22 to 43 psi. At this pressure range, the average evaporator temperature is close to 32°F. The clutch pressure cycling switch is located on the suction (low pressure) side the A/C system.

The circuit shown above also uses a high pressure cutoff switch which will be located in the high pressure side of the system. The high pressure protection switch is wired in series with the pressure cycling switch.

High Pressure Switches

Notes:

SECTION 6 • HVAC CONTROL SYSTEMS   109

An A/C request signal enters the PCM, and if all the input parameters are correct, the PCM will ground the control winding in the compressor clutch relay and the compressor will operate. This data can be read on a scan tool.

Scan Tool Data Showing A/C Request

Four Pin Pressure Switch

Besides controlling the compressor clutch, some systems will use pressure switch inputs to operate cooling fans and control air management doors. The image on the left shows a four pin switch that will open the compressor clutch circuit if pressure gets too high.

In that case, a set of contacts will close. When the contacts close, the PCM will see voltage go to zero. The PCM will turn off the A/C compressor clutch, and turn the cooling fan on high speed.

Four Pin Pressure Switch in Vehicle

The diagram below shows a constant control relay module (CCRM) that interfaces between the PCM and the switch inputs.

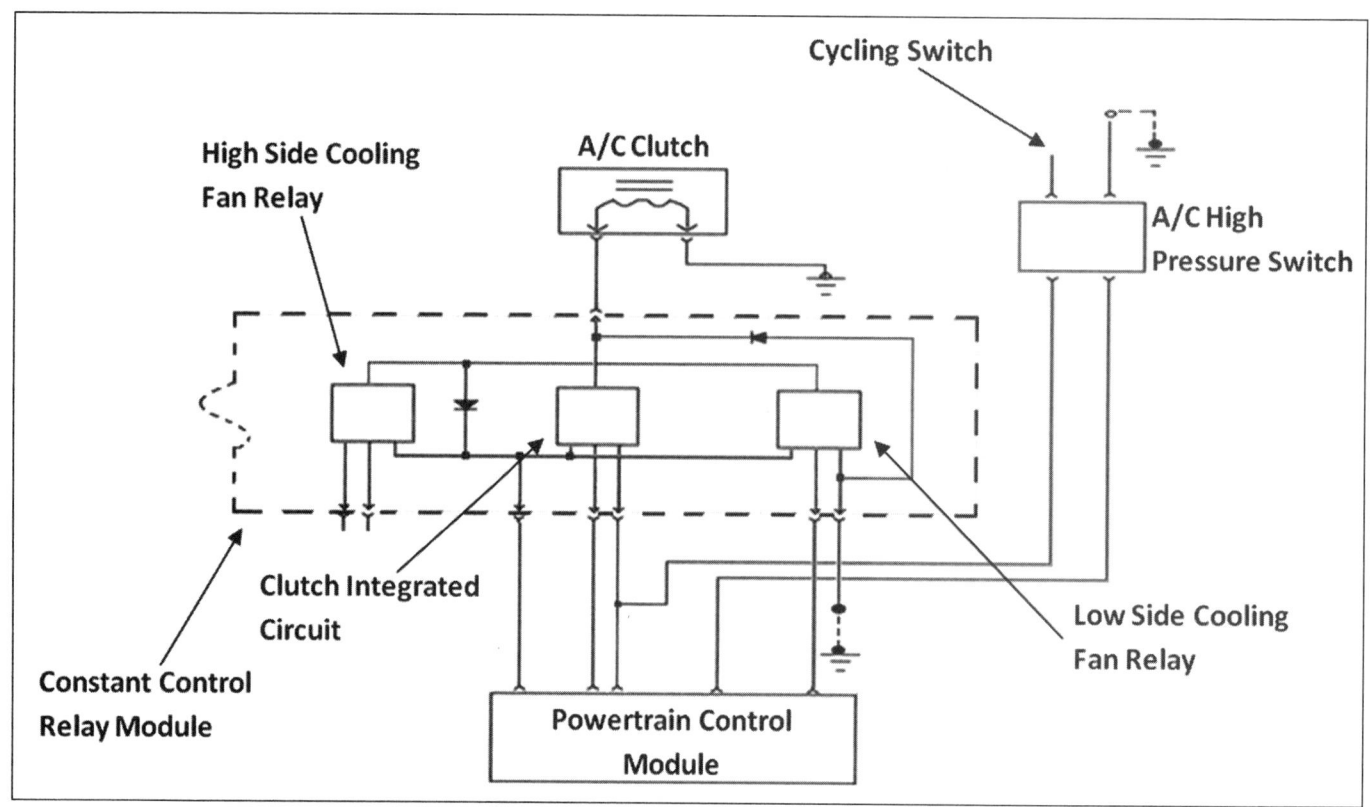

Constant Control Relay Module Diagram

As seen below, pressure switches will appear on scan tool data lists.

Reviewing the scan tool data helps to determine whether the switch is operating as designed.

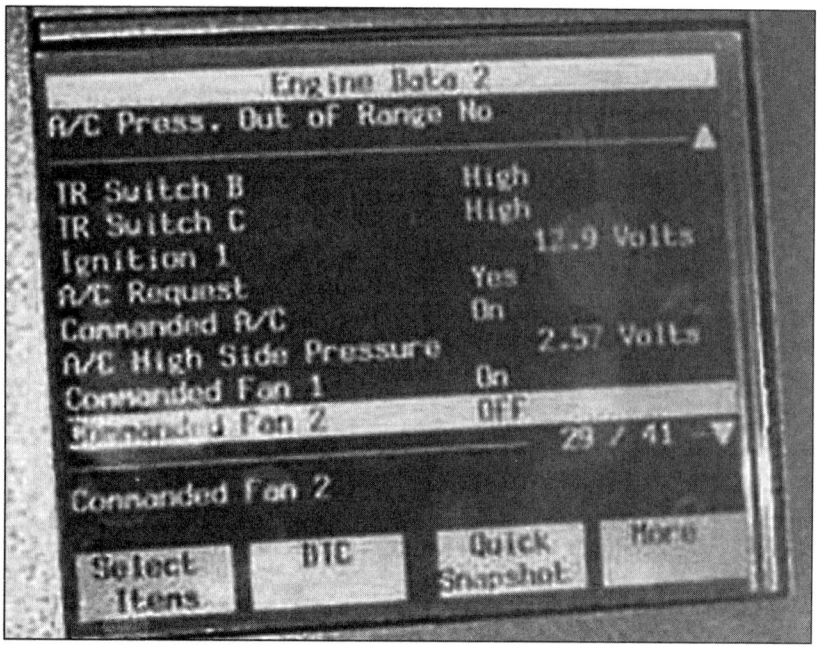

Pressure Switch Status on Scan Tool

SECTION 6 • HVAC CONTROL SYSTEMS

Air Conditioning Pressure Sensor (ACP)

The ACP will convert high side pressure into a voltage value. The value will determine if cooling fan speed should be increased or if the compressor clutch should be turned off due to very low or very high system pressure.

Air Conditioning Pressure Sensor shown in vehicle

The ACP sends a voltage reading to the PCM, which will open the control circuit of the A/C relay, energize a cooling fan relay, or pulse the cooling fan control module to run the fan at a higher speed.

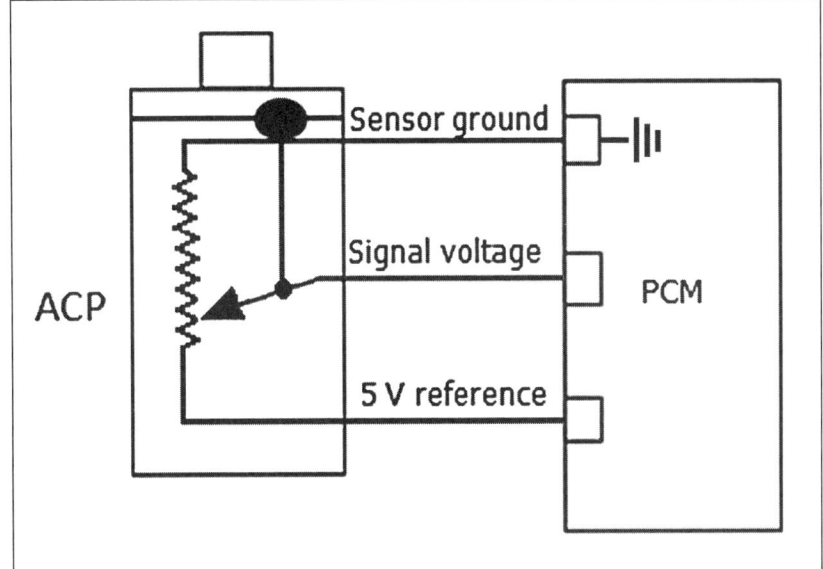

ACP Control Diagram

ACP voltage and pressure can be read with a scan tool.

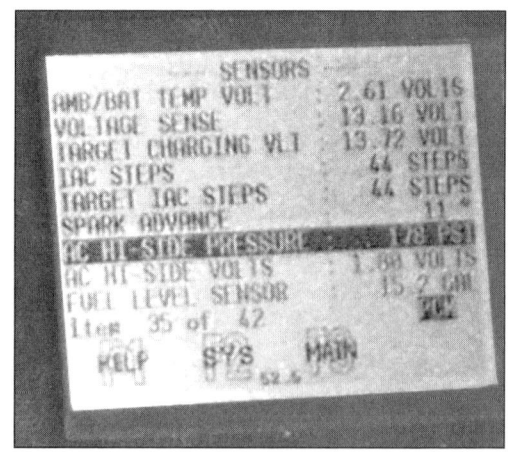
ACP Voltage and Pressure Reading

Evaporator Temperature Sensing Devices

Thermistors are used to sense evaporator temperature. These devices change resistance according to temperature. As the temperature increases, resistance decreases; less resistance increases the amount of voltage flowing in the sensor circuit.

Evaporator Temperature Sensor

This evaporator temperature sensor is located downstream from the evaporator and senses the temperature inside the evaporator case.

This temperature reading is sent to the HVAC module through the CAN bus.

Evaporator Case Air Temperature Sensor

Notes:

SECTION 6 • HVAC CONTROL SYSTEMS

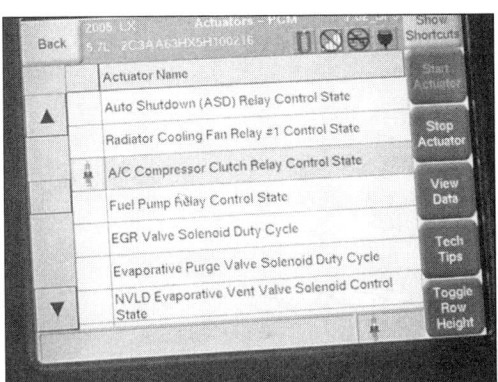

Scan Tool Showing Compressor Clutch Relay State

The CAN message tells the PCM to turn the compressor clutch on or off.

In the circuit below, notice that the evaporator temperature switch does not have a direct path to the compressor clutch; it is simply another input to the PCM. Notice also that there are three fuses (one of which is in the fuse block, which is not shown) that could affect clutch operation if they fail.

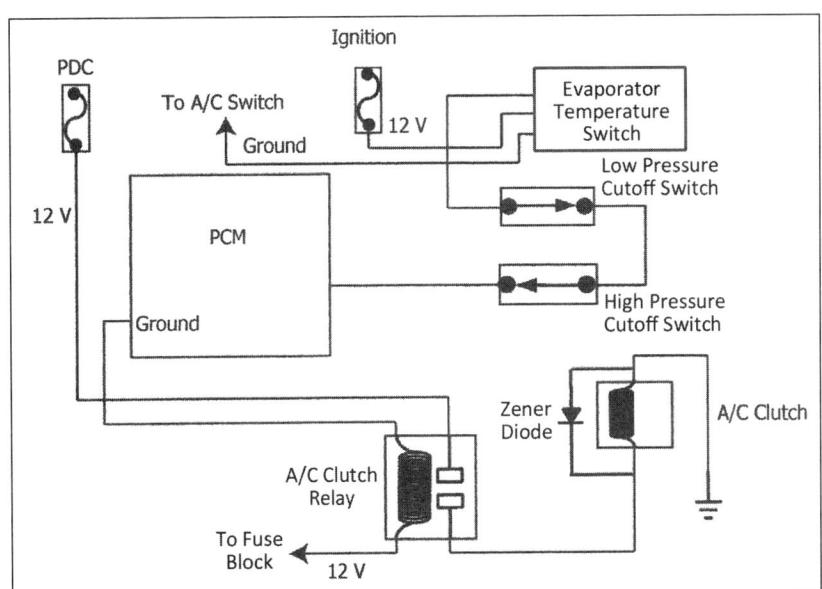

Compressor Clutch Electrical Circuit Showing Evaporator Temperature Switch, Pressure Switches, Relay and PCM

Change in voltage in the temperature switch's circuit relates to temperature. The PCM uses this information to turn the compressor clutch off and on.

This circuit also uses two separate protection switches: one for low pressure and the other for high pressure.

Notes:

Another evaporator switch design uses two wires attached to a probe. The probe is inserted directly into the fins on the evaporator. In this vehicle, the temperature data is sent to the body control module (BCM).

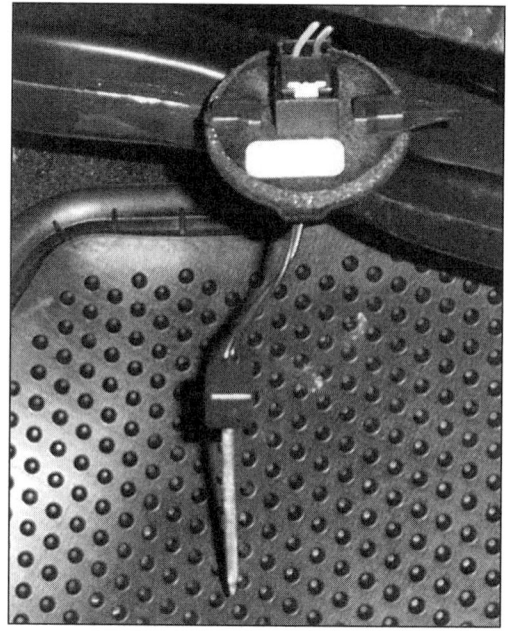
Two-wire Evaporator Switch with Probe

The BCM sends a serial data message to the PCM. The PCM controls the compressor clutch relay.

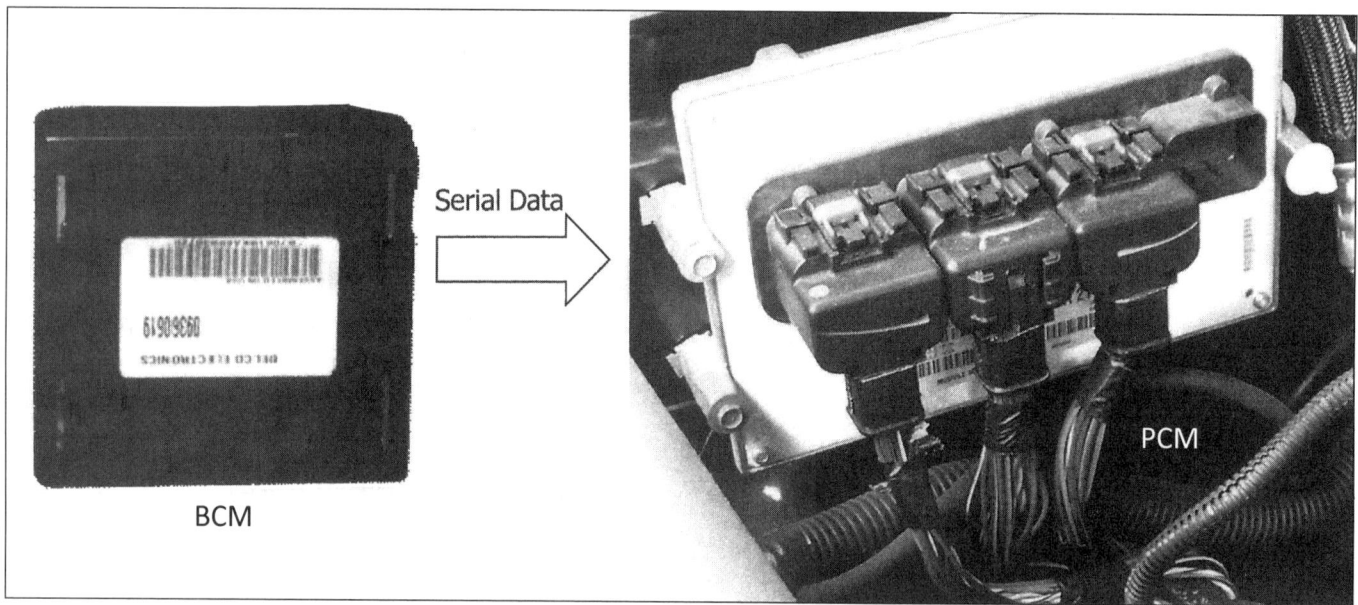
BCM Messaging PCM

Notes:

SECTION 6 • HVAC CONTROL SYSTEMS

A/C Pressure Sensor

This system also uses an A/C pressure sensor to monitor high side pressure and will turn off the compressor clutch if system pressure is too low or too high. The ACP will control cooling fan operation as well.

Variable Displacement Compressors

Variable Displacement Compressor

The advantage of a variable displacement compressor is that it does not cycle off and on. Cycling the compressor effects idle speed and, as is sometimes an operator concern, as the change in load can feel like an engine misfire. Another advantage is that compressor output can be matched to heat load, which improves fuel economy and lowers tailpipe emissions.

Variable displacement compressors use a control valve to change position of their wobble plates. See "Modern Automotive HVAC Systems" Volume 1 for an in-depth description of variable displacement compressor operation. We will provide a brief description here of mechanical variable compressors, as a lead-up to describing electronically controlled ones.

Control Valve on Compressor

The control valve senses pressure on the suction, or low pressure side of the system.

As evaporator temperature increases, low side pressure increases. The control valve will direct system low side pressure into the compressor crankcase. Compressor internal cylinder pressure will now be greater than compressor crankcase pressure. This causes the compressor to increase piston stroke which increases compressor output.

As the evaporator cools down, system low side pressure drops. The bellows in the control valve now bleeds high side pressure into the compressor crankcase. Crankcase pressure is now greater than compressor cylinder pressure, which reduces piston stroke and compressor output.

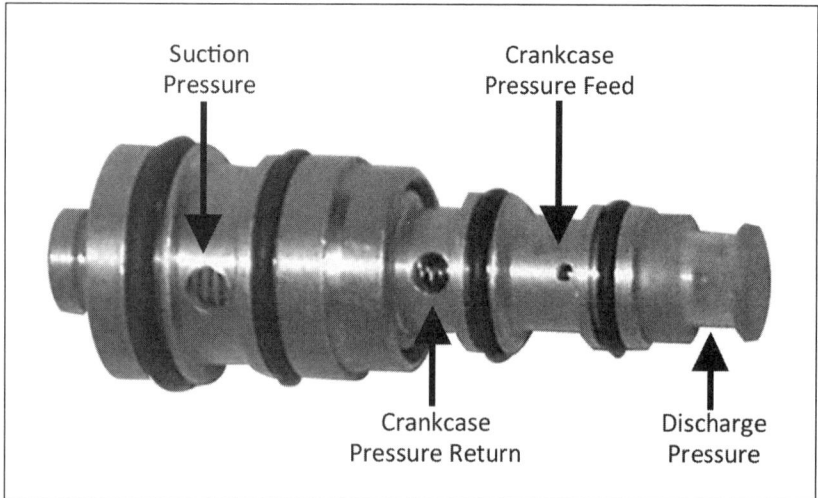

VDC Control Valve Ports

The control valve is constantly moving to maintain the correct temperature without cycling the compressor clutch. Correct refrigerant charge is critical for the control valve to function properly.

The current trend is to replace mechanical control valves in variable displacement compressors with electronic valves.

Some variable displacement compressors have no electromagnetic clutch, and the compressor operates anytime the engine is running. These clutchless compressors use an electronic control valve to regulate compressor output. The compressor is designed to retain more oil to insure proper lubrication during minimum output operation. A control unit receives inputs from various sensors and adjusts compressor output based on ambient conditions and heat load. Another advantage of this design is reduced weight (by eliminating the clutch assembly) and improved tailpipe emissions and fuel economy, because the amount of cooling perfectly matches heat and humidity load.

Electronic Control Valve on Compressor

SECTION 6 • HVAC CONTROL SYSTEMS 117

Worksheet 5 – Section 6

Tasks: Check/Diagnose HVAC System Inputs and Outputs
Perform Interactive (Function) Tests
Retrieve any Current or History DTCs Present

Tools and Materials Needed:

- MACS HVAC Systems, Volume 2 - Electrical and Electronic Systems Operation Manual
- Late model vehicle
- Vehicle service information
- Scan tool

Vehicle to be used:

Year _____ Make _____ Model _____

VIN _____

Engine Type _____ Displacement _____

Procedure:
Using an available vehicle, Section 6 of the MACS HVAC Systems, Volume 2 - Electrical and Electronic Systems Operation Manual as a reference, vehicle service information, and a scan tool, perform the following:

1. Navigate to and review all data specific to the inputs and outputs in the HVAC system.
2. Review and perform all interactive (function) tests available for the vehicle's A/C system.
3. Retrieve any current or history DTCs present.
4. Record the results below.

Type of scan tool used: _____

Describe the inputs and outputs checked using the scan tool: _____

_____

_____

Which interactive (function) tests were performed using the scan tool? _____

_____

_____

Were any stored DTCs found? _____

Were any problems identified in the vehicle? _____

© 2012 MOBILE AIR CONDITIONING SOCIETY   Modern Automotive HVAC: Electrical and Electronic Systems

Section 6 Review – HVAC System Controls

1. Technician A says cycling the A/C compressor clutch is a common way of preventing evaporator freeze-up. Technician B says system pressure is used to control the clutch on some vehicles. Who is correct?
    - A. Technician A
    - B. Technician B
    - C. Both Technician A and Technician B
    - D. Neither Technician A nor Technician B

2. True or False: If system pressure gets too high, the high pressure switch in some A/C systems will open the compressor clutch circuit and also turn on a cooling fan.
    - A. True
    - B. False

3. Which of these statements is/are correct?
    A. The air conditioning pressure sensor (ACP) typically monitors high side system pressure.
    B. The air conditioning pressure sensor (ACP) signal to the powertrain control module (PCM) determines whether or not the compressor clutch receives power.
    - A. Statement A is correct
    - B. Statement B is correct
    - C. Both statements A and B are correct
    - D. Neither statement A nor B is correct

4. Technician A says an evaporator temperature sensor may be an example of a thermistor. Technician B says as evaporator temperature increases, the resistance of the sensor decreases. Who is correct?
    - A. Technician A
    - B. Technician B
    - C. Both Technician A and Technician B
    - D. Neither Technician A nor Technician B

5. True or False: A variable displacement compressor uses an air conditioning pressure sensor (ACP) to cycle the compressor clutch on and off.
    - A. True
    - B. False

Notes:

Section 7: Blower Motors and Cabin Filters

BLOWER MOTOR DESIGNS

The blower motor is located in the plenum assembly (usually under the dashboard) and its job is to push or pull air through the evaporator and heater cores, and on through the ductwork to the various outlets.

Blower motors use various means to regulate blower speed.

Blower Motor

Some blower motors use a small hose that directs air from the plenum into the motor to cool it.

Blower Motor Showing Cooling Hose

A blower switch will have several positions.

When a slower blower speed is selected, the voltage will be lowered so the blower motor runs at a slower speed. This is accomplished through the use of resistor(s).

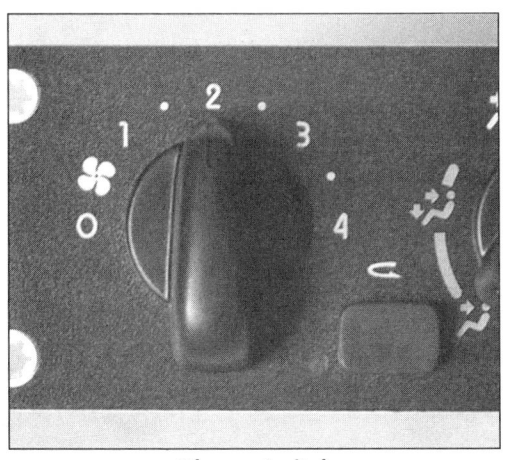
Blower Switch

Blower speed control resistors become hot during operation so they are usually located in the airflow of the blower motor in the plenum for cooling purposes.

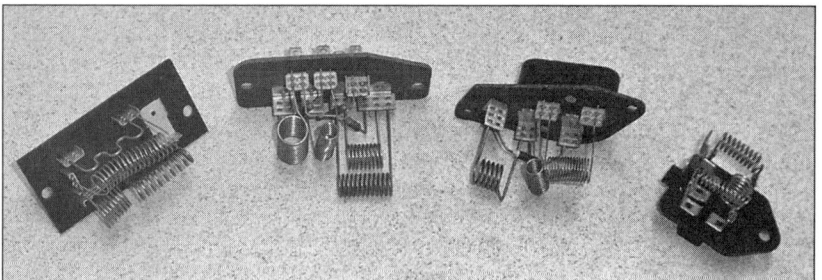

Blower Motor Resistors

Many resistors are equipped with a thermal limiter. The thermal limiter will open if there is an airflow restriction, excessive current draw from the blower motor, or a thermal shock from a rapid temperature change; for example, snow melt water entering the plenum air inlet in the winter, or water from a heavy rain downpour, or from a car wash. If a thermal limiter opens, the blower motor will either stop working or may only run at maximum speed. The thermal limiter is part of the resistor assembly and the entire resistor will have to be replaced.

Blower Resistor with Thermal Limiters

SECTION 7 • BLOWER MOTORS & CABIN FILTERS

Blower resistors come in various designs which include a "credit card" style.

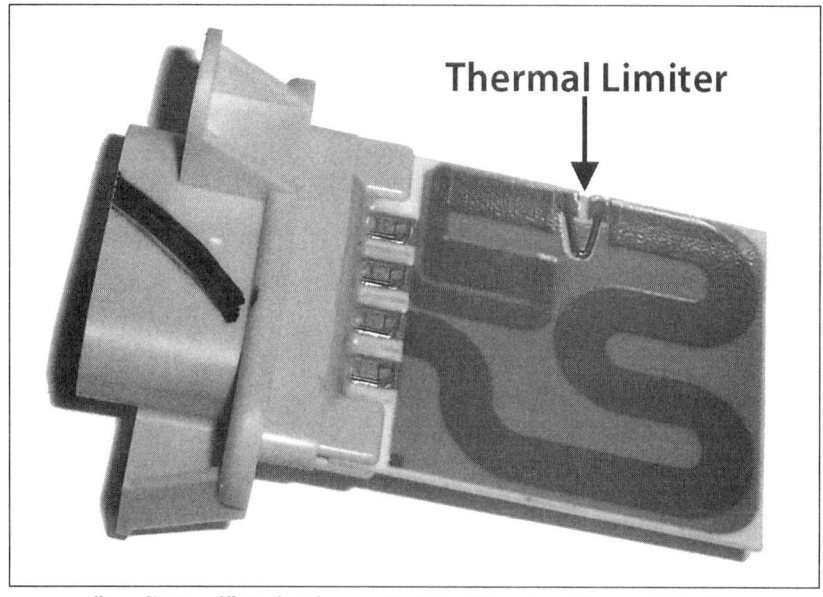

"Credit Card" Style Blower Resistor Showing Thermal Limiter

Blower motors often use a relay for high speed operation. The modular design below includes a relay for high speed operation. If any section of the assembly fails, the entire unit must be replaced.

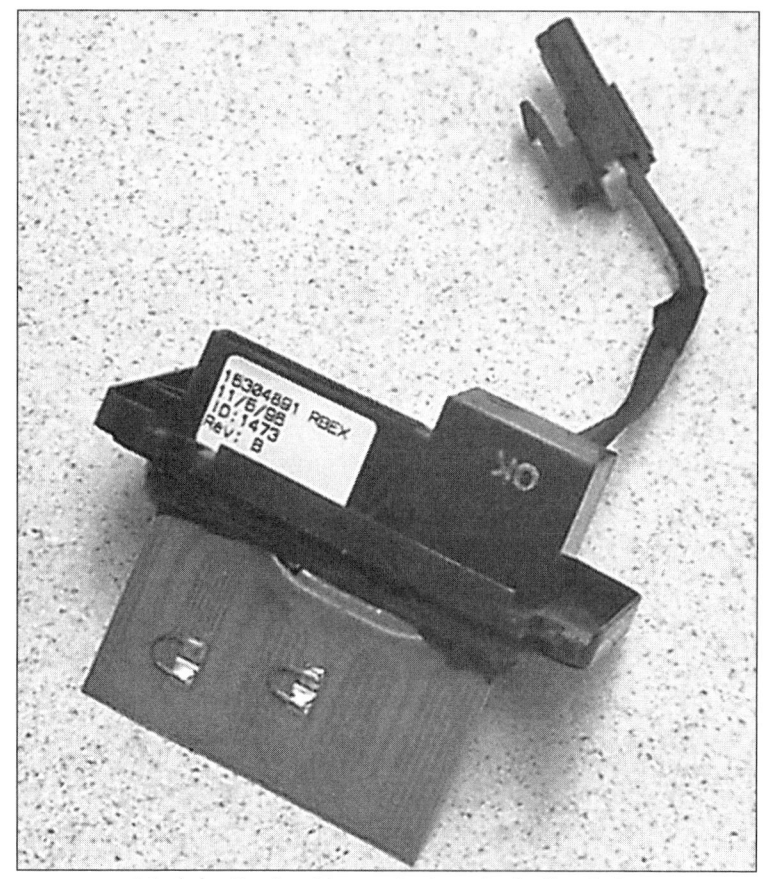

Modular Design Blower Resistor Including Relay

Power Modules and Pulse Width Modulation

Solid state components are also used to control vehicle blower motors. The advantage to solid state control is that a wide range of blower motor speeds are available.

Power modules are usually found on automatic temperature control system (ATC) designs. The power module will sometimes control the compressor request signal as well.

Like fixed resistors, power modules are usually located in the blower motor airflow to keep them cool. If airflow is restricted, the module may fail.

Power Modules

To eliminate high temperatures during operation, many manufacturers have started using brushless blower motors that use pulse width modulation to operate blower speeds.

The brushless blower motor uses magnets and transistors that are pulsed in sequence. When the like poles of the magnets are lined up, they repel each other, causing the motor to turn.

Both the power-module controlled and the brushless motor designs are controlled by pulse width modulation (PWM).

Brushless Blower Motor Incorporating Power Module

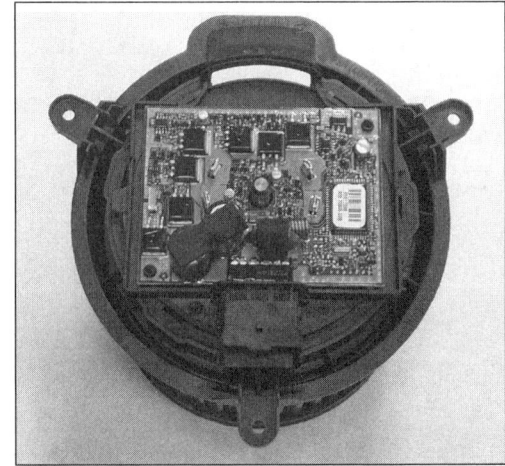

Notes:

Pulse Width Modulation (PWM)

Pulse width modulation is often referred to as duty cycle. A signal will be sent at a specific frequency, measured in units called hertz (Hz). One Hz equals one cycle per second, 100 Hz equals 100 cycles per second, and so on.

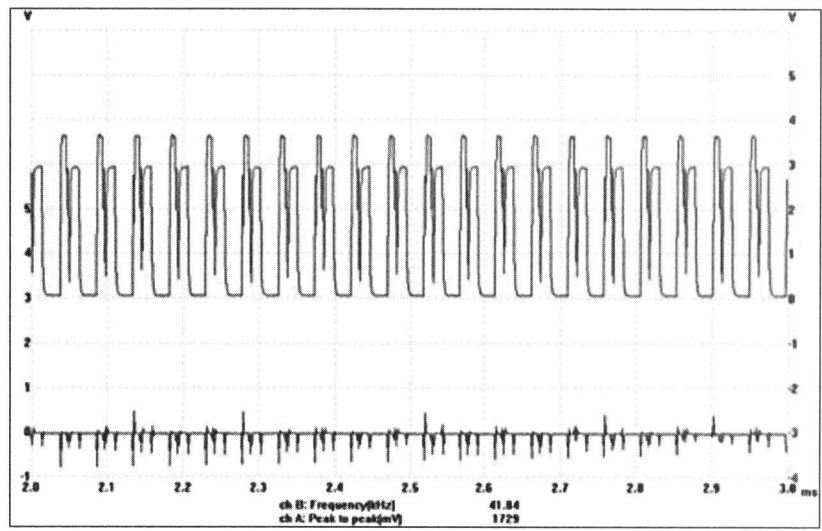

Pulse Width Modulation Readout

The duty cycle is the percentage of time that the circuit is turned on, and will vary depending on a number of parameters.

The DMM on the left shows the blower motor operating at 46% duty cycle, which means the blower motor is operating at below half its maximum speed.

A good quality multimeter will be capable of testing Hertz and pulse width modulation.

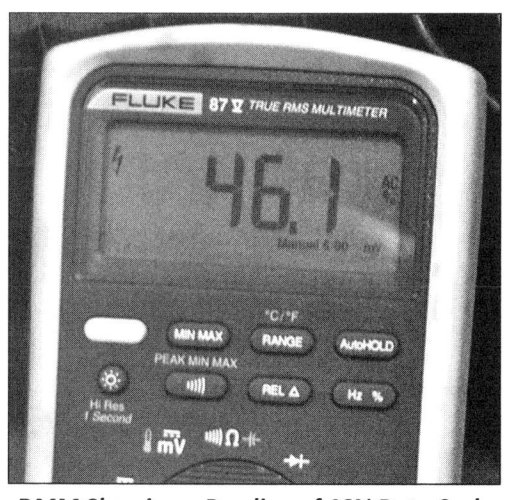

DMM Showing a Reading of 46% Duty Cycle

Notes:

The Hz reading will remain the same in any blower position. Hertz is a fixed rate, and duty cycle will vary from 0% to 100%. The DMM shows 1981.0 Hz as the frequency of the signal.

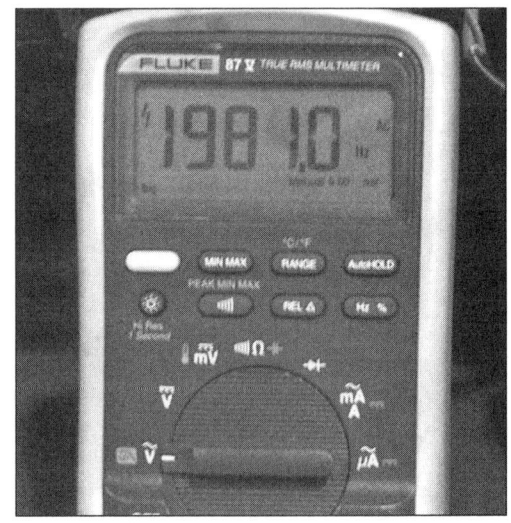

DMM Showing Blower Motor Hertz Reading

Blower Motor Diagnostic Tips

- Allow a motor to run for five minutes before performing a current draw check.
- Poor grounds can lead to motor failure and can be a source of noise on radios.
- Loose and dirty connections can lead to motor and power module failure.
- Check the blower wheel (squirrel cage) for cracks, or signs of slipping on the motor shaft.
- If the thermal limiter on a resistor fails, check motor current draw, and inspect the cabin filter and evaporator for restrictions.

Cabin Air Filters

Cabin air filters are standard on many vehicles and optional on many more. Their purpose is to remove dust, pollen, and odor causing matter, etc. from the air inside the vehicle. The filter is a maintenance item, and many owners are unaware that their vehicles even have one.

If the cabin filter becomes restricted, it will affect airflow though the vents. The restriction will cause air volume to decrease. Although servicing the filter is a maintenance schedule item, cabin filters should always be checked during HVAC system service and troubleshooting.

Cabin Air Filter with Restricted Airflow

SECTION 7 • BLOWER MOTORS & CABIN FILTERS

Worksheet 6 – Section 7

Tasks: Identify the component used for blower motor speed control
Locate the component on the vehicle/confirm the type
Measure duty cycle for all blower speeds

Tools and Materials Needed:
- MACS HVAC Systems, Volume 2 - Electrical and Electronic Systems Operation Manual
- Late model vehicle (NOTE: different vehicles will be needed for this task)
- Vehicle service information
- A digital multimeter capable of measuring frequency and duty cycle

Vehicles to be used:

Year _____ Make _____ Model _____

VIN _____

Engine Type _____ Displacement _____

Year _____ Make _____ Model _____

VIN _____

Engine Type _____ Displacement _____

Procedure:
Using two available vehicles, Section 7 of the MACS HVAC Systems, Volume 2 - Electrical and Electronic Systems Operation Manual as a reference, vehicle service information, and a digital multimeter capable of frequency and duty cycle, perform the following:

1. Using the service information, identify the type of resistor (wire – credit card – modular) used on a vehicle to control blower motor speed.
2. Using the component locator in the service information, locate the resistor on the vehicle and confirm the type of resistor used.
3. Using the service information, a vehicle using pulse width modulation to control blower motor speed, and a digital multimeter capable of measuring frequency and duty cycle:
   a. Look up the duty cycle specifications for all blower motor speeds.
   b. On the vehicle, measure the actual duty cycle for all blower motor speeds.
4. Record the results below.

Vehicle 1:
What type of resistor is used to control blower speed? _____

Was this confirmed on the vehicle? _____

Vehicle 2:
What were the duty cycle specifications given in the service information? _____

Low speed _____ Medium speed 2 _____ Medium speed 3 _____ High speed _____

Were these same values found when measuring on the vehicle? _____

Section 7 Review – Blower Motors and Cabin Filters

1. Technician A says the resistor used to control blower motor speed must be located in the plenum in order to dissipate the heat it generates. Technician B says an indicator that the resistor's thermal limiter has failed is that the blower motor will only operate on low speed. Who is correct?
    A. Technician A
    B. Technician B
    C. Both Technician A and Technician B
    D. Neither Technician A nor Technician B

2. True or False: A relay is sometimes used to control low speed blower motor operation.
    A. True
    B. False

3. Which of these statements is/are correct?
    A. Pulse width modulation eliminates the use of a resistor to control blower speed.
    B. A brushless blower motor offers the advantage of a lower operating temperature.
        A. Statement A is correct
        B. Statement B is correct
        C. Both statements A and B are correct
        D. Neither statement A nor B is correct

4. Technician A says signal frequency increases as duty cycle increases. Technician B says a scan tool must be used to check duty cycle. Who is correct?
    A. Technician A
    B. Technician B
    C. Both Technician A and Technician B
    D. Neither Technician A nor Technician B

5. True or False: A blocked cabin air filter can cause airflow through the vents to decrease.
    A. True
    B. False

Notes:

Section 8: Air Delivery Systems

When A/C became a popular option on vehicles in the mid to late 1970s, the systems were fairly simple, with the exception of some high level vehicles, which were often the test bed of things to come.

The control systems were cable actuated, and eventually, vacuum controls were introduced. Most systems were equipped with a heater control water valve, also cable or vacuum controlled.

Automatic temperature control (ATC) systems had a range of controls: vacuum, electromechanical, and pure electronic devices. They were complicated for the time and often not reliable.

THE IMPACT OF ELECTRONICS ON HVAC SYSTEMS

As time progressed, so did the HVAC systems. Systems eventually began to become part of the electronic revolution, and the switch to electronic controls began.

The new millennium has led to the need for more environmentally friendly vehicles. This includes HVAC system impact on tailpipe emissions.

Modern HVAC systems consist of two main designs; manual and automatic control. The automatic design can be divided into semi-automatic and fully automatic. Many designs now offer individual controls for the driver, passenger, and rear seat occupants as well.

MANUAL CONTROL SYSTEMS

The air delivery system controls the movement of heated and cooled air into and throughout the passenger compartment. The HVAC housing is the plenum unit located behind and beneath the instrument panel. It contains the evaporator and heater core, and the blower motor assembly and the blower speed control device.

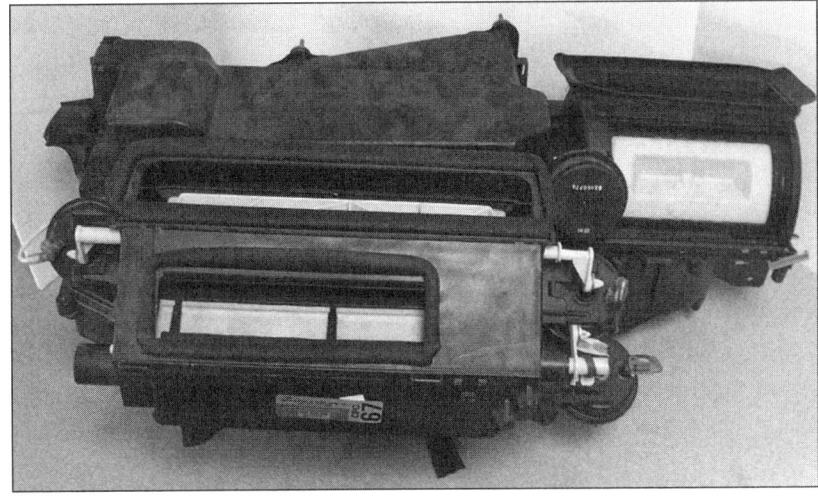

Plenum Assembly

The plenum houses the air doors and door actuators that direct airflow to the correct ductwork. The doors may be controlled by cables, vacuum, or electrical actuators. Single zone systems are usually equipped with three doors:

The recirculation door – The recirculation door determines whether outside air is used in the plenum, or if the air in the passenger compartment is recirculated.

The recirculation door is usually located in the plenum air inlet near the bulkhead and beneath the cowl air inlets.

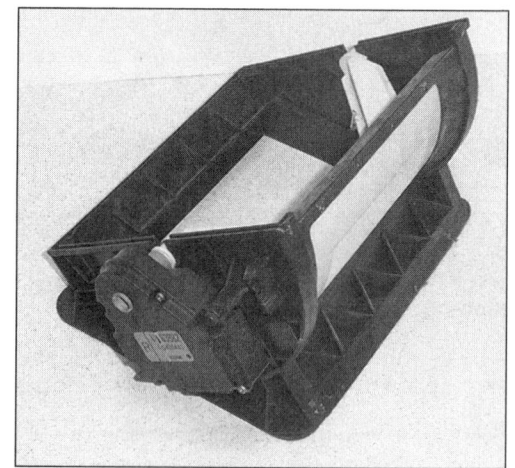
Recirculation Door Assembly

The blend door – the blend door determines the temperature of the air flowing through the passenger compartment.

If the A/C is operating, the air is dehumidified and cooled. The more air the blend door directs through the heater core, the warmer the air entering the passenger compartment.

Blend Doors

Mode doors – The mode doors determine where the air will be distributed. Most systems use at least two mode doors.

One door opens and closes the defrost outlet. The other door switches between the heat and vent/normal outlet.

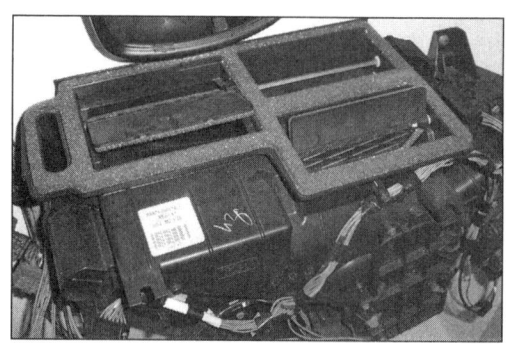
Mode Doors in Plenum

Notes:

SECTION 8 • AIR DELIVERY SYSTEMS

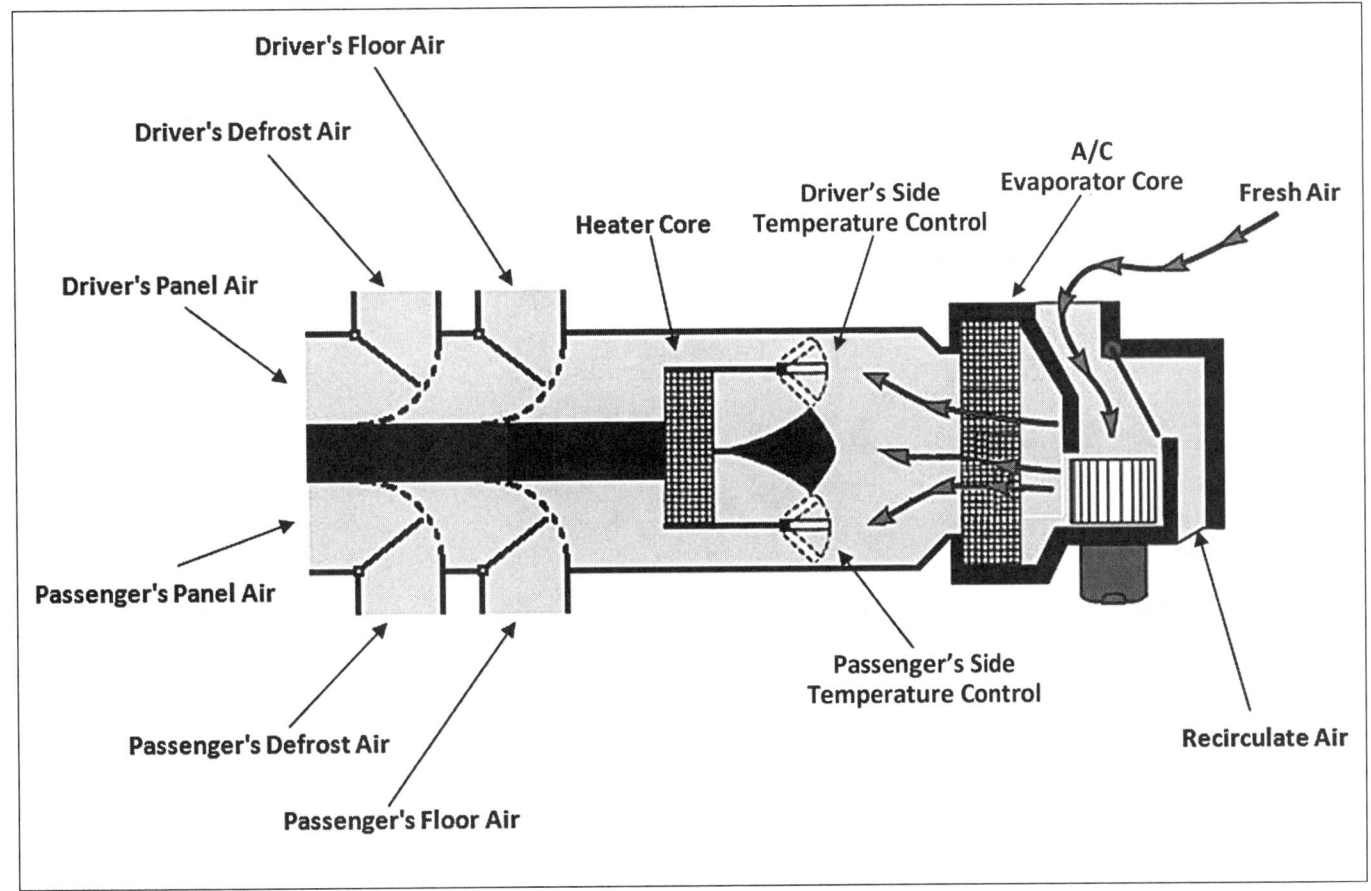

Dual Zone A/C System Diagram

Dual zone systems operate in the same manner as single zone systems. However, most dual zone systems use two blend doors; one for the driver side and the other for the passenger side. This design allows for separate temperature settings on each side of the vehicle.

The plenum contains a drain that allows the moisture that condenses on the evaporator during normal A/C operation to drain out of the HVAC housing. A possible occurrence is when a drain becomes blocked with debris, preventing the condensate from draining. One complaint might be that the accumulated water can be heard sloshing as the vehicle turns, or water may drip on an occupant's foot. Another might be the odor of mildew. There are deodorizer products available to eliminate the odor.

Many plenums will be equipped with a cabin air filter.

Notes:

Operator Interface

All HVAC systems have a main component for controlling temperature, air distribution, and air speed from the outlets. This component is called the control head. It houses the various switches, knobs, levers, and electronic components that adjust the HVAC system. The control head has a wiring harness for backlighting and for various inputs and outputs between the operator and the HVAC system. Wires, mechanical cables, vacuum lines or a combination of the three can be attached to a control head.

Typical Control Head

The number and types of switches will vary between make and model. Some examples are:

- A/C on-off switch: requests compressor clutch engagement
- Temperature selector: adjusts outlet air temperature
- Blower motor switch: multi-position switch that controls blower motor speed and air volume
- Mode selector: routes airflow to different outlets and through various ducts
- Recirculation switch: closes the outside air inlet for maximum system output.

Notes:

SECTION 8 • AIR DELIVERY SYSTEMS

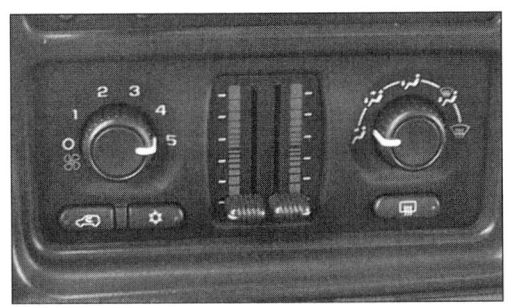
Mode Controls

Mode Controls

Airflow delivery is selected on the control head. Mode selections may include: MAXIMUM (RECIRC), NORMAL (VENT), BI-LEVEL, FLOOR (HEAT), and DEFROST.

When the mode selector is moved from the off position, the blower motor and the A/C clutch circuits are usually activated.

Controls may also be included for rear A/C if equipped, and left and right occupant temperature control on dual zone systems.

MODE DOOR CONTROLS

Inside the plenum assembly are doors or flaps, which change position to allow or block airflow to the outlets. Mode doors can be controlled by cables, vacuum servos, or electric motors.

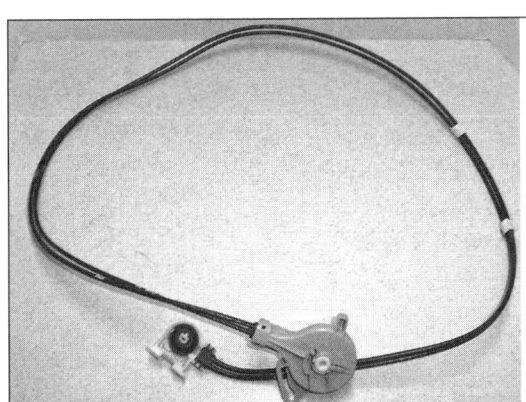  

Mode Door Controls

Many newer vehicles send an electrical signal to an actuator which moves the flapper door to the commanded position.

Mode doors can be flapper type, barrel or film design.

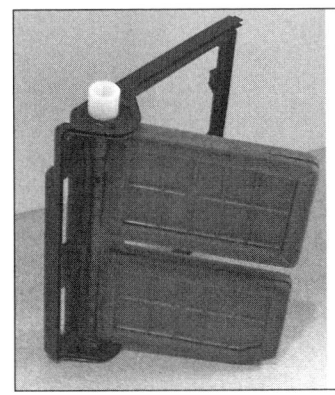  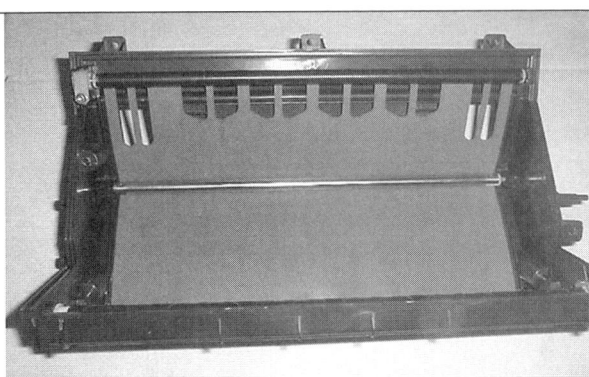

Mode Doors

Notes:

Actuator Motors

Actuator motors used in HVAC systems can be one of four designs, depending on vehicle manufacturer, system design, year and model of the vehicle:
- Tri-state
- Bi-directional
- Three wire
- Two wire

A tri-state actuator is a five wire design. Three of the five wires are used for the feedback circuit. The other wires are for ignition voltage and HVAC control head requests. The actuator receives voltage from the control head. Depending on the selection made, the logic circuits inside the motor will provide voltage to drive the motor in the correct direction; 0 volts will move the motor one way, 5 volts will drive the motor in the other direction, and when the signal wire reads 2.5 volts, the motor stops rotating. These are often called "smart actuators."

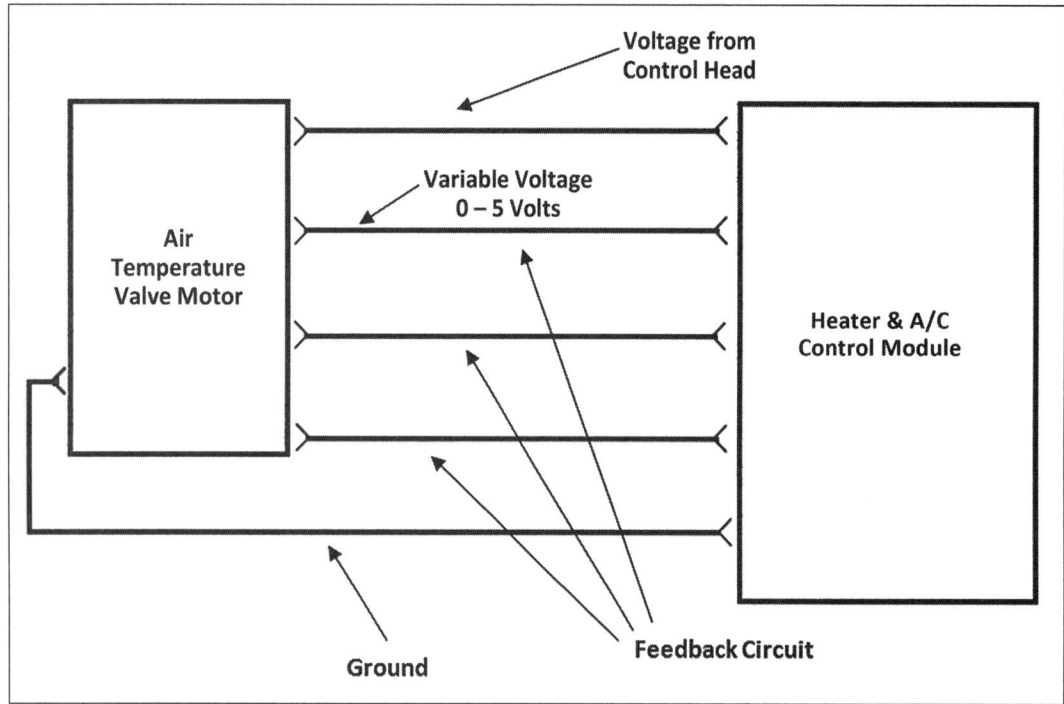

Tri-State "Smart" Actuator Motor

Notes:

SECTION 8 • AIR DELIVERY SYSTEMS

Bi-directional actuators use three wires for circuit feedback. The other two wires are the positive and negative circuits that drive the motor. These circuits are controlled by the HVAC control head and move the motor direction based on the selections made at the control head. They are sometimes referred to as "dumb actuator" circuits.

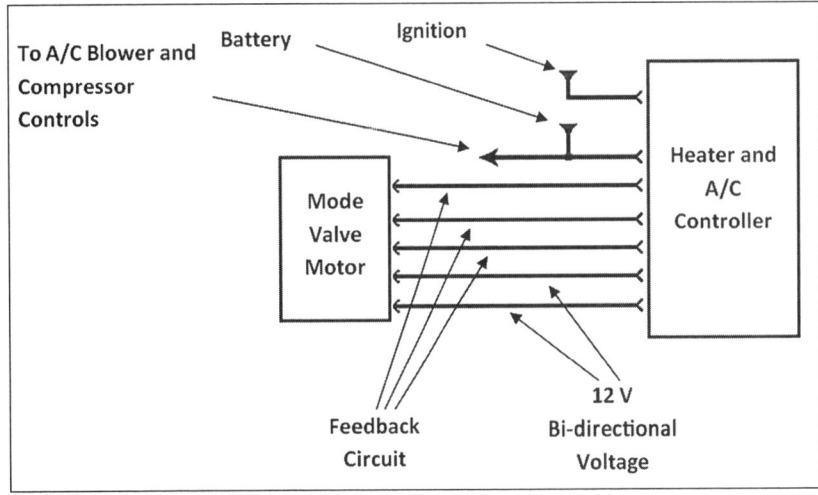

Bi-directional Actuator Motor

Three wire actuators have a power, ground, and an input wire from the HVAC control head. These actuators use a preprogrammed logic chip containing all the information to drive the motor in the requested direction. When a position change is requested by the vehicle operator, a circuit in the control head sends voltage to the actuator motor. As the motor moves, a potentiometer in the actuator compares the motor voltage to the output voltage from the control head. When both voltage readings are the same, the actuator motor stops. There is no feedback to the control head with this design.

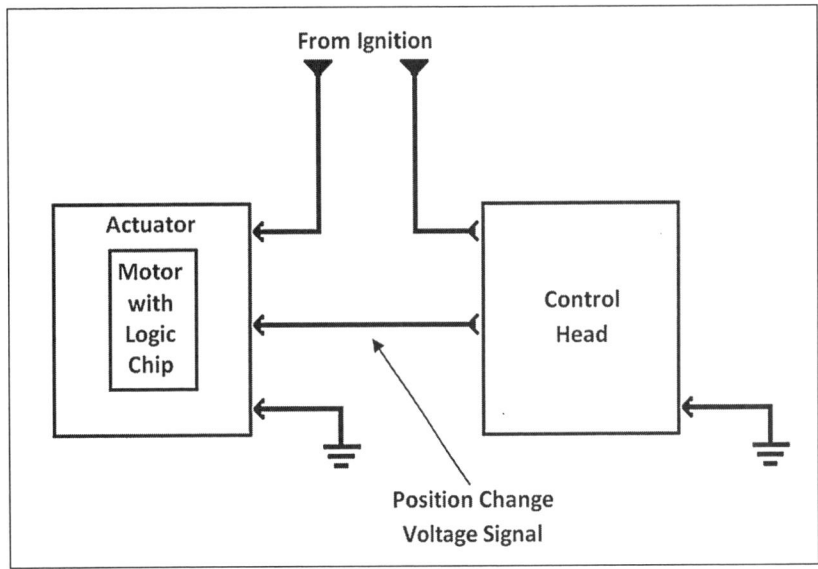

Three Wire Actuator Motor

Two wire actuators create electrical pulses when the commutator rotates across the brushes of the motor. The HVAC control head, which has pre-programmed logic and actuator endpoint references, counts the electrical pulses as the motor moves the door through its sweep from one end to the other end. The actuator endpoints will change as the door seal wears, so if the endpoint counts become too large, a DTC will be set. If the HVAC system loses power, or if a component is replaced, the endpoints must usually be relearned through a calibration process.

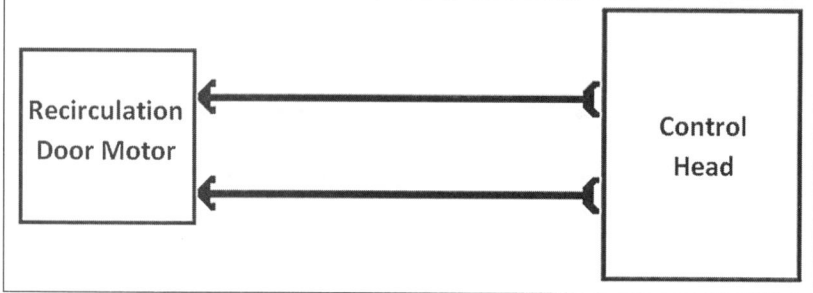

Two Wire Actuator Motor

Actuator Diagnosis

When diagnosing HVAC actuators, always check the door for binding or restriction, caused by a distorted, worn or damaged plenum. Check for restrictions that may be caused by a foreign object that is lodged in the door sweep, or a broken crank arm on the door assembly.

Do not operate an actuator that is not attached to the door on the plenum. If the door is not attached, the motor can drive past its limits, which usually results in damage to the actuator.

Actuator motor operation can be checked with a digital multimeter. Using service information and wiring diagrams for the vehicle, find the correct connector pins for the feedback, power, and ground circuits on the actuator. Carefully back probe at the pins, taking care not to pierce the wiring insulation or cause damage to the connector pins. With the meter set on the DC volts scale, move the HVAC selector knob and watch for a voltage change as the door position is commanded to change.

There should be a voltage change as each position is selected; in the image to the right, the voltage is shown for full cold.

Notes:

Voltage Shows "Full Cold"

SECTION 8 • AIR DELIVERY SYSTEMS

Voltage Change When Turned to "Warm"

With the temperature knob in the middle position the voltage should change.

Voltage Change When Turned to "Hot"

When the temperature knob is in the full hot position, the measured voltage should change again.

These voltage readings will not give the exact position of the door. However, they will indicate that the door is moving through a complete sweep from one endpoint to the other.

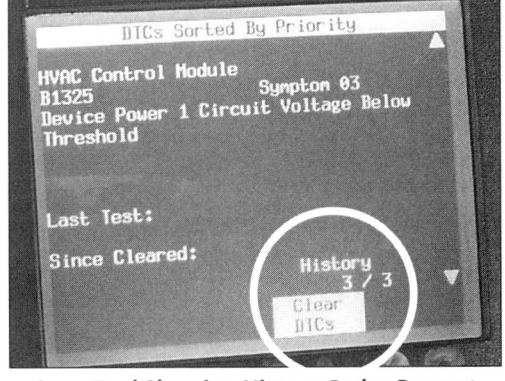
Scan Tool Showing History Codes Present

BINDING ACTUATORS

If an actuator binds inside the HVAC plenum, the control module will attempt to overcome the restriction several times before it shuts down the circuit. If the binding clears on the next activation, the control module will perform a calibration and set a history DTC.

Some vehicles require as long as thirty seconds of binding before setting a DTC.

Notes:

Actuator Calibration

When an actuator is replaced or power to the system has been lost or interrupted, calibration will usually be required. Calibration can be performed with a scan tool or without a scan tool. The procedure will vary with each vehicle manufacturer; consult the proper service information before attempting the process.

When using a scan tool, follow the instructions on the screen after entering the correct vehicle information and entering the proper function prompt on the scan tool menu.

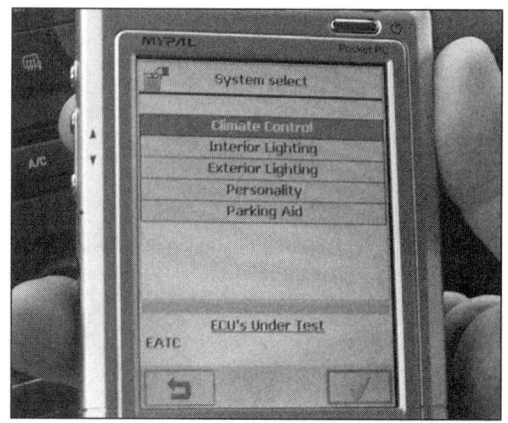

Scan Tool Used for Calibration

The scan tool will indicate when the calibration is complete. A fully charged vehicle battery is essential for a successful calibration to take place.

Some vehicles require the use of a laptop computer to interface with the system's electronics. Due to the amount of data and the fast speed at which data changes, a scan tool may not be fast enough to work with these modern designs.

Laptop Used for Calibration

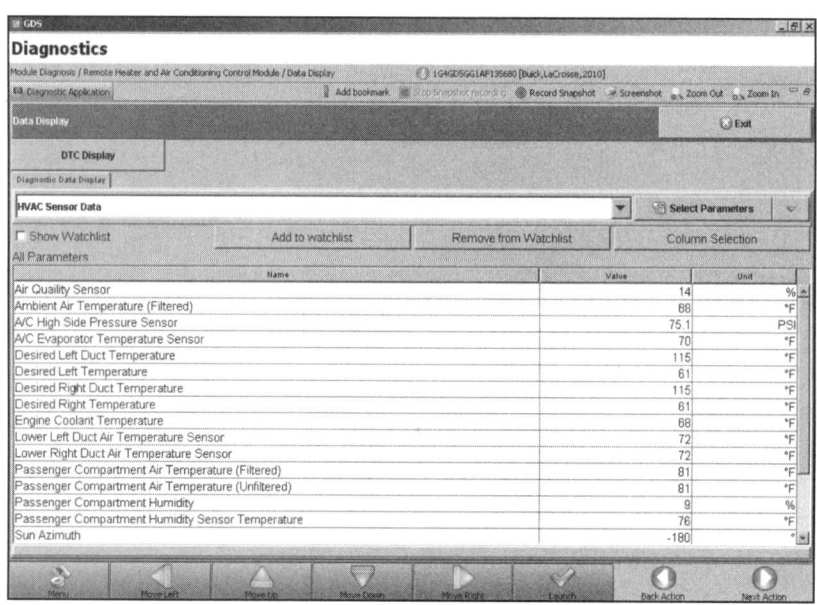

Calibration Program Readout

SECTION 8 • AIR DELIVERY SYSTEMS 137

Calibration Performed through Control Head

Some vehicles can be calibrated through the HVAC control head. The process for the example vehicle shown here is as follows:

- If the vehicle is equipped with rear A/C, the rear motors will be calibrated as well. With the ignition switch in the RUN position, press the power and recirculation buttons at the same time. When the power and recirc LEDs begin to flash, the calibration process has begun. The process will take three minutes maximum. When the LEDs stop flashing, calibration is complete. If the LEDs continue to flash, a DTC has been set and a scan tool will be required to read the DTC. The LEDs will continue to flash with a code present and the vehicle must be driven over three miles to stop the flashing, even though the DTC is still present.

Still, other vehicles can be calibrated simply by removing a specific fuse. A typical procedure is as follows:

- The Ignition must be OFF
- Remove HVAC fuse #1 from left I/P fuse block.
- Wait 60 seconds
- Reinstall the fuse
- Turn the Ignition ON
- Wait 60 Seconds for calibration to complete.

Removing the HVAC Fuse

Notes:

Manually controlled HVAC systems can be successfully diagnosed using either a scan tool or a multimeter. Calibration can be achieved using a scan tool, through the control head, or by fuse removal. The correct service information for a particular make and model vehicle is essential for proper repairs. Even if the control head looks the same, or the vehicle name plate is the same, running changes occur, and the wrong data could be applied to the vehicle being serviced.

AUTOMATIC TEMPERATURE CONTROL SYSTEMS (ATC)

Unlike manually operated systems, ATC systems are designed to "set and forget." They allow the A/C system programs to automatically maintain cabin temperatures. They also automatically direct airflow to the most logical location, based on the temperature setting selected. ATC systems usually have an override feature of automatic operation per the operator's input.

On most systems, if either maximum cold or maximum heat is selected, the blower motor will run on high speed until the temperature selector is moved from either maximum position.

ATC systems come in a variety of designs; some are semi-automatic, where temperature is set to a specific value and the system automatically maintains the desired temperature. The operator has the option of controlling the air delivery mode and blower speed.

Automatic Temperature Controlled (ATC) System

Semi-automatic ATC System

SECTION 8 • AIR DELIVERY SYSTEMS 139

ATC System with Rear Seat Controls

Another variation of the ATC system is rear seat controls. Rear seat passengers can control air volume and direction.

ATC System Rear Seat Controls also Featuring Temperature Adjustment

Other rear seat designs may allow temperature adjustment as well. As long as the front HVAC controller is in any mode except defrost, the passengers can either operate the unit in manual or allow the automatic settings to take control.

Front ATC Control Head also Containing Rear System Controls

Some rear seat system allow their temperature settings to vary quite a bit cooler or warmer from the front settings.

Most vehicles equipped with rear controls will have a master control on the front control head.

The front control is the master and can override the rear controls.

Notes:

The rear controls will be in command of rear HVAC functions when front control head selections allow. Often, when a front control head is replaced, the vehicle will revert to front control only. The HVAC system must be reprogrammed to operate properly.

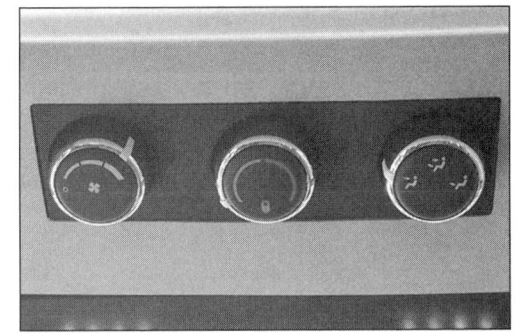
Typical Rear Controls

Many SUV-type vehicles have a self-contained rear plenum assembly to supply conditioned air to the rear of the vehicle. Although the control pieces are serviced separately, the refrigerant and coolant plumbing are tied in with the front system. If refrigerant or coolant is removed from the front unit, the rear unit is affected as well.

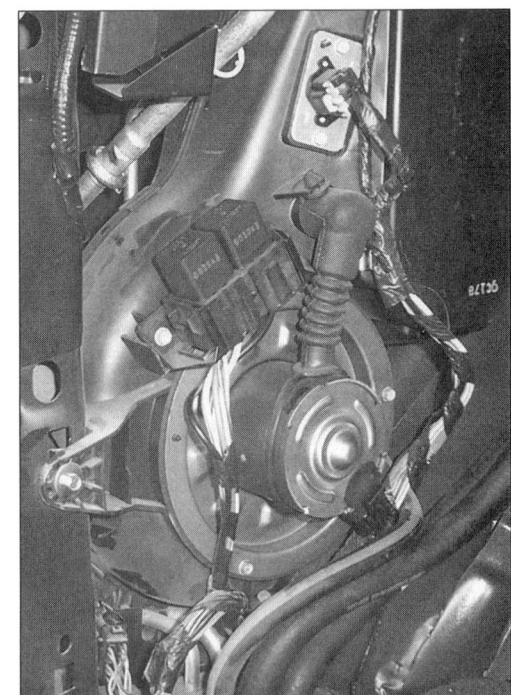
SUV Self-contained Rear Plenum Assembly

Notes:

SECTION 8 • AIR DELIVERY SYSTEMS 141

As seen in the diagram below, ATC systems have additional sensor requirements.

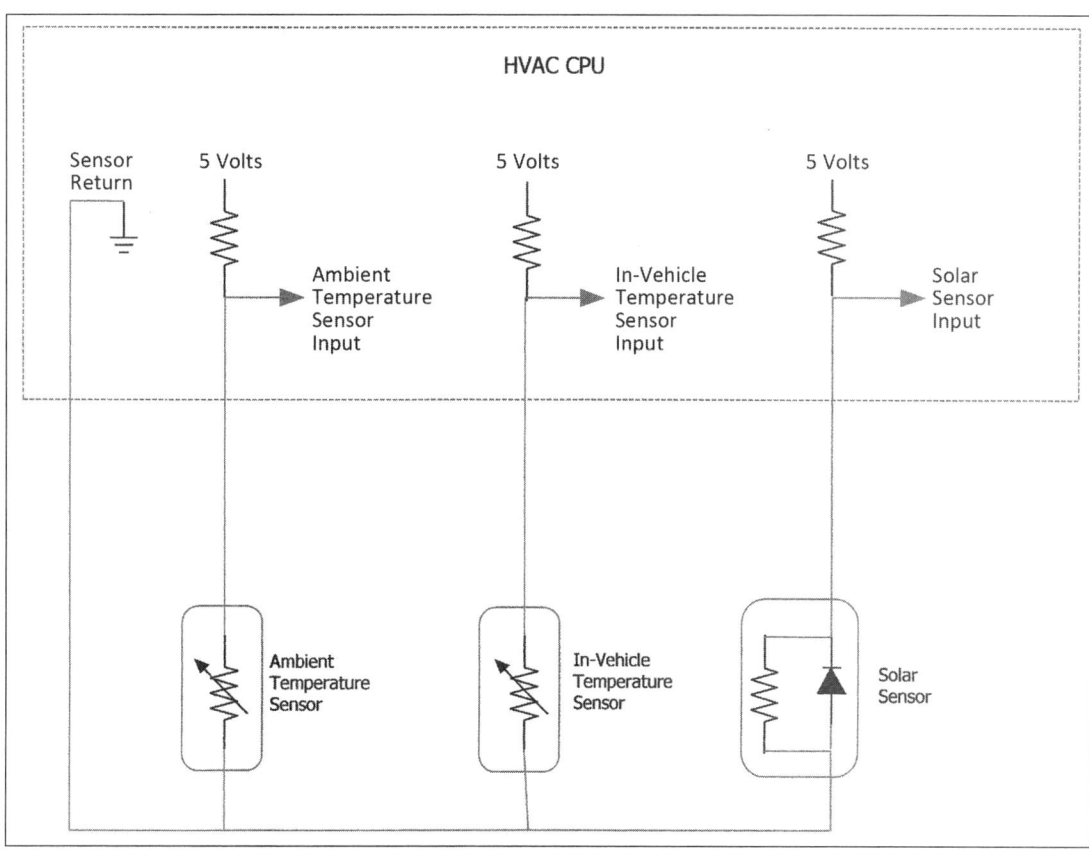

ATC System Diagram showing Additional Sensors

The temperature sensors are thermistors and the solar sensor is either a photo-resistor or photodiode design.

The ambient temperature sensor is located outside the vehicle.

This sensor is a thermistor and can be tested with an ohmmeter. With the sensor disconnected, watch for resistance changes with temperature changes. It can also be tested with a voltmeter; with the ignition on, back probe the sensor terminals. Voltage should vary between one and five volts as temperature changes.

Ambient Temperature Sensor

Notes:

In-vehicle temperature sensors are usually located behind the dash panel or in the headliner or overhead console. They may be thermistor-type sensors, or may be infrared-type sensors. Thermistor-type sensors usually have either an electric fan built in, or use a venturi from the blower motor to pull inside air across the sensor.

Thermistor-type sensors can be checked with an ohmmeter when disconnected. The resistance value for the sensors will be found in the vehicle service information.

Thermistor-type sensors can also be tested with a voltmeter. Back probe the sensor connectors and watch the voltage change with temperature change.

Refer to vehicle service information for test procedures for infrared-type sensors.

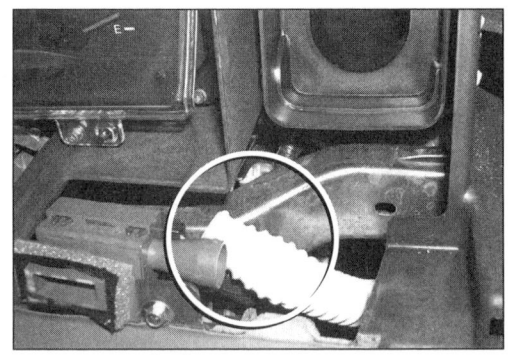
In-Vehicle Temperature Sensor

In-Car Temperature Sensor with Built-in Electric Fan

Solar, or Sun Load Sensors

The solar, or sun load sensor, detects the heat load of the sun, and is used to adjust the amount and direction of the cooled air through the dash vents. Dual zone systems use two sun load sensors, one on each side, usually on top of the dashboard.

The solar sensor uses a light-sensitive photo cell. When the sensor is in direct light, the voltage signal will be low. As the sensor is shaded, the voltage will increase. This sensor will not provide accurate resistance values; the most effective test is with a voltmeter. The normal voltage range is between zero and five volts.

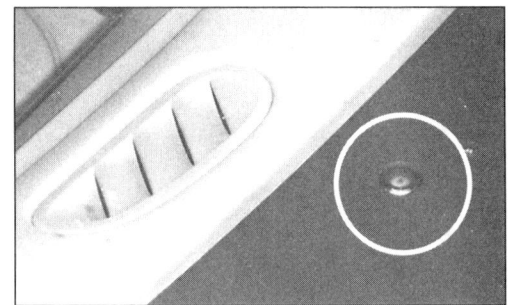

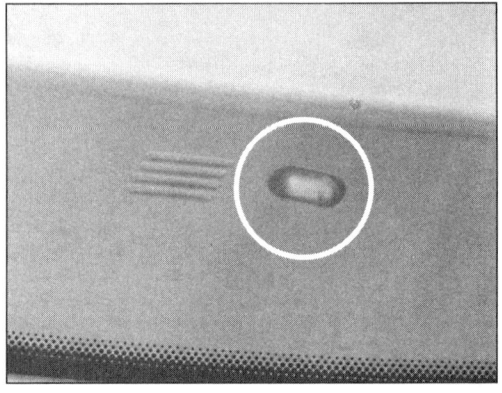

SECTION 8 • AIR DELIVERY SYSTEMS

Additional Inputs

Many (most modern) ATC systems may utilize additional inputs from the following sensors and devices:

- Engine coolant temperature sensor
- Crankshaft position sensor
- Throttle position sensor
- A/C pressure sensor
- Vehicle speed sensor
- Evaporator temperature sensor
- Power steering pressure sensor

Inputs from these devices help to determine the duct outlet temperature, air delivery, blower speed, and compressor operation.

Data Lines

ATC systems communicate over various data lines, depending on vehicle year, model and platform. Some systems use single wire serial lines, others will use multiplexing and a twisted-pair data line.

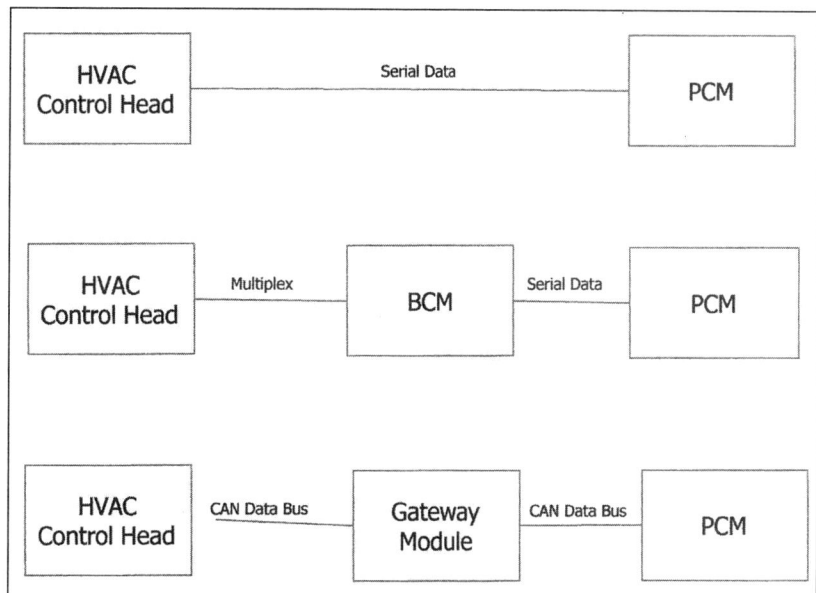

Examples of ATC Communications

Most late model vehicles use a CAN bus for faster communication and decision making. Use of a scan tool is essential when working on ATC systems.

AIR DELIVERY SYSTEMS • SECTION 8

Air Delivery

Many older ATC systems use a programmer to control the air delivery modes and the duct output temperature. The programmer can be all electronic or may use electro/vacuum solenoids for actuator control.

The diagram below shows a typical air delivery layout found on many vehicles.

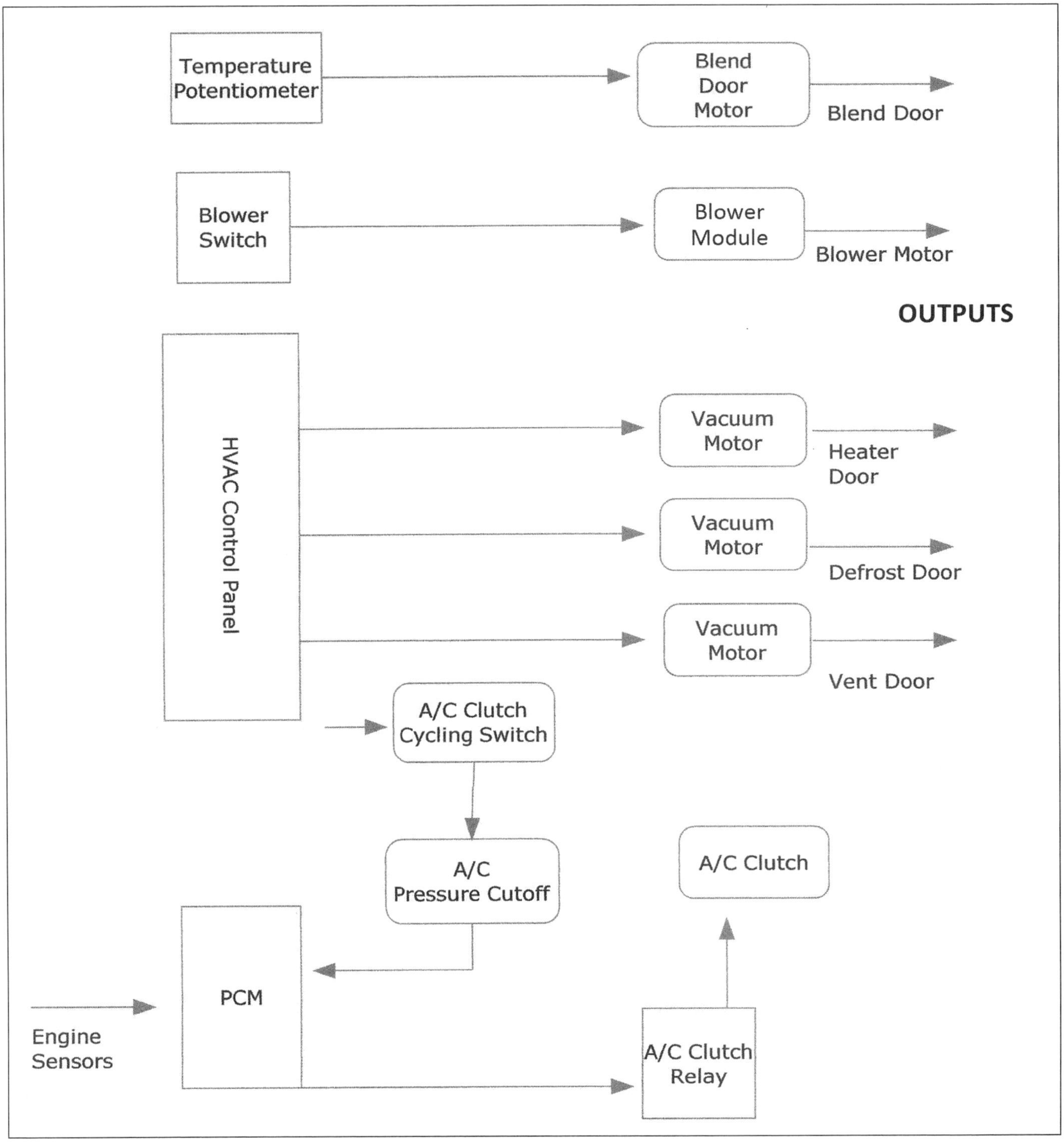

Typical Air Delivery Diagram

SECTION 8 • AIR DELIVERY SYSTEMS

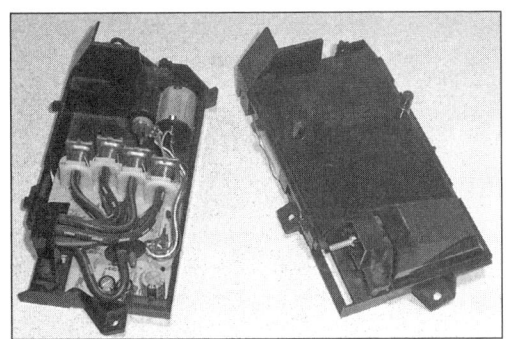

ATC Programmer

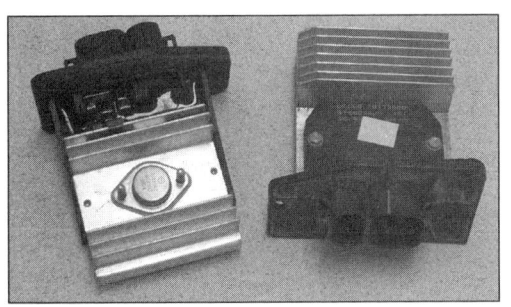

Blower Control Modules

This type of programmer uses vacuum for the air delivery doors and an electric motor for the temperature door. It is serviced as a complete unit.

Blower Controls

The blower motor control module is a solid state device with a power transistor positioned in the evaporator airflow which keeps the transistor cool. The module receives command inputs from the HVAC ECU.

The blower speed is controlled by pulse width modulation (PWM) and the microprocessor not only supplies the control signal but monitors the blower motor output through a feedback circuit.

Notes:

Common ATC Designs

Vehicle manufacturers use various ATC designs to meet the needs of different makes and models in their lineups. Variations are commonly identified by where the microprocessor is located. It can be located:

- In the programmer
- In the body control module
- In the HVAC control head

Microprocessor in the programmer: Two types are used. A working programmer has all the control components built in, while a delegating programmer uses a separate vacuum solenoid box and blend door actuator.

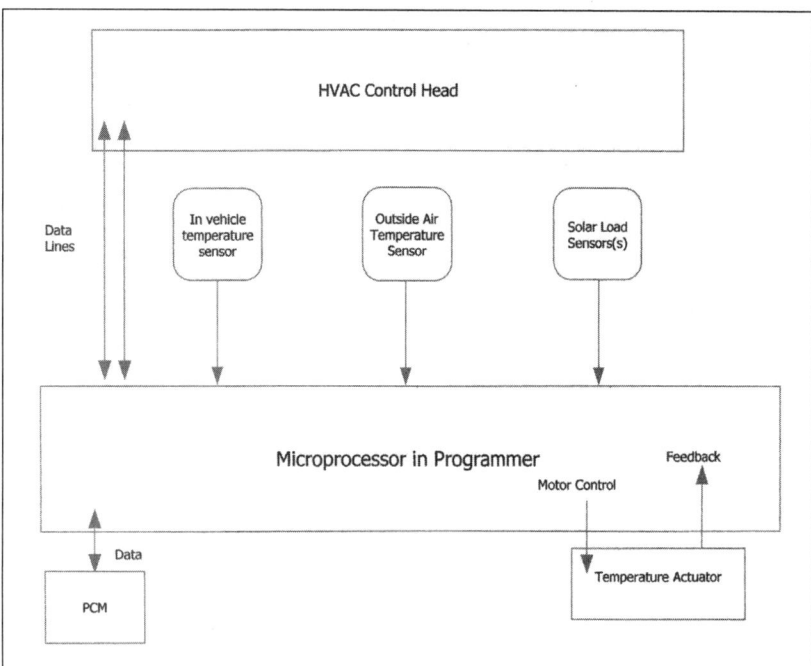

One Example of Microprocessor in the Programmer

The programmer makes decisions based upon inputs from:

- Control head
- Sensors
- Powertrain control module

SECTION 8 • AIR DELIVERY SYSTEMS

Another design is the microprocessor in the body control module (BCM). With this design, the HVAC control head serves as an input and the display.

The BCM contains the control logic; it receives ATC inputs, controls outputs, and communicates this information to the PCM.

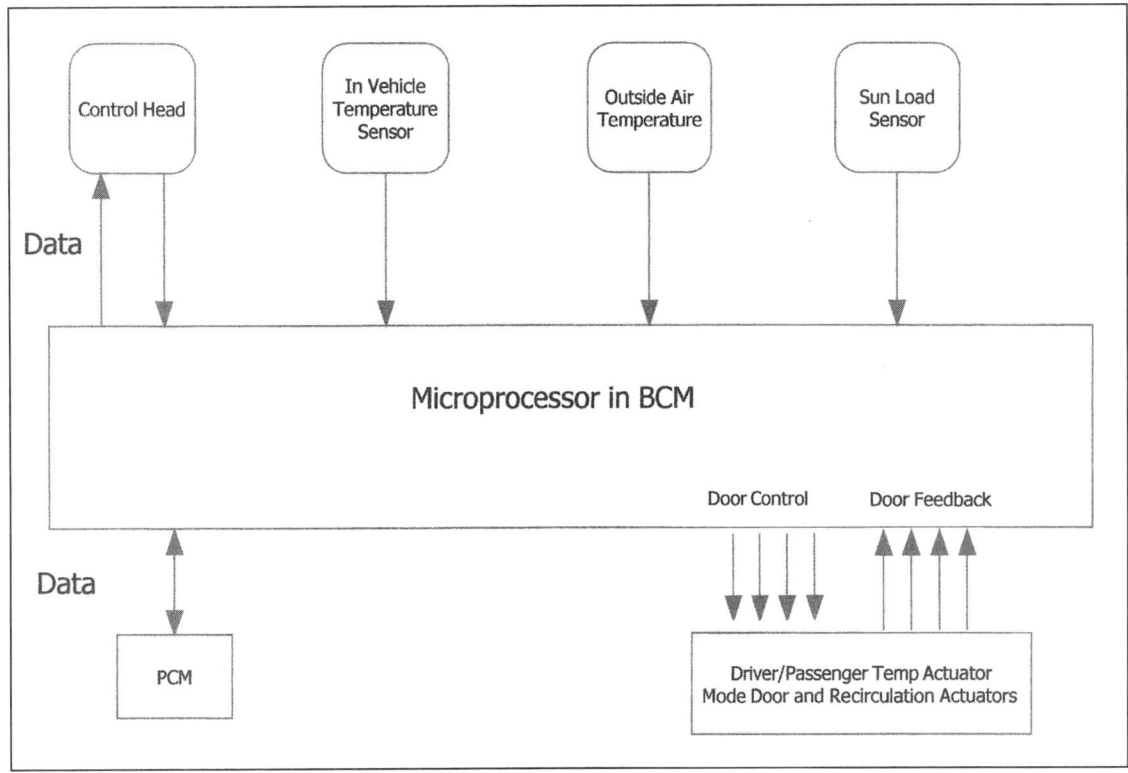

Microprocessor in the BCM

A third design is the microprocessor in the HVAC control head. The control head receives all inputs, and makes all output decisions.

Microprocessor in the HVAC Control Head

The control head may have the in-car sensor built in. The sensor may be either a thermistor or an infrared design.

As shown in the diagram below, the control head signals the PCM for an A/C clutch request and also receives inputs.

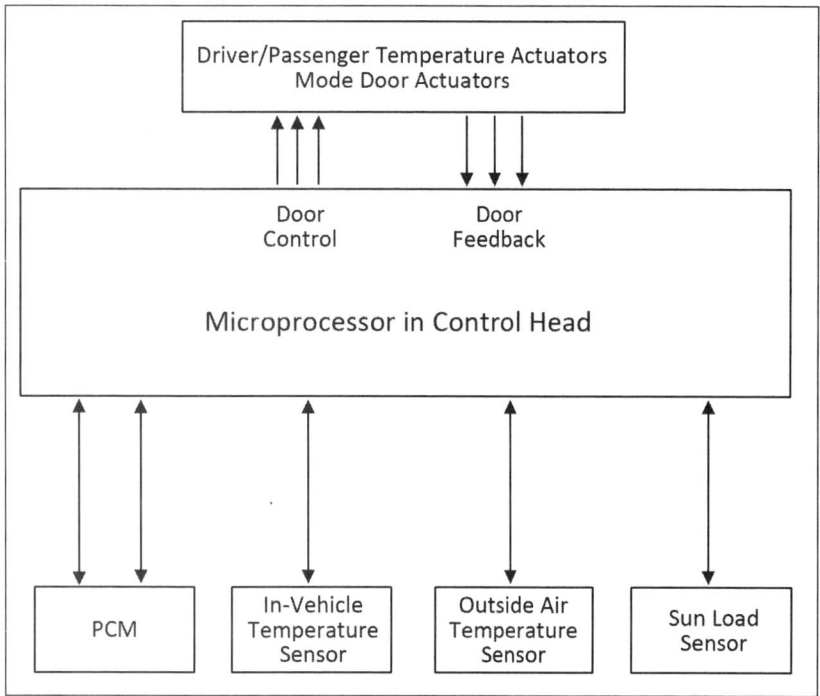

Control Head to PCM Clutch Request Diagram

Most ATC systems will set DTCs when sensor signals are out of range, or if communication on the data lines is lost. When a DTC sets, the HVAC display or the driver information center will usually display a message, turn on a warning light, or the temperature display may flash.

Service information for the vehicle is essential to properly diagnose and repair the ATC system.

Notes:

SECTION 8 • AIR DELIVERY SYSTEMS

Notes:

ATC Diagnostics and Calibration

Although the use of a scan tool and multimeter are necessary to diagnose and possibly calibrate ATC systems, some designs allow the technician to extract DTCs and perform calibrations using buttons on the control head, or by removing and reinstalling fuses.

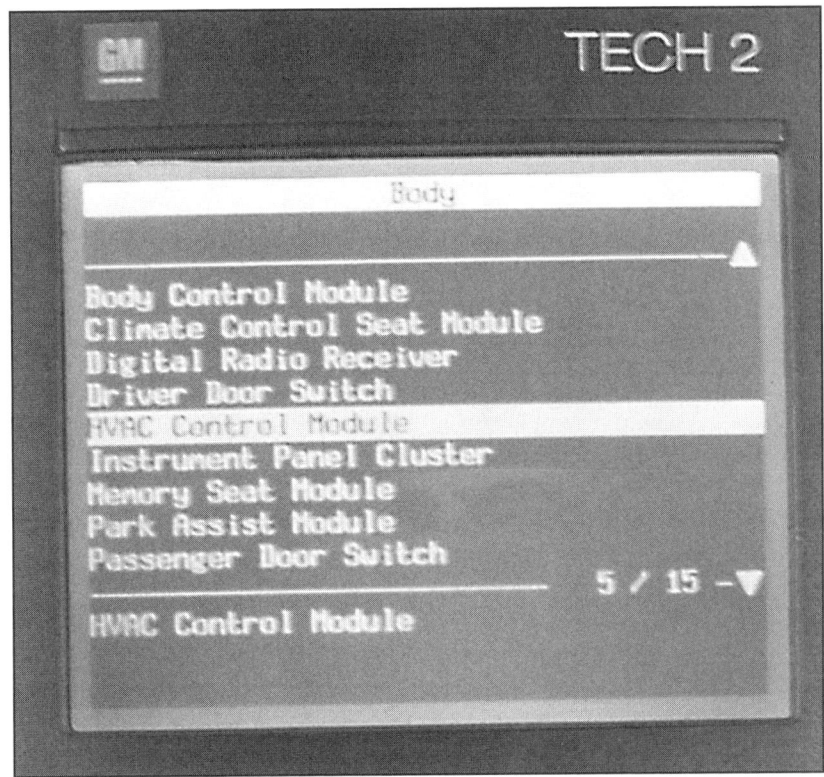

Accessing HVAC Control Module on Scan Tool

Below is the procedure for certain Chrysler LH vehicles. The engine must be running and at normal operating temperature.

1. Set temp to 75°F. Press and hold: Floor, Mix and Defrost buttons; when display blinks release the buttons.

2. After the system runs through diagnostic tests, any codes present will be displayed one at a time. Press the panel button to scroll through the codes. If there are no DTCs, the temperature display will return to 75 degrees F.

1) Pressing Floor, Mix and Defrost Buttons Simultaneously • 2) Press Panel Button to Scroll through DTCs

Next is the process for some late model Ford vehicles.

To enter the self-test:

1. Ignition key on, interior temperature must be between 40° F and 100°F.
2. Press: Off & Defrost at the same time, release and press Auto.
3. Blower icon will flash while the system is tested.
4. At the end of the self-test, all segments will light if no DTCs are present.
5. Always exit self-test by pushing the OFF button.
6. Leave the ignition on for 60 seconds for all actuators to recalibrate.

Press Off and Defrost, Release, then Press Auto

Notes:

SECTION 8 • AIR DELIVERY SYSTEMS

If there are DTCs present, the LCD will display the following:

1. "00 00" will display if there are DTCs; then the DTCs will be displayed.
2. 21 DTCs are available.
3. To retain the DTCs press any button except Defrost.
4. Clear the DTCs by pressing the Defrost button; the display will blink, then all the segments will light in the LCD.
5. Always exit self-test by pushing the OFF button. Leave ignition on for 60 seconds for all actuators to recalibrate.

Pressing Defrost Button to Clear DTCs; Pressing Off Button to Exit Self-Test

Notes:

A typical Chrysler minivan self-test procedure is detailed below.

1. Ambient temperature must be a minimum of 70° F.
2. Engine must be running at normal operating temperature.
3. Push POWER and RECIRC Buttons at the same time until the delay and recirculation graphics on the control head blink on and off.
4. The graphics will stop blinking when the test is complete if no DTCs are present.
5. If the graphics continue to flash, calibration failed or a DTC is set. A scan tool must be used to read the DTCs.
6. The graphics will continue to flash until actuator calibration is complete or the DTC is cleared with a scan tool.

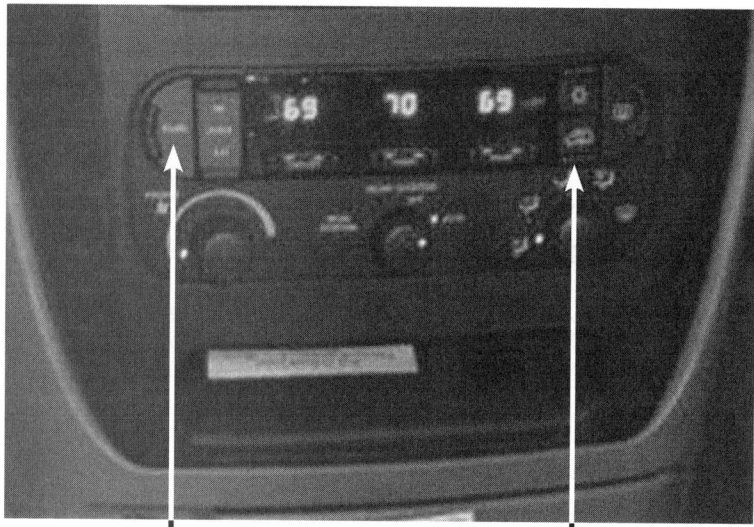

To Enter Self-Test, Press Power and Recirc Buttons

Due to the large variety of ATC systems found on various makes and models, it is vital that the proper tools and service information be used during diagnosis and repair procedures. Specific service information is critical for the correct specifications and testing procedures as well as the correct wiring diagrams.

Scan tools are required to access and clear trouble codes and also to perform calibration.

Multimeters are required to check sensor values and to perform pinpoint tests, as the tests will often include checking resistance values and checking for voltage signals, as well as power and ground.

Notes:

SECTION 8 • AIR DELIVERY SYSTEMS

HYBRID HVAC

It is beyond the scope of this book to provide detailed information on repair of hybrid HVAC systems. As such, we will concentrate the discussion on safety and service precautions. The following information serves as a preface for the more in-depth training required for hybrid HVAC systems.

Keep in mind: HIGH VOLTAGE can be FATAL!

⚠ **DANGER**

HIGH VOLTAGE You will be killed or hurt.

Before servicing:
- Remove ignition key and shut off main switch.
- Check voltage at junction board terminal.
- Always wear insulated gloves and use insulated tools.
- Carefully read and follow service manual instruction.

Hybrids Require Extra Precautions Due to Electrocution Risks

There are two safety items that must be used when working on hybrid vehicles:

- Class 0/1000 Volt Gloves
- Category III/1000 V Multimeter

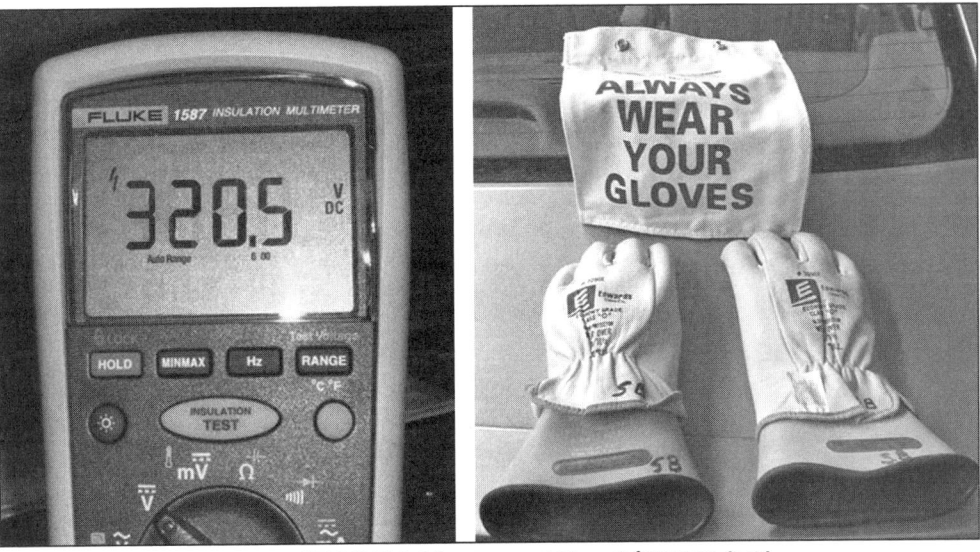

Category III/1000V Multimeter and Class 0/1000 Volt Gloves

Notes:

Always be careful of any component that has an orange cable connected to it and be careful of the orange cables themselves. Even a pinhole in one of these high voltage cables can allow a high voltage leak.

Be Careful of Orange Cables on Hybrid Vehicles

Always disconnect the high voltage batteries before any work that involves removing or servicing the A/C system components.

Keep in mind: HIGH VOLTAGE can be FATAL!

Always follow the manufacturer's recommended procedures for disconnecting the high voltage circuit.

Typical High Voltage Battery Disconnect

SECTION 8 • AIR DELIVERY SYSTEMS

Many hybrids use electric motor driven A/C compressors that require special lubricant. Note the label indicating the oil required for this particular vehicle.

Hybrid Vehicle A/C System Information Label

Electric Motor Inside Hybrid Vehicle A/C Compressor

If incorrect oil is used, the refrigerant system may become conductive. The electronics on the vehicle will detect the voltage leakage, and this will lead to the shutdown of the A/C compressor and a DTC will set.

Hybrid Oil R/R/R Device

To prevent cross-contamination of oils, a separate or specified refrigerant recovery/recycling/recharging machine is recommended for servicing hybrid vehicles. However, if the amount of hybrid repairs in a shop is limited, a device is available that can remove the oil from the service machine refrigerant lines. This device connects to the service hoses of the R/R/R machine.

With the oil removed from the refrigerant, the R/R/R machine can be safely used on hybrids with electric driven compressors.

Worksheet 7 – Section 8

Tasks: Perform Actuator Calibration:
- Using a scan tool
- Without using a scan tool

Tools and Materials Needed:
- MACS HVAC Systems, Volume 2 - Electrical and Electronic Systems Operation Manual
- Late model vehicle (NOTE: several different vehicles may be needed for this task)
- Vehicle service information
- A scan tool

Vehicles to be used:

Year: _____ Make _____ Model _____

VIN _____

Engine Type _____ Displacement _____

Year: _____ Make _____ Mode _____

VIN _____

Engine Type _____ Displacement _____

Procedure:

Using two available vehicles, Section 8 of the MACS HVAC Systems, Volume 2 - Electrical and Electronic Systems Operation Manual as a reference, vehicle service information, and an available scan tool, perform the following:

1. Perform actuator calibration using a scan tool.
2. Perform actuator calibration without using a scan tool.
3. Record the results below.

Vehicle 1:

Type of scan tool used: _____

_____

What were the steps involved in calibrating the actuators using the scan tool? _____

_____

Was the calibration successful? _____

Vehicle 2:

What were the steps involved in calibrating the actuators without using the scan tool? _____

_____

Was the calibration successful? _____

_____

SECTION 8 • AIR DELIVERY SYSTEMS

Section 8 Review – Air Delivery Systems

1. Technician A says the blend door determines where the air is directed: floor vents – dash vents - defrost. Technician B says a dual zone system uses two blend doors. Who is correct?
   A. Technician A
   B. Technician B
   C. Both Technician A and Technician B
   D. Neither Technician A nor Technician B

2. True or False: With a tri-state actuator, the motor only rotates in a clockwise direction.
   A. True
   B. False

3. Which of these statements is/are correct?
   A. One way to calibrate an actuator is to operate it with it not attached to the door.
   B. A digital multimeter can be used to check actuator operation.
      A. Statement A is correct
      B. Statement B is correct
      C. Both statements A and B are correct
      D. Neither statement A nor B is correct

4. Technician A says a scan tool may be used to perform diagnostics on an automatic temperature control (ATC) system. Technician B says a binding door may set a DTC. Who is correct?
   A. Technician A
   B. Technician B
   C. Both Technician A and Technician B
   D. Neither Technician A nor Technician B

5. True or False: Any oil of the recommended viscosity can be used in a hybrid vehicle A/C compressor.
   A. True
   B. False

Notes:

Section 9: Glossary

Actuators – Output devices that receive electrical signal commands and act to change the system being controlled.

A/D Converter – A circuit which translates an analog signal into a digital value.

Alternating Current (AC) – An electric current which reverses direction in the conductor. The flow in the conductor is created by repeatedly changing the polarity of the source field.

Alternator – A type of generator used on vehicles to produce electric current. Its AC output is rectified.

Ambient Temperature – The temperature of the air outside the vehicle.

Ammeter – A test instrument which measures current flow in a circuit.

Ampere (amp) – The unit of measure for electric current flowing in a circuit.

Analog Signal – A continuous but changing signal; voltage, current, pressure, etc.

Armature – The rotating part of a generator or motor.

Battery – A group of two or more cells connected together for the production of an electric current by converting chemical energy into electrical energy.

Binary – A numbering system using a base number of 2. In the binary system, the only two digits are 0 and 1.

Brush – A conductor, usually made of carbon, arranged to make contact with a rotating surface, such as an armature in a motor or generator.

Cable – An assembly of one or more conductors enclosed in a protective sheath.

Capacitor – A device for holding or storing an electric charge.

Circuit – A path provided for current flow.

Circuit Breaker – A device, other than a fuse, for automatically opening an overloaded circuit.

Closed Circuit – A circuit which is uninterrupted from the current source back to the current source.

Computer – Any device capable of accepting information, comparing, and processing that information, then supplying the results of these processes in the form of an output.

Conductor – A wire or other metallic object.

Continuity – A continuous path for the flow of electrical current.

Current – The movement of free electrons along a conductor.

Data – Information used as a basis for mechanical or electronic computation.

Digital – Using numbers expressed in digits and in a certain scale of notation to represent variables.

Diode – A semiconductor which permits current to flow in one direction only, and used in rectification and voltage spike suppression.

Direct Current (DC) – An electrical current which flows in one direction only.

E – Symbol for voltage or emitter.

Electricity – The movement of electrons from one body of matter to another.

Electromagnet – A soft iron core which is magnetized when an electric current is passed through a coil of wire surrounding it.

Feedback – The return of energy from one point in an electrical system to a preceding point, as from output to input.

Field Coil – A coil of insulated wire forming a part of one of the fields electromagnets.

Frequency – The number of cycles of a periodic phenomenon in a given time, usually per second.

Fuse – A device containing a soft piece of metal which melts and breaks the circuit when it is overloaded.

Fuse Link – The current carrying portion of a fuse which melts when the current is greater than a specified amount.

Generator – A device that produces an electric current through magnetism.

Ground – The connection made in the grounding circuit or to a common conductor for one part of a circuit.

Hertz (Hz) – A measurement of frequency (cycles per second).

Impedance – The total opposition a circuit offers to the flow of alternating current. It includes resistance and reactance and is measured in Ohms.

Induction – The process by which an electrical conductor becomes electrified when near a charged body.

Infinite – Having no limits, boundless.

Input Device – Any component in a circuit that provides information to a controller or computer about the status of another component, system, or condition.

Notes:

SECTION 9 • GLOSSARY

Insulator – Non-conductive material used for protecting wires in electrical circuits.

Jumper – A short length of wire used as a temporary connection between two points.

Kilo – A prefix meaning 1,000.

Light-Emitting Diode (LED) – A diode that generates light.

Load Device – Any component in a circuit that performs some type of work. Examples include lamps, solenoids, coils and motors.

Magnet – Any body with the property of attracting iron and steel.

Magnetic Field – The field produced by a magnet or a magnetic influence.

Meter – An electrical or electronic measuring device.

Micro – A prefix meaning one-millionth.

Microprocessor – An electronic device that, on a single chip, contains all of the components necessary to analyze incoming data according to a predetermined program. The microprocessor can display the data or use it to control other devices.

Milli – A prefix meaning one-thousandth.

Modulate – To vary or change an existing condition, e.g. speed, temperature, pressure etc.

Module – A self-contained assembly of electronic components and circuitry.

Motor – An electromagnetic device used to convert electrical energy into mechanical energy.

Multimeter – A test instrument that can measure voltage, current, and resistance.

Multiplexing – A system that enables the transmission of several messages over a channel or circuit. A method that allows several controllers or computers to communicate with each other and share information.

Ohm – A unit of electrical resistance.

Ohmmeter – An instrument for measuring resistance.

Ohm's Law – The law that states one volt is required to push one amp through one ohm of resistance. If two of the three values are known, the unknown value can be found.

Open Circuit – A circuit which is not complete.

Output Device – Devices whose operations are controlled by a controller or computer based on commands received from that controller or computer.

Parallel Circuit – A method of connecting units in an electrical circuit. In a parallel circuit there is more than one path for power and ground and all units are connected positive to positive and negative to negative.

Photodiode – A semiconductor diode in which the reverse current decreases whenever the unit is illuminated.

Photoresistor – A light-sensitive semiconductor resistor, its resistance decreases when the unit is exposed to light.

Photovoltaic – A substance which will generate a voltage when exposed to light.

Positive Temperature Coefficient (PTC) – Description of certain types of thermistors. Their resistance decreases when temperature increases.

Power – The rate at which work is done.

Pulse – An abrupt change in voltage which conveys information to a circuit.

Pulse Width Modulation (PWM) – A method of output control in which a signal is turned on and off for a specific duration to precisely control the operation of an output device. Usually represented in percentage.

Random-Access Memory (RAM) – A computer memory in which the data can be retrieved at a speed which is independent of its location in the memory.

Read-Only Memory (ROM) – A computer memory that is pre-programmed and used primarily for information retrieval applications.

Rectifier – A device in the electrical system used to convert alternating current to direct current.

Regulator – A device used to limit the output of an alternator by controlling the current and voltage.

Relay – A device using a low current circuit to control a high current circuit by opening and closing a set of switch contacts. A relay allows a high current circuit to be remotely controlled by a low power switch and wiring.

Resistance – Opposition to the flow of an electric current.

Scope – Abbreviated term for an oscilloscope.

Semiconductor – A group of materials having conductivity between metal and insulator.

Sensing Device – Any type of device that provides an input to a controller or computer regarding the status or operation of a system or component. Examples includes temperature, pressure, and position sensors and switches.

Notes:

SECTION 9 • GLOSSARY

Series Circuit – A circuit in which the components are consecutively connected positive to negative and all current must flow through all components.

Short Circuit – An unintentional routing of a circuit, bypassing part of the original circuit.

Solenoid – A tubular coil containing a movable core which moves when the coil is energized.

Solid-State Device – A term used to describe a device that performs some type of function but has no moving parts. Diodes and transistors are examples of solid state devices.

Supply Voltage – The voltage obtained from a power source to operate a circuit.

Switch – A device used for opening and closing or changing the connections in an electrical circuit.

Terminal – A device attached to the end of a wire or a connector for the convenience in making electrical connections.

Thermistor – A solid-state semiconductor device of which the resistance changes with temperature.

Transformer – A device for transforming an electrical current to a higher or lower voltage without changing the supply voltage.

Transistor – A semiconductor device often used for high-speed switching. Capable of controlling a high-current with a low-current circuit.

Variable Resistor – A wire-wound resistor with a sliding contact for changing the resistance.

Volt – A unit of measure of the electrical pressure in a circuit.

Voltage Drop – The difference in voltage between two points, caused by the loss of electrical pressure as current flows through a resistance.

Voltage Regulator – A device which maintains the output voltage of a device at a predetermined value.

Voltmeter – An instrument for measuring electrical pressure.

Watt – The unit of measuring electrical energy. The value of watts is the result of multiplying amps by volts.

Zener Diode – A semiconductor device which switches the current through it rapidly whenever the applied voltage decreases. Also called an avalanche diode.

Notes:

Notes:

Notes:

Notes:

To order the study manual and test:
Visit www.macsw.org

You have several options via the Internet.
You can order the test and take it online, or order the test online to be sent to you in the mail.
The study manual can also be downloaded from the MACS website. You can also arrange a live class or webinar.

Call or Fax Phone: (215) 631-7020
Fax: (215) 631-7017

Call in your order, or fax it with your credit card number.

Mail Send this form to P.O. Box 88, Lansdale, PA 19446 with credit card information or a check/money order.
Orders without payment will not be processed.

Please allow 10-14 days for processing and mail delivery.

Then, Take the NEXT Step and Stay Educated and Informed; Become a MACS Member!

Certified Technician Introductory Membership

- Receive seven issues of ACTION™ Magazine
- Receive the *MACS Monthly E-Newsletter*
- Receive **MACS Service Reports** via e-mail only
- Receive member discounts on the MACS convention
- This is a non-voting membership

Tests available in English or Spanish. Please specify which tech(s) needs Spanish.
Order form is on the other side . . .

*Contributions or gifts to MACS Worldwide are not deductible as charitable contributions for federal income tax purposes. Fees for educational materials may be deductible as an ordinary and necessary business expense. Check with your tax advisor. Charges for international shipping vary. Please allow 10-14 days for delivery. Sales tax applies to PA shipments (6%). 7/2009. Prices subject to change.

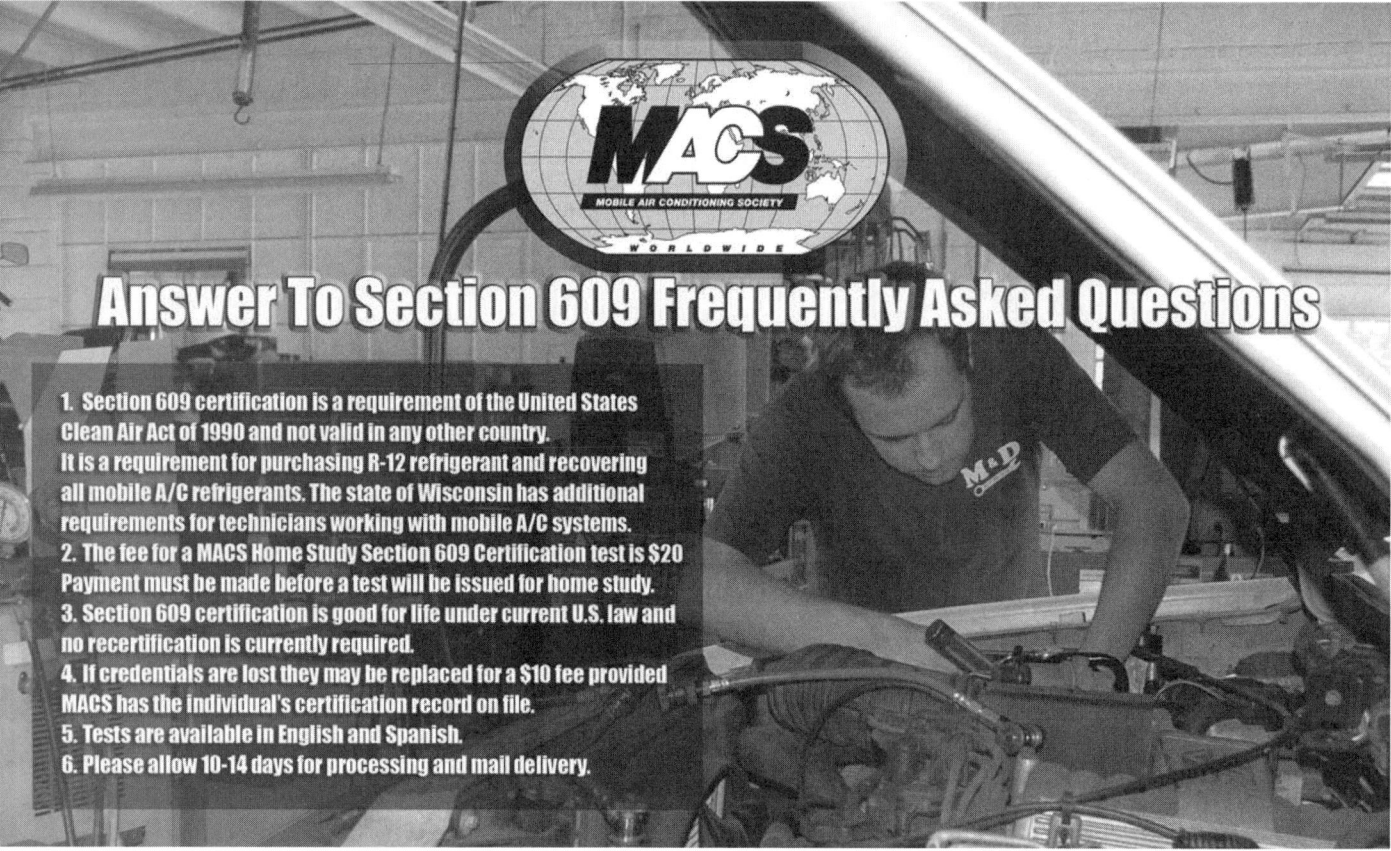

Answer To Section 609 Frequently Asked Questions

1. Section 609 certification is a requirement of the United States Clean Air Act of 1990 and not valid in any other country. It is a requirement for purchasing R-12 refrigerant and recovering all mobile A/C refrigerants. The state of Wisconsin has additional requirements for technicians working with mobile A/C systems.
2. The fee for a MACS Home Study Section 609 Certification test is $20. Payment must be made before a test will be issued for home study.
3. Section 609 certification is good for life under current U.S. law and no recertification is currently required.
4. If credentials are lost they may be replaced for a $10 fee provided MACS has the individual's certification record on file.
5. Tests are available in English and Spanish.
6. Please allow 10-14 days for processing and mail delivery.

(More information available at www.macsw.org)

To request Section 609 certification tests, please fill out the following information and return to MACS Worldwide with payment. You may mail, fax or email this form but it must be accompanied by $20 for each test requested.

$20 per test

1st Tech: _____ Email address: _____
❏ $20 per Certification Test
❏ $10 MACS Membership*

2nd Tech _____ Email address: _____
❏ $20 per Certification Test
❏ $10 MACS Membership*

3rd Tech: _____ Emailaddress: _____
❏ $20 per Certification Test
❏ $10 MACS Membership*

4th Tech: _____ Email address: _____
❏ $20 per Certification Test
❏ $10 MACS Membership*

5th Tech: _____ Emailaddress: _____
❏ $20 per Certification Test
❏ $10 MACS Membership*

6th Tech: _____ Email address: _____
❏ $20 per Certification Test
❏ $10 MACS Membership*

(Attach list if necessary)

See other side for Membership Details

Shop / Company Name _____

Mailing address: _____ City/State/Zip: _____

Area Code/Phone: _____ Fax: _____

MACS Worldwide P.O. Box 88 Lansdale, PA 19446
Phone: 215/631-7020 • Fax: 215/631-7017 • email: info@macsw.org

❏ Check/MO# _____ for $ _____ Charge my: ❏ Mastercard ❏ Visa ❏ AMEX ❏ Discover
Card# _____ Name On Card _____ Ex. Date _____
CVV2/Sec Code _____ (3 or 4 digit # on front or back of card) _____
I give MACS permission to fax and email me: ❏ YES ❏ NO

* See other side for Membership details. Contributions or gifts to MACS Worldwide are not deductible as charitable contributions for federal income tax purposes. Fees for educational materials may be deductible as an ordinary and necessary business expense. Check with your tax advisor. Charges for international shipping vary. Please allow 10-14 days for delivery. Sales tax applies to PA shipments (6%). 7/2009. Prices subject to change.